A Revolution in Economic Theory

Ajit Sinha

A Revolution in Economic Theory

The Economics of Piero Sraffa

palgrave
macmillan

Ajit Sinha
Azim Premji University
India

ISBN 978-3-319-30615-5 ISBN 978-3-319-30616-2 (eBook)
DOI 10.1007/978-3-319-30616-2

Library of Congress Control Number: 2016947370

Printed on acid-free paper

This Palgrave Macmillan imprint is published by Springer Nature
The registered company is Springer International Publishing AG Switzerland

For

Alice

The joy of my life

Foreword

For many years now, Ajit Sinha has been writing on the nature and significance of Piero Sraffa's approach and contributions to economic theory. He began by formulating his interpretations on what was available in the public domain—in Sraffa's case, these were relatively thin pickings as far as quantity but not quality was concerned—and then by exhaustive archival research once the Sraffa Papers at Trinity College, Cambridge, were eventually opened to scholars.

The result of these labours is this present book which is a mature coming to fruition of many years of deep musing. Most importantly, Sinha perceived that Sraffa's approach to economic theory could not be understood unless you realised that Sraffa's philosophy and economics were indissolubly mixed, that Sraffa was as much a genius as a philosopher, as he was a critical yet constructive economist. The result is an historical analytical account of the nature of Sraffa's ideas and their significance for pure economic theory.

Sinha has a fine understanding of the history of our subject and of Sraffa's absorption of it from his undergraduate days on. All these strands come together in *A Revolution in Economic Theory*. Sinha's thesis is already a highly controversial take on the approach and the contributions of one of the greatest scholars of the twentieth century. Here, he has presented a serious sustained argument which should be treated with respect by other scholars, and especially by those who disagree with Sinha's interpretation.

GC Harcourt
Emeritus Reader in The History of Economic Theory, Cambridge, 1998; Emeritus Fellow, Jesus College, 1998; Professor Emeritus, Adelaide, 1988; Visiting Professorial Fellow, UNSW, 2010–2016.

Preface

Arguably Piero Sraffa (1898–1983) was one of the most enigmatic and philosophically the most sophisticated minds in the history of economic science. He has been credited for 'the most consequential ideas' of the *Philosophical Investigations* by Ludwig Wittgenstein, who put him high on his short list of geniuses. Wittgenstein had regular discussions with Sraffa for more than a decade during 1930s and 1940s in Cambridge, England, and on many occasions he told his friends that those discussions 'made him feel like a tree from which all branches had been cut' (see Monk 1990, p. 261). Thus the philosophical sophistication and sharpness of Sraffa's mind is beyond doubt. At the early age of 27–28, Sraffa published two articles (1925, 1926) that challenged the established Marshallian hegemony on economic theory and consequently gave birth to the literature on 'imperfect competition'. However, he quickly lost interest in such a project. Apart from a book review of Hayek's *Prices and Production*, written at the request of Keynes, in 1932 and his magisterial editing of *Works and Correspondence of David Ricardo* in 11 volumes, most of which was published during 1951–52, Sraffa mostly remained silent until he published his slender classic, *Production of Commodities by Means of Commodities: Prelude to a Critique of Economic Theory*, in 1960. This book was in the making from late 1927. It is less than 100 pages long and reads like an example of minimalist art in economic prose. After this, Sraffa did not publish anything except a short response to Sir Roy Harrod's review of his book in 1962.

In the 'Preface' to his book, Sraffa declared: 'It is, however, a peculiar feature of the set of propositions now published that, although they do not enter into any discussion of the marginal theory of value and distribution [i.e. the orthodox economic theory], they have nevertheless been designed to serve as the basis for a critique of that theory.' The book, however, was mostly received as an enigma. Harrod echoed the sentiments of many leading economic theoreticians of the time when he wrote in his review: 'The publication of this book is a notable event.... A reviewer would be presumptuous if he supposed that he could give a final assessment of the value of its net product, or even single out what may prove to be its most lasting contributions. Before that result could be achieved, much prolonged consideration and reconsideration would be required' (1961, p. 783).

By 1965–66 a controversy over the orthodox theory of 'capital' between the two Cambridges, University of Cambridge, UK, and Cambridge (MIT), USA, came to head. Although Sraffa himself did not participate in the controversy, one proposition from his book was used by a group of younger-generation Cambridge-educated economists, who had come to be known as 'Sraffians', to beat back the orthodox position.[1] This success was hailed as the crowning glory of Sraffa's great work, but it came at a very high cost. The proposition in question related to the re-switching of techniques of production, which proves that the notion of 'aggregate capital' prior to the determination of prices of commodities is illogical. The orthodoxy interpreted Sraffa's re-switching proposition as his main contribution to economic theory, they accepted its truthfulness and argued that modern general equilibrium orthodox economics need not aggregate capital independently of prices. Hence, the Sraffa-critique of the orthodox theory was not fatal but rather minor and, therefore, the book on Sraffa could be closed. The Sraffians felt highly annoyed. They maintained that the re-switching proposition hits at the heart of the orthodox economic theory, and some Sraffians are perhaps still busy

[1] *Quarterly Journal of Economics* (1966, 80).

trying to prove that the re-switching proposition is fatal to the orthodox theory even with the notion of disaggregated capital.[2]

The canonical Sraffian interpretation of Sraffa's book is that it re-establishes the theoretical paradigm of classical economists such as Adam Smith and David Ricardo as well as Marx on a logically more solid foundation, and that there is a sharp distinction between the theoretical paradigms of the classical school and the neoclassical school that came to dominate economic theory after the 1870s. This has given rise to a lively debate on the history of economic thought that has been now going on for more than three decades regarding the question of whether there was continuity or a paradigmatic break between the Classicists and the Neoclassicists.[3]

Leaving aside the question of how to interpret the Classics, it is, in my opinion, extremely important to begin re-interpreting the nature of Sraffa's contribution to economic science. The common mistake, that the 'Sraffians' as well as the leading orthodox theorists have made with regard to the nature of Sraffa's contribution, is that he is read within the well-established frame of discourse in economic science without any concern for the philosophical underpinnings of his contribution to economic theory. This has led to a profound misunderstanding of the nature of Sraffa's contribution. I concur with Amartya Sen that 'Sraffa's economic contributions … cannot, in general, be divorced from his philosophical understanding' (2003, p. 1240).

In this book, I argue that Sraffa was interested in changing the nature of the fundamental questions that economic theories ask. For example, the question of why '*x*' has a price but air is free, requires an answer in terms of discovering the essential *cause* of the phenomenon of price, that is, why does *anything* have a price? Here the question about a particular '*x*' presupposes an answer in universal or general terms. On the other hand, the question: why is '*x*' sold for $2/kg. today in a particular market? requires an explanation or rather a *description* of a particular event that has happened. Here the question is not concerned with why '*x*' has

[2] See articles by P. Garegnani and B. Schefold in Kurz, H.D. (ed., 2000) and also Schefold (2008) for an immanent critique of this approach.

[3] See Sinha (2010a) for my position on this issue.

a price but rather how it turns out that '*x*' has a particular price—how it is *related* to $ as 1 kg for 2, or 1 of '*x*' for 2 of '*y*'? Unfortunately in the history of economic theory the two questions have always been conflated and there has been a general tendency to answer the second question in terms of the first. Sraffa, however, was careful to distinguish the two questions as completely different in nature. Furthermore, Sraffa also distinguished the problem of why '*x*' has increased in price from $2 to $3 from the question of why '*x*' is sold at $3. The first question needs an answer in terms of a discovery of a *cause* that explains the *change*. However, the second question, as mentioned above, requires an answer in terms of a *relation* (a logical relation), that is, why '*x*' must relate to $ or other commodities '*y*', '*z*' and so on in a precise quantitative association at one moment. The first case is *mechanical* in nature whereas the second is *geometrical*. In the second case, the problem of causation does not arise because time is absent from the problem—hence the explanation must be a *description* of what exists. Sraffa maintained that any answer to the question of change in terms of causation must always be uncertain in nature, and therefore it is highly problematic to make an assumption of a functional relation between two or more variables.

Sraffa's project of building a geometrical description in opposition to causal explanation (either essentialist or mechanical) led him to a complete rejection of any role for demand or human psychology in his theory. His commitment to purging psychology from economics was based on his firm conviction that a scientific theory cannot be built on the basis of *unobservable* variables. This led Sraffa to reject 'counterfactual reasoning'—a point first highlighted by Amartya Sen (1978)—particularly the ubiquitous 'marginal method' which is based on the quintessentially unobservable concept of *notional change* at the margin.

When it comes to the fundamental question of methodology, Sraffa sharply distinguished his position from the dominant atomistic method of analysis. He looked at 'a system of production' as a unified whole and not as a combination of individual industries or firms. Thus the coal industry has no independent existence without the iron industry and vice versa if they need each other as inputs in their production. Hence the determination of prices cannot be understood in terms of 'cost of production', in which an arrow can be drawn from the left hand side to the right hand side of the equation of an industry. In this case prices must be determined as a solution of a simultaneous equation problem, in which no arrow of *causation* can be drawn.

The result of this approach was truly revolutionary. Sraffa succeeded in showing that, on the basis of observed input-output data of an interconnected system of production, and by simply arranging them, the rate of profits of the system (which *must* be uniform) can be determined without knowledge of the prices, if the wage rate is given from outside the system. In this context, prices have only one role in the system, and that is to consistently account for the given distribution of the net output in terms of wages and the rate of profits (the introduction of rent of land does not make any difference to the result). Prices, in this context, do not carry any information that prompts 'agents' to adjust their supplies and demands to bring about equilibrium in the market. The questions of *equilibrium* as well as *market structure* are simply irrelevant to the problem. The fundamental peg on which Sraffa's theory hangs is the assumption that either wages or the rate of profits is *given* from outside the system of equations, a proposition he considered to be characteristically 'classical' in opposition to the modern economic theory where the size and the distribution of the net income are simultaneously determined with prices.

Unfortunately both the followers of Sraffa, led by Pierangelo Garegnani, as well as his critics, led by Paul Samuelson, read his theory to be an equilibrium theory of prices in a competitive market economy. The contention of this book is that this interpretation was built on a false understanding of Sraffa's condition of the uniform rate of profits across industries. My arguments and evidence are designed to show that the condition of equal rate of profits in Sraffa's system of equations is a *logical necessity*, or a mathematical property, of his equation system once wages are taken to be given from outside. If my argument is accepted then it becomes incumbent on those interested in pure economic theory to take a second look at Sraffa's contribution and investigate what could be built on the new foundation provided by him.

The book begins with a long chapter entitled 'Prologue'. It is designed to bring the reader up to speed with the literature that existed before Sraffa embarked on his revolutionary project—a literature with which Sraffa intensively, although implicitly, engaged in his book. In subsequent chapters, I follow a chronological order in charting the development of Sraffa's thought, which culminates in his book, *Production of Commodities by Means of Commodities.*

This book is heavily based on Sraffa's unpublished notes which are housed at the Wren Library, Trinity College, University of Cambridge. Since most of these notes are hand-written and Sraffa had a habit of going back and annotating them, they are obviously not very neat. In quoting from these notes I have followed the publisher's advise to change single underlines to italics and double underlines to single underlines along with italics. In the case of squiggly underlining, we have kept it as in the original and all Sraffa's double quotation marks are changed to single quotation marks. Sraffa had a habit of using both parentheses and large or square brackets in his notes, so I have used only middle brackets or braces for my insertions. All the parentheses and large brackets are Sraffa's own and at times when Sraffa uses more than one word for an expression as alternatives by writing them above or below that word, I have put them in parentheses. All the citations from Sraffa's unpublished notes are shown by the file numbers given to 'Sraffa Papers' by the archivist Jonathan Smith, such as (D3/12 …) etc.

I take this opportunity to thank the Institute of New Economic Thinking (INET) and Centre for International Governance and Innovation (CIGI) for a grant to support my research for this book. Without it I could not have made several visits to the Wren Library at Trinity College, Cambridge, to study Sraffa's archive and to give this matter my singular attention. I thank Professor Lord John Eatwell, the current literary executor of Sraffa's unpublished papers, for granting me permission to publish from Sraffa's unpublished archive. I am grateful to Jonathan Smith, the archivist of the Wren Library, for his most generous help; the same goes for all his staff at the Wren Library. No words of thanks can convey my sense of gratitude to Professor Geoffrey Harcourt, who has been a pillar of intellectual support throughout, for his offer to write the 'Foreword' to this book and for his very constructive comments and suggestions on various drafts. Professor Samuel Hollander's intellectual honesty and broad-mindedness have been inspirational to me. Even though my earlier book, *Theories of Value from Adam Smith to Piero Sraffa*, consistently takes issue with his interpretations of Adam

Smith, Ricardo and Marx, he applauded my efforts most generously as a 'splendid achievement'. I thank him for his continuing friendship and encouragement and for his highly constructive comments on the draft of this book. I am also greatly indebted to Professor John King for very helpful suggestions and comments on the first draft of the book, which led to a substantial rewriting of the 'Preface' in particular. Many thanks to Professors Arthur Gibson, Sanjay Reddy, Stefano Zambelli and Shantha Bhushan for several discussions on the mathematical properties of Sraffa's equations, and to Nerio Naldi for discussions on Sraffa's biography, for suggesting some important references and for translating some from Italian to English. Riccardo Bellofieori also helped me understand some of Sraffa's notes that were written in Italian, for which I thank him. I am grateful to Alex Thomas and Paul Zarembka for their comments on an early draft and Indrani Bhattacharjee for her comments on the chapter on Sraffa and Wittgenstein. I would also like to thank Romar Correa and Andres Lazzarini for being very helpful in finding some references.

Finally, I must thank my parents-in-law, Annette and Guy Maugier, and my wife, Anne, for taking care of our daughter Alice during most weekends and holidays so that I had time to write this book.

Ajit Sinha
Bangalore, India

Contents

1

Prologue

The Classical Paradigm

Why do certain things have value or price and are not free as air? The classical economists thought it prudent to distinguish between two kinds of goods that are not free: one is fixed in supply and the other can be increased or reproduced. They thought that the goods that are fixed in supply do not play any significant role in the economic life of society. Therefore, they can be left out of consideration of a theory that seeks to explain the phenomenon of price as an aspect of our economic life. As early as 1776, Adam Smith introduced the problem in terms of a rule of exchange between two hunters in 'the early and rude state of society':

> In the early and rude state of society which precedes both the accumulation of stock and the appropriation of land, the proportion between the quantities of labour necessary for acquiring different objects seems to be the only circumstance which can afford any rule for exchanging them for one another. If among a nation of hunters, for example, it usually cost twice the labour to kill a beaver which it does to kill a deer, one beaver should naturally exchange for or be worth two deer. It is natural that what is usually the produce of two days or two hours labour, should be worth double of what

A. Sinha, *A Revolution in Economic Theory*,
DOI 10.1007/978-3-319-30616-2_1

> is usually the produce of one day's or one hour's labour. (Smith 1981, p. 65)

What Smith does not care to clarify in this relationship, however, is the question of the instruments (or the weapons, in this case) that must have been used to kill the deer and the beaver. If we assume that the two hunters must have used some weapons, however crude, then the question arises: were those weapons made by the hunters themselves or by somebody else? If we assume that the weapons used were fashioned by the respective hunters themselves, then the question arises: did they or did they not need any instruments to fashion those weapons? And if they did need some instruments, then again the question arises: were those instruments produced by the respective hunters themselves or by someone else? And so on. If our answer to this series of questions at every step is that the respective hunters built all the instruments themselves then we must conclude that the whole process of killing the deer and the beaver started with the hunters working against nature with their bare hands to fashion the first instrument without any help from any man-made artefact. Let us start with the assumption that the respective weapons become useless after killing two deer or one beaver, and for the next kill the whole process must start all over again. In this scenario a *linear* chain of labor-time from scratch to the final production of dead deer and beaver can be laid down and total labor-time spent in their production can be calculated. In the case where weapons remain efficient for killing many deer and many beavers, we will have to devise some rule for depreciating the labor-time from the weapons to the single deer and the single beaver to arrive at the calculation that 'it usually cost twice the labour to kill a beaver which it does to kill a deer' (*ibid.*).

But even after arriving at this calculation our problem is not solved. Since it takes twice the amount of time to kill a beaver that it does to kill a deer, it is obvious that the beaver hunter has to go hungry for twice as long as the deer hunter before he can consume. Thus, if the beaver hunter receives two deer in exchange for his one beaver, then the question arises: why would he not switch to hunting deer and exchanging it for beaver, if he desires to consume some beaver? And since the same logic would hold for all beaver hunters, why would they continue to hunt beaver?

The point is that it makes no sense for a group of hunters to specialize in hunting beaver unless there is some reward for going hungry for twice as long as the deer hunters. And any economic reward for going hungry for twice as long would amount to one beaver exchanging against *more than* two deer. Thus Adam Smith's simple rule must break down, even in a 'nation of hunters'.

This is the sort of reasoning that lies at the heart of most of the post-classical (Austrian and neoclassical) critique of classical 'labor theory of value' and its proponents' explanation of the existence of a positive rate of interest in a capitalist system since Nassau Senior (1836). The fundamental feature of such reasoning is its *linear narrative*. An economic activity has a definite *beginning* and a definite *end*. Production of any commodity has a purpose and that purpose is *consumption* or satisfaction of human desire, which defines the end point. Similarly, production of any good for consumption can be traced back to a point at which laboring activity is unassisted by any produced means of production. In other words, capital investment can be reduced to only wage advances. This identifies a well-defined beginning. Thus in our example of deer and beaver hunters, the beaver hunter *must* exchange more than two deer for a beaver to compensate for the longer time that it takes to produce a dead beaver starting from scratch than to produce a dead deer. This extra quantity of deer for the extra time is the interest on the extra capital, which is measured by the extra time invested in the beaver industry. Thus capital can be measured by *time* or the *period of production* that a productive activity takes from its well-defined beginning to its end.

There is, however, another scenario that may explain Adam Smith's claim. Because deer and beaver hunting are specialized activities in this 'nation of hunters', it may be that weapon making and the instruments that help in making weapons and the instruments that help in making other instruments and so on are all specialized activities. In other words, there is no productive activity that a worker (or a hunter) undertakes that is not assisted by some instrument that has been acquired by *exchange* from some other specialized worker. In this scenario no one starts from scratch. All the workers and the hunters work for a day (or a year) after which, in the evening market (or the annual market), they exchange their final products with others' so that what has been used up in production is replenished and the surplus output is consumed (or reinvested) in the mix they mutually desire. In this case no one makes more or less sacrifice than the others, which is their daily (or yearly) labor, and therefore Smith's simple rule of exchange applies: 'It is natural that what is usually the produce of two days or two hours labour, should be worth double of what is usually the produce of one day's or one hour's labour.'

To illustrate this point further, let us take an example from Sraffa (1960) and suppose that there exists a society that produces three commodities in the manner given below:

$$90\text{t.iron} + 120\text{t.coal} + 60\text{qr.wheat} + 3/16\text{labor} \rightarrow 180\text{t.iron},$$
$$50\text{t.iron} + 125\text{t.coal} + 150\text{qr.wheat} + 5/16\text{labor} \rightarrow 450\text{t.coal}, \textit{and}$$
$$40\text{t.iron} + 40\text{t.coal} + 200\text{qr.wheat} + 8/16\text{labor} \rightarrow 480\text{qr.wheat}.$$

After a production cycle is over, the three workers, or the several workers in the three industries, find themselves in possession of exclusively iron or coal or wheat. To renew the production process for another cycle or the year they must exchange their commodities with each other. What must be the exchange ratios between the three commodities such that the system can reproduce itself? If this society is made of only workers, as Adam Smith's society of hunters, then all the income generated in this society must be appropriated by the workers. In this case we can write the equations for price determination in this system as:

$$\begin{aligned} 90p_i + 120p_c + 60p_w + 3/16w &= 180p_i. \\ 50p_i + 125p_c + 150p_w + 5/16w &= 450p_c \\ 40p_i + 40p_c + 200p_w + 8/16w &= 480p_w, \end{aligned} \tag{I}$$

where p_i, p_c and p_w represent prices or exchange ratios of the respective commodities and w represents the remuneration of the workers per unit of their labor. By putting any of the ps equal to one, say $p_w = 1$, we can solve for the values of p_i, p_c and w. In this scenario, it turns out that the exchange ratios between iron, coal and wheat—that is, $p_i : p_c : p_w$—must be in proportion to the labor contents of one 1 ton of iron: 1 ton of coal:

1 qr. of wheat. The value of total *w* must be equal to the value of 165 tons of coal plus 70 quarters of wheat, that is, exactly the total value of the net output of the system. Thus Adam Smith's proposition regarding income and prices in a nation of hunters is completely satisfied. The point to note here is that the prices in this scenario are completely determined by the specification of how net output or total net income is distributed. Once we specify that all the workers must receive equal pay for equal direct labor-time spent in production, which exhausts the total net output, it leaves no room for any psychological factor such as the initial sacrifices made to acquire the original means of production to be brought into the picture.

This scenario is *circular* in contrast to the earlier *linear* one. In this case there is no definite beginning because reducing any production process to its direct and indirect labor will always leave some *commodity residue*. For example, we can collect direct and indirect labor in the production of iron given by

$$90\text{t.iron} + 120\text{t.coal} + 60\text{qr.wheat} + 3/16\text{labor} \rightarrow 180\text{t.iron}$$

by replacing 90 tons of iron by (45 t . iron + 60 t . coal + 30 qr . wheat + 3/32 labor) and then again replacing 45 tons of iron by (22.5 t . iron + 30 t . coal + 15 qr . wheat + 3/64 labor) and so on. By making similar substitutions for 120t.coal and 60qr. wheat, we can see that the quantities of commodities, iron, coal and wheat, become successively smaller and smaller. By reducing the commodity residue to negligible levels we could calculate the total direct and indirect labor-time embodied in a commodity, although the commodity residue never completely vanishes. Therefore, there is no well-defined 'beginning' of the production process. One serious implication of this is that, even if wages become zero, there is a finite maximum to the rate of profits beyond which it cannot rise because there will always be some positive capital in the form of materials or produced means of production. However, in the linear scenario, since all capital can be reduced to wage advances only, the rate of profits must rise to infinity when wages become zero. Furthermore, there is no definite end to an economic process in the circular scenario—production merges into reproduction. There is no hierarchy of goods of 'lower order' or 'higher order' or 'consumption' and 'intermediate' goods in the process of production. And finally, the exchange ratios or prices of commodities are explained solely on the basis of *objective* data.

This is what Sraffa (1960) refers to as the 'classical standpoint from Adam Smith to Ricardo' in the 'Preface' to his book. It should, however, be kept in mind that this is a reconstruction of the classical standpoint by Sraffa. Both Adam Smith and Ricardo were interested in finding the *ultimate cause* of *changes*, whether in the wealth of a nation or the distribution of income over a period of time, and thought that they could locate the sole cause of such changes by reducing production to the primordial relation of man and nature. In this context they did try to reduce all capital to wages advanced by the capitalists with no commodity residue remaining. As we shall see in Chap. 6, this was Sraffa's own reading of Smith and Ricardo in summer 1927.

Now, let us get back to Adam Smith's story. After recounting the 'natural' rule of exchange in a society of hunters of deer and beaver, he quickly abandoned his proposition that '[i]t is natural that what is usually the produce of two days or two hours labour, should be worth double of what is usually the produce of one day's or one hour's labour' on the grounds that once a class of capitalists and landlords arrive on the scene and ask for a share in the total net output, this simple rule of exchange that is valid for a society of only laborers no longer holds. In other words, the change in the rule to account for the appropriation of the net output demands a change in the rule for exchange of commodities. Ricardo thought that Adam Smith was too quick in abandoning his original proposition.

Ricardo ([1821] 1951) argues that it was a mistake on Adam Smith's part to have abandoned his original proposition that relative value of commodities are determined by relative direct and indirect labor-time expended on their production when the net output is divided between wages and profits. He showed that, if the ratios of direct to indirect labor-time needed to produce all the commodities are the same, then a positive rate of profits would not affect the exchange ratios of commodities determined on the basis of embodied labor ratios. In other words, the labor-time ratios would predict the correct exchange ratios even if the society was not made up only of laborers but was divided between capitalists and laborers and there were positive profits in the system.[1]

However, this conclusion would not hold when the ratios of direct to indirect labor of various industries are not uniform, which is the general case. This is because, if wages are lowered by 10%, the total income released to be transferred to the capitalists of each industry would be in proportion to the share of the direct labor employed in that industry however the total capital employed in the industry is measured by the direct plus indirect labor employed in the industry. Therefore, if the ratios of direct to indirect labor-time are not uniform across industries then prices determined by labor-time ratios would generate unequal rate of profits across industries. But Ricardo, following Adam Smith, strongly held the view that such situations cannot hold for long in a competitive capitalist system because movements of capital in search of the maximum rate of profits must lead to a uniform rate of profits across industries in the long run. This can happen only if the price ratios or the exchange ratios of commodities deviate from their labor-time ratios.

Ricardo acknowledged this difficulty but did not think that it was a good enough reason to abandon the 'labor theory of value'. He argued that the requirement of a uniform rate of profits in the general case only introduces a 'modification' to the strict 'labor theory of value', but he did not go on to show how these 'modified' exchange ratios are determined on the basis of the labor-times embodied in the commodities. Instead, he modified his theoretical stance. He proposed that given the 'modified' exchange ratios, whatever they might be, any *change* in those exchange ratios can be traced back to changes in the total labor-time required to produce the commodities. Thus labor-time is the *sole cause* that explains *changes* in the price ratios of commodities.

But this 'modified' hypothesis does not solve the original problem. It is clear from our example that prices or exchange ratios must change with changes in wages if the condition of a uniform rate of profits is to be maintained in the general case. So how could Ricardo argue that the sole cause of change in prices is labor-time? In his published book,

---

[1] Rent of land did not make any difference to this proposition, since in Ricardo's theory rent does not play any role in determining prices.

Ricardo tried to get away from this problem on the grounds that even large changes in the rate of profits or wages have very minor effects (not more than 6–7%) on the prices, so this cause could be practically ignored. However, from his unpublished notes it is clear that he did not think that this was a satisfactory argument. In Sinha (2010a, b) I have argued that Ricardo went on to entertain the idea that the effect of changes in wages on prices is solely due to the fact that we have to arbitrarily choose a commodity as a unit of measure to quantify changes in wages and prices, but no matter which measuring yardstick one chooses it is itself affected by the very changes it is supposed to be measuring. He thought that if one could find an 'invariable measure of value', in the sense that the measuring standard would not be affected by changes in wages, then one could show that wage changes have no effect on prices of commodities when they are measured against *this* measuring standard.

This hypothesis, however, is logically untenable. Suppose that there are three commodities *a*, *b* and *c* that exchange in the proportion 1:2:3 when wages are equal to 1 and the exchange ratio of commodities *b* and *c* changes to 2:4 when wages become 0.9. If we assume commodity *a* to be such a commodity that it is not affected by changes in wages, how could it be possible for *a* to keep on exchanging for 2 units of *b* and 3 units of *c* after the change in wages? That would contradict the fact that after the change in wages 2 units of *b* exchanges against 4 units of *c*. Sraffa (1951) has a different interpretation of Ricardo on this issue, which we will discuss in detail in Chap. 6.

Marx ([1894] 1991) criticized Ricardo for losing sight of the major problem and getting bogged down by a secondary matter. For Marx, the question of the deviation or rather the *difference* between the equilibrium price ratios and the 'labor-time' ratios is more important than the question of the *cause* of *changes* in the price ratios. Marx argues that a commodity has 'value', which is an absolute category and is measured by the direct and indirect labor-time needed to produce it. He then divides the value of a commodity into three distinct components: $c+v+s$, where c represents the value of the means of production used in producing the commodity (that is, the indirect labor-time which Marx called 'constant capital'), v represents the value of wage goods advanced to the workers (which Marx called the 'variable capital') and s represents the difference between the total labor-time worked and the value of the wage goods advanced (which Marx called the 'surplus value'). Thus the direct labor-time is divided into two parts: one part represents the wage advances and the other part represents the labor performed over and above the value of the wage basket received by the workers.

Marx first argues that the price ratios of commodities deviate from their labor-value ratios in a systematic way, which could be explained on the basis of his value analysis. According to him, the total surplus produced in the economy is equal to the sum of all the surplus-values produced in individual industries. This total surplus is then divided among the individual industries according to an equal rate on their individual capital investments such as (c_i+v_i) for industry *i*. Thus $\Sigma s_i / \Sigma(c_i + v_i) = r$ (say) defines the average rate of profits in the system and the 'price of production' of a commodity is then defined by $p_i = (c_i + v_i)(1 + r)$. Given these prices of production, the equilibrium price ratios only represent the ratios of prices of production of any commodity against price of production of the commodity produced by the average 'organic composition of capital', that is, $\Sigma c_i / \Sigma v_i$ (or C/V), of the system. This has the same rate of profit in the value system and in the system of prices of production, and therefore has no reason to deviate from its value. Thus, in the general case, the prices of commodities will systematically differ from their value ratios although they are derived from the labor-values of commodities. In these calculations the sum of profits must come out to be equal to the sum of surplus-values and the sum of prices of production must come out to be equal to the sum of values. Thus, the competitive mechanism seems to only displace individual profits from their surplus-values and individual prices of production from their values, and creates an *appearance* that disguises the true *essence* of the system.

There is, however, one serious problem with this analysis, as Marx soon realized (Marx 1991). Once it is acknowledged that prices of production deviate from their values, then the relevant measure of capital must also be in terms of prices of production and not in terms of values. Thus r is not necessarily the correct measure of the average rate of profits in the system, as $(C + V)$ is not necessarily the correct measure of total capital. In other words, Marx's system of equations is not well defined. Once we allow prices of production to appear on the left hand side of the equations as well, then we are back in Ricardo's world and Marx's analysis of a singular commodity as value loses all analytical significance—we are in the world of relative prices and profits. Once values are replaced by unknown prices of production on the left hand side of the equations, it becomes clear that Marx's system of equations is underdetermined, that is, it has more unknowns to solve than it has independent equations. In this system an extra equation for the *numéraire*— the measuring yardstick—can be added from outside the system and then the equations can be solved for an equal rate of profits and relative prices. If one puts the condition that total prices of production must equal total values in the system, which satisfies Marx's yardstick of maintaining the aggregate deviations of prices of production from value to be zero, then there is no reason to assume that the total profits in the system would come out to be equal to total surplus-value. So Marx's value analysis of a commodity no longer appears to reveal the *essence* of relative prices and profits.

In a nutshell, the fundamental theoretical problem that classical economics seems to be grappling with is the relation of labor-time as an activity with cost of production on the one hand and the notion of 'surplus' on the other. This relationship apparently has two aspects to it. On the one hand, labor-time appears to represent the 'cost' of production; for example, Adam Smith's 'toil and trouble', which he measures in terms of labor-time, is definitely a cost from the point of view of the laborer. On the other hand, it appears that Ricardo uses the measure of labor-time as a surrogate for the technique of production and his proposition regarding determination of value or changes in value relates to the technique of production in use. But then Ricardo's representation of the technique is highly incomplete. For example, in agricultural production it is obvious that air, rainfall and above all the energy of the sun play the most decisive roles in production, yet they do not appear explicitly in Ricardo's description of the technique of agricultural production. Thus the technique represented by Ricardo is not a scientific representation of what inputs are consumed to produce an output. Ricardo only takes into account those inputs that already have positive price for the producer. Therefore, they are 'costs' to the producer. But the problem is that labor-time represents an *activity* and, although it can be thought of as a 'cost' to the laborer (as Adam Smith did), it cannot be thought of as a 'cost' to the capitalist. So, from the point of view of the capitalist, the 'cost' of laboring activity is the *wages* paid to the laborers. Thus Ricardo finds himself time and again driven to reducing all costs to wages by going back and back in the production chain on the assumption that at some finite point all material means of production can be reduced to wages (the surrogate for the idea of primordial exchange between man and nature). But then how does one account for the profits received by the capitalists? Adam Smith had solved this problem by suggesting that the rate of profits could be treated as the conventionally determined 'cost' of production and rent could be explained, following Physiocrats, by the notion of a 'gift of nature'; that is, the free elements that enter into produced goods represent the excess of goods over and above all the goods used up in production, which creates the 'surplus' income category (see Sinha 2010a for details). This, however, does not solve the problem satisfactorily because it is not clear why the 'natural' elements remain free when they are a part of the inputs, but take on a positive value when they become a part of the outputs. In any case, for Ricardo profits are 'surplus', that is, they are over and above all the costs incurred by the capitalists: 'The remaining quantity of the produce of the land, after the landlord and the labourer are paid, necessarily belong to the farmer, and constitutes the profits of the stock' (*op. cit.*, p. 112). So the problem for Ricardo is how to account for profits on the side of the equation that only represents 'costs'. He was never able to resolve this problem satisfactorily, as is evident from his response to Malthus: 'Mr. Malthus appears to think that it is a part of my doctrine, that the cost and value of a thing should be the same;–it is, if he means by cost, "cost of production" including profits.' (*op.cit.*, p. 47). But the problem is that if profits are treated as 'costs' then they cannot be treated as 'surplus', that is, whatever is left after paying all the costs. It is a great credit to Marx that he recognizes that the central theoretical problem with classical economics lay in the confusion between the concept of laboring activity and its cost. He thought that new concepts were needed to resolve the problem. He argues that wages cannot be interpreted as the ultimate cost of laboring activity simply because a given wage can be associated with a range of labor-time as an activity. For Marx, what matters is 'human labor'. Commodity exchange in a market economy only represents the interconnectivity of human labor and therefore values of commodities represent only human labor. So now a distinction between cost and value can be drawn: value of a commodity represents human labor whereas costs represent prices the producers pay for their inputs and the difference between value and costs represents the surplus, which explains the surplus income category. But to be able to subtract costs from value, Marx had to measure costs in the same unit as value, that is, in terms of human labor. But if the prices of the commodities that the producer uses as inputs are different from their values then one needs to know those prices prior to determining the surplus, and this was the problem that Marx was never able to resolve. As we shall see, these were the issues Sraffa was intensely thinking through during the the period from 1927 to 1931.

As we have mentioned above, all these theories assume that the rate of profits in the system must be uniform. The idea was first established by Adam Smith and later accepted by Ricardo and other classical economists, and by Marx without much reconsideration. According to Adam Smith, if a productive activity generates wages, profits and rent as three distinct categories of income, then the price of every commodity produced by this productive activity must be constituted by the respective shares of wages, profits and rent that it represents. He further argues that in a modern capitalist society there exist a natural rate of wages, a natural rate of profits and a natural rate of rent at any given point of time. These natural rates are determined by the long-term economic and socio-historical dynamics of the system and are not affected by the supply of or the demand for commodities at that point of time. These *given* natural rates (that is, the distribution of income) determine what Adam Smith calls the 'natural prices' of commodities by adding up the direct and indirect 'natural' wages, profits and rent. In other words, 'natural prices' account for the given national income identities. After arguing that 'natural prices' are determined by the *given* 'natural' rates of wages, profits and rent, Adam Smith, however, does not go on to argue that prices *must* be at their 'natural' levels. Instead, he argues that prices at any given point of time are determined by the prevailing state of demand and supply in the market, which he calls their 'market prices'. The 'natural prices' are supposed to be the 'centers of gravitation' of the 'market prices'. Although Adam Smith's 'additive theory of value' proved to be highly controversial in classical literature,[2] his idea of the 'natural price' and his description of the relationship between the 'market' and the 'natural' price was almost universally accepted.

According to Adam Smith (1981, pp. 73ff.), there are fixed 'effectual demand' points for every commodity, which correspond to the quantities that would be demanded, given the real income generated in the economy, when the prices of commodities are equal to their 'natural prices'. When the output or the quantity brought to market of a commodity is lower (higher) than the given effectual demand point, then the competition among the buyers (sellers) would push the 'market price' of the commodity higher (lower) than its 'natural price'. This would result in at least one of the factors that are used in its production receiving higher (lower) returns than their 'natural rates'. In this circumstance, given competition and free mobility of factors, there would be movement of the factors into (out of) the industries that are receiving higher (lower) than their 'natural rates'. This would increase (decrease) the supply of the commodity and thereby reduce (increase) its 'market price' along with the returns to the specific factors. Thus, there would be a tendency for the 'market prices' to gravitate toward their 'natural prices' and the factor incomes to gravitate to their 'natural rates' as long as 'market prices' deviate from their 'natural prices'. When the 'market prices' become equal to the 'natural prices' then the returns to factors become uniform across industries and equal to their 'natural rates', and thus the *cause* for the movements of 'market prices' ceases and the system comes to its 'centre of repose'.

Clearly what Adam Smith presents is a few broad brush strokes of an argument that there is an inherent tendency in the market for 'market prices' to gravitate towards their equilibrium or 'natural prices' and that those equilibrium prices could be determined independently of the conditions of demand and supply prevailing in the market. Since the classical tradition accepted the truth of Smith's proposition without much investigation, it is incumbent on us to look into the matter a bit more closely. So let us first examine what constraints are required for determining the

[2] See Sinha (2010a, c) for my position on it.

'effectual demand' and its fixity during the process of gravitation of the 'market prices' to their 'natural' levels.

According to Adam Smith, the effectual demand has two aspects to it: (i) it is a demand that is backed by real income and (ii) it is the quantity demanded of the commodity at its 'natural price'. Thus, to determine the effectual demand we need to know two things: (i) the income generated in the economy and (ii) the 'natural price' of the commodity. Although the 'natural rates' of wages, profits and rent can be taken as given, the *total* 'natural' wages, profits and rent can only be determined after we know the scale of the outputs produced. Thus it is implicit in Adam Smith's definition of 'effectual demand' that he must begin with a given set of inputs used and outputs produced in the economy, that is, a given *size* of the economy.

Now, if we apply the given natural rates of wages, profits and rent to the equations of inputs and outputs to determine the 'prices' of the set of outputs produced, would that give us Adam Smith's 'natural prices'? The answer is, not necessarily. The reason for this is that, if the produced outputs are not equal to their 'effectual demands', which would be the usual case, then according to Adam Smith:

> When the quantity of any commodity which is brought to the market falls short of the effectual demand, all those who are willing to pay the whole value of the rent, wages, and profit, which must be paid in order to bring it thither, cannot be supplied with the quantity which they want. Rather than want it altogether, some of them will be willing to give more. A competition will immediately begin among them, and the market price will rise more or less above the natural price, according as either the greatness or the deficiency, or the wealth and wanton luxury of the competitors, happen to animate more or less the eager competition, according as the acquisition of the commodity happen to be of more or less importance to them. [And the converse is the case when quantity supplied is larger than quantity demanded at the 'natural price'.] (Smith [1776] 1981, pp. 73–74)

Here Adam Smith imposes no specific restriction on the 'market prices', such as requiring that the income calculated at the 'market prices' must be equal to the 'natural' income. In other words, when the system is not in equilibrium then it is the 'market prices' that must determine the income in the system. This, however, contradicts his fundamental position that income is determined independently of prices. But more importantly, if the market prices could affect income in the system then the 'effectual demands' registered at any set of 'market prices' could be either higher or lower than they would be when the incomes happen to be at their 'natural' levels. And since the 'market prices' are continuously fluctuating, it would result in fluctuating income levels and thus no fixed effectual demand points toward which the system could be gravitating. Thus, for the fixity of the 'effectual demand' quantities, the 'market prices' must be constrained in such a way that they do not affect the given 'natural' incomes—all they can do is to distribute the given 'natural' incomes unequally (in terms of the rates of wages, profits and rent) among the industries. In effect, Smith's proposition implies that the size of the economy or the total employment of labor must remain fixed all through the movement of 'market prices' to 'natural prices'. Otherwise, if industrial rescaling leads to an increase or decrease of the total labor employment in the system then it might have some impact on wages and, therefore, the 'natural prices'.

In addition to this, if the industries were not subject to constant returns to scale (CRS), then the industrial output adjustments toward their 'effectual demands' would change the input-output equations and thus the 'natural' income levels and the effectual demand points. This indicates that Smith must have implicitly assumed CRS for all his industries. And finally, one must also assume that there are no substitution possibilities for the techniques in use. If there were other techniques available then it is likely that fluctuations in industrial rates of profits would lead to switches in techniques, and therefore changes in the 'natural' rates of wages, profits and rent as well as the effectual demands.

Given all these restrictions, one can now describe Adam Smith's argument as follows: given a system of inputs and outputs with CRS prevailing in all the industries and no substitution possibilities, its total labor employed can be reallocated to produce several set of outputs. Any of those sets can be chosen as 'effectual demand' points for the system and if the actual output happens to be a different set from the chosen 'effectual demand' set then the price mechanism (that is, the gravitation mechanism) would guide the system to reallocate its total labor such that the system produces its 'effectual demand' set.

Is this proposition valid? When one thinks of it in terms of a single commodity then the proposition appears to be highly persuasive. However, in a system of a large number of interconnected industries, the matter turns out to be quite complicated. Dupertuis and Sinha (2009) have shown that in a system of three or more basic goods, that is, goods that are directly or indirectly used as inputs in the production of all goods, the mathematical probability of the system converging to the center of gravitation from its neighborhood by following the classical gravitation mechanism is zero. This should not come as a surprise, since classical gravitation mechanism allows trade to take place at disequilibrium prices which change the incomes of the participants in the exchange. If that is so, then can the classical theory of 'natural prices' remain meaningful after discarding the *mechanism* by which the system is supposed to converge to its 'natural prices'? We will let Sraffa answer that question.

The Post-classical Paradigm

The previous section has summarized the state of the classical approach to the theory of value and capital when it came under a frontal attack in the early 1870s from major works by William Stanley Jevons (1871), Carl Menger (1871) and Leon Walras (1874). The three theses had a similar basis but were developed independently of each other. All set out to establish a *subjective* theory of value in direct opposition to the classical *objective* theory. For example, Jevons declared that '*value depends entirely upon utility*' ([1871] 1957, p. 1). He proposed this hypothesis in direct opposition to the '[p]revailing opinions [that] make labour rather than utility the origin of value' (*ibid.*, p. 1). The three trail blazers argued that a thing is valuable or commands something valuable in return not because it is produced by labor but because it is *scarce* in relation to how much people would like to have it. So price of a commodity is simply a rationing device. They maintained that people want something only because it gives them utility. According to them, classical economists had also understood that point when they had admitted that the use-value of a commodity is essential for it to have any exchange-value, but they could not build their theory on the basis of use-value because they thought utility could not be measured. Now, the challengers proposed that differential calculus provided them with a tool to overcome this limitation. Jevons argued that, although total utility derived from a commodity may not be measurable, its marginal utility is and it is the measurement at the margin that is only needed in order to work out a rigorous theory of prices based on utility. This approach quickly gained wide acceptability in the profession. Leaving aside the well-known history of the modern theory of price determination, here we concentrate on its explanation for profit/interest as an income category—the issue Sraffa was mostly concerned with.

Their explanation rests on the linear narrative that a production process has a definite beginning and end. For example, Jevons argues that: 'all employments of capital resolve themselves into the fact of time elapsing between the beginning and the end of industry' (*op. cit.*, p. 229). In his view, the single purpose of capital is to make the laborer work while the output is still awaited; thus *time* is the *essence* of capital. Now, if the laborer could begin from scratch and produce something useful in one year, then the total capital needed would be the advance of the wage goods to the laborer for a year. But if the laborer needs some implement to produce the useful commodity and it takes one year to produce that implement, then whether the implement is produced by some other worker or the laborer himself, the total capital needed for production would be wage advances for two years: one for producing the implement and the other to produce the useful good. Jevons argues that the purpose of capital is only to extend the average time of commencement from scratch to the final production of the consumption good in this manner. He, however, recognizes that: 'It is true that in modern industry we should seldom or never find the same man making the spade or plough, and afterwards using the implement. The division of labour enables me, with much advantage, to expend a portion of my capital in purchasing the implement from someone who devotes his attention to the manufacture, and probably expends capital previously in facilitating the work'. But then he goes on to erroneously add: '*But this does not alter the principles of the matter*' (*ibid.*, pp. 226–27, emphasis added).

So, why should anyone invest more capital to extend the period of production? For example, let us suppose that it takes the laborer one year to produce 1 ton of corn on a plot of land by starting from scratch, then why would a capitalist add any implement to the production if it makes the period of production two years? The answer is that the addition of the implement must increase the total output of corn from one ton to more than two tons, which provides the source of interest on capital investment. So how is the investment of capital measured and the rate of interest on that capital investment determined? In our example, at the beginning of the production of corn the total investment is equal to the wages of labor for two years and at the time of the harvest it is zero, so on average the total investment over the two years is equal to the total wage bill for one year. Thus the formula for the average investment at any point of time can be written as $\frac{1}{2}t.w$, where t is the amount of years and w is the wage bill for a year. Jevons argues that, given w, a rise in t amounts to a rise in the average investment and it is continuously and positively related to output, that is, $x = F(t)$, $F'(t) > 0$ and $F''(t) < 0$. From here on, he reasons that the rate of interest must be $F'(t)/F(t)$, that is, '[t]he interest of capital is, in other words, *the rate of increase of the produce divided by the whole produce* ...' (*ibid.*, p. 246, original emphasis). Jevons identifies $F(t)$, the initial output with total capital investment on the grounds that if $F(t)$ is maintained during the process of extending the period of production then this could be done only if the total $F(t)$ was exhausted as wage advances.

As the reader will have noticed, Jevons measures capital by taking the simple average over the total time of investment, which amounts to assuming simple interest over the total period of time of capital investment. Jevons, however, is aware that this is strictly speaking incorrect, but he erroneously thinks that introduction of compound interest is only a matter of mathematical complication and does not change the terms of the problem: 'Thus when the whole expenditure is ultimately the same, the amount of investment is simply proportional to the time. The result would be more serious if the accumulation of compound interest during the time were taken into account; but the consideration of compound interest would render the formula very complex, and is not requisite for the purpose in view' (*ibid.*, p. 236).

Menger also looks at the production process of any good of 'lower order' (that is, consumption goods) as a long linear chain of goods of higher and higher orders (that is, intermediate and fixed capital goods) that over the periods of time convert into goods of lower order. The values, and therefore the prices, of higher order goods are 'imputed' from the prospective values and prices of the lower order goods they help to produce or convert into over a period of time. But how is this imputation done? To be able to impute values to goods of higher order one needs to first understand the notion of capital and the determination of the returns to capital or the rate of interest on capital. According to Menger, the existence of the goods of higher order and an increase in the use of goods of higher order in the production process implies lengthening the period of production. And this lengthening in the period of production is introduced by economizing individuals only because it increases the quantity of consumable goods produced: '… by making progress in the employment of goods of higher order for the satisfaction of their needs, economizing men can most assuredly increase the consumption goods available to them accordingly—but only on condition that they lengthen the periods of time over which their provident activity is to extend in the same degree that they progress to goods of higher order' (*ibid.*, p. 153). Thus, it is the lengthening of time and its relation to increase in the quantity of outputs of lower order goods that gives rise to interest on capital. Menger, however, does not specify exactly how the rate of interest is determined, although he makes some allusions to the subjective rate of discount of future consumption. Once the origin of interest is understood, Menger simply takes the rate of interest as given and argues that the total aggregate value of all the high order goods used to produce the consumption good is equal to the prospective value of the consumption good minus the rate of interest payable on the capital used to produce the consumption good.

This line of reasoning found its most advanced and sophisticated form in Böhm-Bawerk's (1884) *Capital and Interest.* Böhm-Bawerk accepts Jevons's and Menger's position that capital and changes in its quantity can be measured by the 'period of production' and the lengthening of the 'period of production', or what he called 'roundabout way of production'. He also accepts that such lengthening of the period of production is associated with an increase in output. But then he contends that this is not enough to explain why there is interest on capital. Böhm-Bawerk argues that a mere rise in physical output due to an increase in the length of production does not explain why the *value* of the physical output must always be higher than the *value* of capital and it is the difference in the *values* and not quantities that must explain the existence of interest on capital. In other words, Böhm-Bawerk maintains that the 'productivity of capital' theories fail to explain why competition does not reduce the total value of the product to the level of total value of capital used to produce the product. He provides the missing link in the argument by introducing a psychological dictum that human beings value an economic good more today than a promise of it tomorrow. In other words, there exists a positive discount for the prospective value of goods in the future. Thus, from this point of view, if a good takes five years to produce and after five years when it is finished its value is $1,000, then in its first year of production the promise of $1,000 after five years must mean less than $1,000. And therefore, the 1/5th of this commodity that is produced in the first year must mean less than $200. How much less would, of course, depend on the psychological discount rate the worker puts on future consumption. However, every year the real value of one year of production would rise but remain lower than $200. Thus, if wages are paid every year for five years to the exact amount of the value produced it will total less than $1,000. And it is this difference in value that explains interest. In other words, even if workers are paid full values of their production over the entire period of time there still would remain something for interest on capital investment. Thus the origin of interest lies in the psychological trait of human beings to discount future consumption over present. In the end, Böhm-Bawerk argues, or rather puts his faith in the proposition, that, given at a moment the total labor supply, the total capital in money terms and the condition of full employment of both labor and capital, one can arrive at the general equilibrium of the system that would simultaneously determine the rates of wages and interest as well as the 'period of production' of the technique that would be chosen as the most profitable one.

Although Böhm-Bawerk's psychological dictum is accepted almost as a truism in orthodox economic theory, the idea of discount of future consumption over present is not all that obvious. Let us suppose that an individual has an option of receiving $10,000 today or $1,000 every year for ten years. Now, if a positive rate of interest exists then it is obvious that the person would prefer $10,000 today over $1,000 per year for ten years. However, if the rate of interest is zero then the person may prefer the alternative option because it protects her from the temptation of frivolous expenditures up front and guarantees her a steady income for ten years. Some people may be even prepared to pay a small fee for saving their current income for future consumption. The point is that discounting of future consumption is obvious rational human behavior only if a positive rate of interest exists. Thus it cannot be used to explain the origin of interest.

Wicksell ([1901] 1934) closely follows Böhm-Bawerk but recognizes the complications created by compound interest in determining the value of capital by the simple average time of total capital investment. Wicksell also rejects Böhm-Bawerk's criticism of Jevons and Menger that their productivity of capital argument alone cannot explain interest income because it fails to prove that the value of capital will be necessarily lower than the value of the consumption goods it helps produce. He argues that, since their argument assumes a stationary state of equilibrium (including Böhm-Bawerk's own), the prices must remain constant before and after the marginal change in capital, thus the productivity argument is sufficient to explain the difference in values of capital and the product. He, however, argues that when a system increases its period of production it *simultaneously* increases the wage rate and thus some of the savings that were destined for deepening or increasing the period of production of capital investment get absorbed by the rise in wages. Therefore, the marginal product of labor must be less than $F'(t)/F(t)$, as calculated by Jevons and accepted by Böhm-Bawerk.

Wicksell also argues that in a competitive capitalist system it is a logical requirement that the production function must be linear and homogeneous, otherwise accounting for the total income produced and its distribution according to the marginal productivities of factors of production would not match (Euler's theorem). He then wanted to prove that, in a competitive capitalist system, an increase in the amount of capital (or its value given constant prices) is necessarily related to an increase in the amount of product (or the value of product given constant prices).

In other words, he wanted to prove that the marginal productivity of capital is positive. In this context, in his review of Dr. Gustaf Akerman's *Realkapital und Kapitalzins* written in 1923, Wicksell (1934) realized that this proposition can be proved only on the *assumption* that an increase in wages always brings an increase in the period of production, given that all the functions are continuous. Now, this is the consequence of the Jevons–Böhm-Bawerk theory. But Wicksell (1934, Appendix 2) shows that to prove the presupposition of their theory one needs to assume the consequence of the presupposition. In other words, the whole argument goes in a circle. Wicksell shows that if this *assumption* is not maintained then it cannot *a priori* be ruled out that changes in wages and changes in period of production can have opposite signs. Let us suppose that output 'p' is a function of capital 't', that is, period of production, and 'h', the number of current labor, that is, $p=f(t, h)$. Moreover, $p=w+t(dp/dt)$; where w is the total wage bill given h and dp/dt is the marginal productivity of capital, which must be equal to the rate of interest in equilibrium. Taking h to be fixed, we can write the production function as $p=f(t)$, where $f'(t)>0$ and $f''(t)<0$. Now, $d(w/p)/dt=p(dw/dt)-w(dp/dt)$. Since $w=p-t(dp/dt)$, we have $dw/dt=-t(d_2p/dt^2)$. Therefore, $d(w/p)/dt=-pt(d_2p/dt^2)+t(dp/dt)^2-p(dp/dt)$. Clearly the first two terms on the right hand side of the equation are positive but the last term is negative. Hence the sign of $d(w/p)/dt$ cannot be determined *a priori* unless more information about the production function is available. In other words, a logical possibility of $d(w/p)/dt<0$ cannot be ruled out. From this it follows that wages and the period of production are not uniquely determined by each other, and that wages may have two or more values for the same value of capital and *vice versa*. Although Wicksell's original argument was made in the context of Akerman's case of fixed capital and its life-time, Uhr (1962) translated it into the case of pure circulating capital and called this result the *Wicksell effect*.

Irving Fisher (1907) had also pointed out a similar problem with Böhm-Bawerk's theory of interest. He argued that his idea of the *average* 'period of production' as a measure of capital suffered from an index number problem. How is one to 'average' the period of production of, say, cloth and iron, even if one knew that the average periods of production for cloth and iron are 2 and 5 years, respectively? What weight must be attached to the two numbers in averaging them? If the weights are attached according to the value of the total amount consumed annually then the rate of interest (as part of the values of the two items) is enmeshed in the calculation of the average period of production. Fisher went on to show (in an appendix) that it would be a mistake to think that one could associate a one-to-one relationship between choice of technique and the rate of interest. He put forward an example in which technique 1 represents a payoff of $5 after 10 years and $100 after hundred years of an application of labor whereas technique 2 issues a single return of $15 after twenty-five years of an application of labor. In this case, it turns out that, 'if the rate of interest is 5%, the $15 alternative will be preferable, whereas if the rate of interest is either 1% or 25%, the other alternative will be chosen' (*ibid.*, p. 353).

J.B. Clark ([1899] 1965) bucks the trend and rejects the idea of measuring capital in terms of 'time'. He argues that in a stationary state which is continuously reproducing itself there is no time-gap between the investment of social capital and the production of consumption goods. He conceptually distinguishes between capital goods and 'capital'. According to him, capital is a value (money-value) that endures during production while capital goods perish. In other words, although the particular physical capital goods are used up in the process of production, at the same time the system is continuously reproducing other capital goods to replace them, and therefore the value of capital initially invested endures through production rather than being used up. Now, in a stationary state one would presume that the system must be reproducing exactly the same capital goods in exactly the same amounts as it is using them up in the process of production—that is, the system is in circular motion. But Clark uses the idea of continuous production and *reproduction* of capital goods to distinguish 'capital' from capital goods. He first uses the metaphor of individual living organisms and the generalization of the notion of 'life' or the particular drops of water in a river and the notion of 'river' itself. Clark argues that, in the same way as individual lives come and go and the drops of water in a river flow by but life and river endure, 'capital' endures in relation to physical capital goods. But this analogy is not apt. In the case of 'life' or 'river', neither 'life' nor 'river' can have a *measure* separately from concrete living organisms or flowing water. In the case of

Clark's abstract notion, 'capital' can be *measured* by the monetary value of the capital goods. The problem is that, if a sum of money is 'capital', then how can it have productivity or marginal productivity that explains the rate of interest?

That is why, after liberating 'capital' from physical capital goods, Clark takes a flight in the deep world of metaphysics and imbues his abstract notion with a *magical power*. 'Capital' is not a generalization but it is a 'real thing', Clark maintains, which has a capacity to change its shape and form in all sorts of ways. In other words, capital is something like the *atma* of Hindu philosophy that never dies but transmigrates (or 'transmutates', in Clark's terminology) from one body to another. Once this magical power is granted to 'capital', it is just a short step for Clark to argue that, with every change in the ratio of total value of capital to total labor employed (leaving land aside), the shape and form of the physical capital changes to ensure full employment of both capital and labor, that is, there is always an appropriate change in the technique of production. When 'capital' per unit of labor rises then every unit of 'capital' has to work with less units of labor, which reduces the average productivity of capital; from this Clark concluded that with every addition of capital the marginal product added to total output would decline. Simultaneously, each unit of labor gets more 'capital' to work with, which increases labor's average productivity and therefore its marginal productivity.[3] In equilibrium when total 'capital' and total labor are both fully employed, their respective marginal productivities determine the equilibrium rate of interest and the wages that exhaust the total value of the net product.

Both in the Jevonsian and the Clarkian traditions the marginal productivity of capital, which is supposed to determine the equilibrium interest

[3] 'It is with the latter test that we are immediately concerned; and what we have been careful to guard against is the notion that, at any one time, there is a difference between the products of different units of labor, as such. Each of them, with its share of the capital, produces one-half of the whole present output of the industry; but a half of the present output is less than was the whole output, when only one man was working with the aid of the entire capital. This reduction measures the product of one-half of the capital, as used by one unit of labor. On the other hand, the whole product, now that the two units of labor are working, is greater than was the whole product with one working; and this addition to the product is due solely to an accession of labor. The amount of the addition measures the product of that labor and of all labor under the present changed conditions' (Clark 1907, pp. 325–26).

rate, is associated with the condition of stationary state. In other words, the idea of change is inextricably associated with the idea of no-change, which introduces the fundamental contradiction in their arguments. All the 'marginal method' does is to dodge the problem rather than solve it. In the Jevonsian tradition the marginal change in capital is measured on the continuous scale of time, which ignores its relation to physical techniques of production, but it still has to ignore the effect of the changes in the rates of interest and wages on prices. In the Clarkian tradition the marginal change in 'capital' is associated with an implicit change in technique of production but its impact on prices is ignored. However, once the *real* change is allowed then the comparison between 'before' and 'after' the change can only be between *two* stationary states (leaving aside the dynamic problem of crossing from one stationary state to another) and not within the same stationary state.

Sraffa pointedly refers to this problem when in the 'Preface' to his book he declares: 'In a system in which, day after day, production continued unchanged in those respects, the marginal product of a factor (or alternatively the marginal cost of a product) would not merely be hard to find—it just would not be there to be found.' And then he goes on to say: 'It is, however, a peculiar feature of the set of propositions now published that, although they do not enter into any discussion of the marginal theory of value and distribution, they have nevertheless been designed to serve as a basis of a critique of that theory' (Sraffa 1960, pp. v–vi).

2

Before a New Beginning

Money Matters

L'Inflazione Monetaria in Italia durante e dopo la guerra[1] was the first major written work by Sraffa on economic matters. This was written in 1920, when Sraffa was barely twenty two years old,[2] as his dissertation for the law degree he obtained from the University of Turin. It was written in Italian and was 64 pages long in typed scripts. A highly noteworthy feature of this dissertation is the author's style of writing. It is written with such authority as befits the world masters of the subject—a feature that remains constant in all his subsequent writings. This is even more remarkable given the fact that Sraffa, by all accounts, was never an outstanding student[3] and that economics was not his major area of study.

[1] An English translation of it by Wendy Harcourt and Claudio Sardoni titled 'Monetary inflation in Italy during and after the war' was published in *Cambridge Journal of Economics*, 1993, pp. 7–26.

[2] Sraffa was born on August 5, 1898 in Turin.

[3] See Naldi (2001) for a detailed account of Sraffa's early life and student career. Luigi Pasinetti (1998) recalls: 'One may well ask how, and where, Sraffa received his education as an economist. To those who were asking him questions on this topic, Sraffa always used to answer in a dismissive way, especially with reference to the time spent at the university. He never gave any impression of valuing in any way his university years' (p. 368).

A. Sinha, *A Revolution in Economic Theory*,
DOI 10.1007/978-3-319-30616-2_2

The dissertation, however, was well appreciated and was awarded the distinction of appearing as an official publication of the University of Turin. Marcello de Cecco, in his 'Introduction' to the English translation of the dissertation, reports that the 'oral tradition has it that Sraffa succeeded in convincing him [Sraffa's thesis director, the legendary Luigi Einaudi] that bringing the lira back to pre-war gold parity was wrong' (1993, p. 1).

The dissertation was a timely intervention in the debate on the Italian government's policy for dealing with the problem of inflation and the fall of the value of lira *vis-à-vis* gold during the war. Apparently a majority opinion in Italy was that the state must follow a policy of revaluation of the lira to its pre-war parity with gold. The practical question that had to be decided, according to this opinion, was whether the revaluation of lira should be done rapidly or gradually over a long period of time. Sraffa argues, on the one hand, that the policy of revaluation has serious downsides. He maintains that revaluation of the lira would most likely lead to economic recession or rather 'crisis', because a contraction in the money supply would lead to a high rate of interest compounded with falling prices, leading to industrial losses due to the necessary time lag between the prices of raw materials that industries have to pay out and the prices they would receive after the sale of their products. Moreover, the real wages of labor would also rise because money wages do not rise or fall instantaneously with the rise or fall in prices. These factors would force many firms to shut down. He further maintains that the policy of gradual revaluation may be even more destructive to the economy than a rapid revaluation because the investors would wait until the deflation reaches the bottom and a long-term expectation of slow deflation may result in a long-term malaise of the economy.[4]

---

[4] Sraffa took Thomas Tooke's evidence before a meeting of the Parliamentary Committee of Inquiry on removing the privilege of the Bank of England on 10 July 1832, as support for his opinion and went on to conclude that 'I think nobody argues that it is right for governments to follow a policy of this kind, that is withdrawing at once, through a loan, all notes issued during the war. At least, I never heard this policy suggested; the damage it causes is too evident. Why, then, should we follow the method of a gradual withdrawal of the issued notes, which would produce even more serious damage?' (Sraffa [1920] 1993, pp. 22–23). It should also be noted that the resolution of Brussels International Finance Conference, which was published in 1920, had also recommended a gradual deflation, 'if and when undertaken' (see Cecco 1993).

On the other hand, Sraffa argues that the case for revaluation is moral rather than economic in nature.[5] It was argued that the state must keep its word in order to maintain its trust with the people, and as it had promised to pay a certain amount of gold in return for its notes (or those of privileged banks) before the war, it must therefore restore the pre-war parity of the lira with gold. The question of the pre-war parity of the lira with gold was not a question of justice for the note holders only but also for the lenders to the state who had lent to the state during the war at the appreciated value of the lira. The creditors, it was argued, deserved to be paid back their loans at the same value, not only for the sake of justice but also for the sake of the ability of the state to borrow in future at a reasonable rate of interest. Furthermore, the argument continued, the people who were unjustly damaged by inflation such as pensioners and other fixed income earners, salary and wage earners, bond holders and money lenders, and so on would be compensated for their losses by a policy of deflation.

On the question of justice, Sraffa's main counter-argument is that when it comes to the lenders to the state it is quite unlikely that those who hold the state's debt bonds after the war are the same people who held them at the beginning of the period of inflation. According to Sraffa, most of the people in possession of the state's debt bonds had acquired them only recently and therefore at a low value of the lira; thus restoring the value of the lira to the pre-war level would amount to a big gift to the current creditors of the state rather than restoring the injustice done to the original lenders.[6] Furthermore, the consequences of this on the state's exchequer would be rather serious as its real debt, in terms of current value of money, would increase about sevenfold at a time when the economy would be contracting and, as a consequence, its revenue would be falling. In the case of wage and salary earners, Sraffa argues that it is true

[5] 'The strongest arguments in favour of the method of restoring payments in metal to the parity before the depreciation of notes are of a moral rather than an economic nature' (Sraffa [1920] 1993, p. 21).

[6] Sraffa cites Fisher's (1920, *Stabilizing the Dollar*, New York, Macmillan) estimates, according to which 'if, in the United States, money were returned to its pre war value, those who had underwritten Liberty Loans, would receive almost twice the value they paid.' Using the same hypothesis, Sraffa estimated that the bearers of Italian Public Debt securities would gain 'more than five times they paid' (Sraffa [1920] 1993, p. 23).

that the fall in money wages may lag behind the fall in general prices but most of the workers do not get to benefit from this because the rise in real wages leads to a shutdown of factories and increase in unemployment.

After making a strong case against revaluation of the lira to its pre-war gold parity, Sraffa argues that there is nothing sacrosanct about the value of lira against gold in the pre-war period. It is as arbitrary as the value that exists today. He argues that 'The value of money is normal when forces which tend to make it change are absent' (p. 24). Thus government policy should simply aim at stabilizing prices, which establishes a new lira–gold parity. In recommending this strategy Sraffa acknowledges that such a policy would have an impact on the exchange rate of the lira with the currencies that maintain a fixed ratio of gold to notes. But given that 'foreign trade is by far the smallest part of a country's total trade, the maintenance of security is much more important in domestic trade than in foreign trade' (p. 26), therefore a policy of 'price stabilization' must be pursued.

Sraffa's dissertation is divided into five sections. The first section carefully establishes the fact that the total money supply from the eve of the outbreak of the war to the current period, that is 30 June 1920, had expanded by almost eight times. This expansion was mainly due to the increased demand for money by the state rather than due to increased demand for money for the purposes of trade. Sraffa, in Section 2, then explains how the money supply could have increased so enormously. He first explains that, in a system of competitive commercial banking where every bank can issue notes, the requirement of convertibility of notes to metals such as gold or silver creates a natural check on money supply. However, these checks did not apply in the Italian case. Instead of all banks having the power to issue notes or checks, only three banks were allowed to issue notes, and the exchange of notes was normally limited to the three banks of issue. He argues that, on the one hand, these three banks, instead of being competitive with each other, were in a close relationship and decided to increase circulation simultaneously, and, on the other hand, during the war the convertibility of notes into gold was virtually suspended.[7] Section 3 establishes the correlation between increase

[7] 'Thus, already before the war, the limit to the issue of notes deriving from the competition among different banks of issue in the same country had been removed. Afterwards, during the war, the

in money supply and price level and its effect on real wages; for example, in the case of Italy, taking 31 December 1913 as the base, the active circulation increased from 100 to 643 in April 1920 and the wholesale price index rose from 100 to 679 for the same period, and while food prices increased by 82.7% from 1914 to 1917 money wages rose by only 29.75% for the same period. Section 4 documents the historical cases of revaluation of currencies after a period of inflation and establishes a correlation between such policies and economic crises that followed.

Although the dissertation is an important contribution to the monetary policy debate in Italy after the First World War, it, nevertheless, bases its argument on the established orthodox theoretical foundations. For example, on the basis of the prevalent quantity theory of money, Sraffa argues that the *cause* of inflation in Italy during the war was the rise in money supply, which, of course, he later corroborates with empirical data that show a close correlation between the price rise and the money supply. He also seems to accept the foundations of orthodox demand and supply price theory because he suggests that a rise in real wages must lead to a fall in the demand for labor, and that the natural value of money is determined by the equilibrium of the forces of demand and supply. However, the point that we must note is that Sraffa considers inflation or deflation as a situation of *disequilibrium* but he is careful to recognize that these phenomena have a time dimension, and once time comes into picture, removal of the causes of disequilibrium does not necessarily take the system back to the original equilibrium position—the up and down movements are not along the same curve.

Sraffa's second major work was published two years later in 1922. This is mainly a work of recent Italian economic history, entitled 'The Bank Crisis in Italy'. It was written on an invitation from Keynes.[8] In this paper Sraffa describes in detail how the intermeshing of large financial and

convertibility of notes into gold was virtually suspended in all belligerent countries. As a consequence, with any external restraint now removed, producing money was left totally to arbitrary decisions of banks and the governments controlling them, a position which they did not fail to take advantage [of]' (Sraffa [1920] 1993, p. 14).

[8]Actually Keynes had invited Sraffa to write an account of the financial crisis in Italy for the *Manchester Guardian Commercial Supplement*, which Keynes was editing. The paper, however, turned out to be too long for a newspaper and therefore it was published in *The Economic Journal*. An abridged version of this paper was published a few months later in the *Manchester Guardian*

industrial interests, given the backdrop of a war economy, had created a serious financial crisis in post-war Italy. This paper attests to Sraffa's acute understanding of practical matters in the functioning of a real economy; it, however, does not have much of theoretical interest.

Theories of Value

Three years later, in 1925 Sraffa published a major paper in an Italian journal, *Annali di Economia*, in which he leaves monetary matters behind and takes up the problem of the theory of value for the first time.[9] In this paper the young Sraffa confronts the newly established orthodoxy of Marshall (1890). It should be noted that Marshall had distanced himself from the 1870s anti-classical movement by suggesting that his contribution was in the classical tradition, in the sense that it made the classical theory of value or prices more general. Marshall argues that classical economists, particularly Ricardo, had understood that the relative prices of goods depend on the demand and supply conditions in the market, although they emphasized the supply side of the equation in the long run as being more important because they assumed constant cost. In this light, Marshall's own contribution was to show that, in general, costs are variable with changes in quantity and therefore both supply and demand play their roles in determining prices, as two blades of a pair of scissors play their roles in cutting cloth. The young Sraffa leaves the demand side of the equation of Marshall's theory as unproblematic—'[t]he "demand function" is based on an elementary and natural hypothesis, that of decreasing utility' (Sraffa [1925] 1998, p. 325)—and concentrates his attack on the notion of variability of costs in his supply function.

Commercial Supplement, which came to the notice of Mussolini and caused Sraffa some considerable political problems.

[9] It is not clear what prompted Sraffa to switch his interest. Sraffa had recently been appointed to a teaching position at the University of Perugia and the preparation for his lectures might have something to do with it. Alternatively, his attendance of Cannan's lectures at the London School of Economics on the history of political economy during 1921–22 might have influenced his interest in such matters. The third possibility is that his interest in fundamental theoretical matters could have been aroused by his friendship with Antonio Gramsci and others of his circle. (see Naldi 2000, for more details on this matter.)

Before we take up Sraffa's argument against Marshall's supply function, it is important to mention his understanding of the classical theory—the representative of which for him is Ricardo. He points out that the idea of increasing and diminishing returns is there in the classical theory, but they appear in contexts other than those of value or price determination, which is the context of resource allocation in a static equilibrium framework: diminishing returns appear in the context of distribution of income and increasing returns appear in the context of production or economic growth in general. Both these contexts deal with aggregate outputs and are separated in theory from the context of relative price determination of commodities. In the context of relative price determination, it is simply assumed that the causes of increasing or decreasing returns are absent, and therefore constant costs prevail with respect to changes in the quantities produced by an industry: 'It can be said that all classical writers accept implicitly, as an obvious fact, that cost is independent of quantity, and they do not bother to discuss the contrary hypothesis' (*ibid.*, p. 325).

Now within Marshall's context of 'particular' or partial equilibrium in a freely competitive market, it is obvious that constant cost supply functions would make the demand blade of Marshall's scissors completely impotent in determining the price of a particular good. All demand could do is influence the quantity produced but, since cost of production was not affected by variations in quantity, its price must be determined exclusively by its cost of production. It is not clear whether Sraffa at this stage believed that the classical context of price determination (or the idea of a center of gravitation) shares Marshall's assumption of partial equilibrium or whether it was framed in a general equilibrium context. If it is accepted that the classical explanation of resource allocation is framed within the context of a general equilibrium (see Smith and Ricardo), then a problem remains: the assumption of constant cost in a general equilibrium framework would, in general cases, require an additional assumption of no substitution possibility in the techniques of production. It remains an open question whether Sraffa, at this time, held that the assumption of no substitution possibility in the techniques of production was part of the classical theory. However, he clearly maintains that 'it is difficult to find an industry in which no possibility is left for substitution' (*ibid.*, p. 333).[10]

Sraffa first takes up the case of diminishing returns or increasing cost. He points out that the idea of increasing cost crucially depends on the idea of substitution. It depends upon the fact that at least one input remains fixed when output is increased. In other words, two things happen: (1) the proportion in which the inputs are combined to produce the output changes, and (2) the size of the industry increases. Sraffa claims that it is the first circumstance that is exclusively responsible for decreasing returns or increasing costs. The second circumstance is responsible for increasing returns or decreasing cost, which in itself does not require a change in the proportions of inputs but only requires an increase in the size of the industry. This distinction is introduced at the outset to counter the mistaken opinion, as propagated by Palgrave in his *Dictionary of Political Economy* (vol. II, p. 583), that both diminishing and increasing returns stem from the same circumstance, that is, the constancy of at least one input when output is increased.

The popular idea is that if one has a homogeneous plot of land of a certain size then in the beginning every additional small 'dose' of labor and capital on land would result in proportionately larger and larger outputs, because the given piece of land would be more thoroughly ploughed and weeded and so on. However, after a point at which the average output from the application of labor and capital reaches its optimum level, any further increase in the dose of capital and labor would lead to a fall in the average output per dose. Sraffa counters this argument by arguing that this unreasonably assumes that the farmer must cultivate the whole plot of land even if it is clearly not in his interest. Instead of cultivating the whole plot of land, a reasonable farmer would cultivate only a part of the

[10] Could classical economists take wages *given* from outside and at the same time maintain a general equilibrium of supplies and effectual demands for all the commodities? If yes, then how could it be denied that if the labor market is not in equilibrium at the *given* wages then it might affect the wages that could lead to substitution of techniques in use? Even if we argue that classical economists assumed that wages were at the 'subsistence' level (a difficult argument to maintain in the face of contrary evidence), the possibility of a rise in wages due to excess demand for labor cannot be denied. Hollander (1973, 1979, 1992) has made such arguments consistently to argue that classical economists did not take wages *given* from outside. See Sinha (2010a) for my alternative position on this issue.

land that optimally combines with the first dose of capital and labor and he will extend the output by increasing cultivation on additional parts of the land in a similar way until the whole plot of land is covered by optimal combination of land, labor and capital. Thus up to this point, the marginal and the average product of every dose of capital and labor would be equal and constant. And it is only after this point is reached that diminishing returns would begin to operate due to the constancy of the plot of land.[11] In other words, increasing returns due to a fixed factor assumes that getting rid of the factor is either impossible or requires cost; that is, the fixed factor has negative marginal productivity throughout the range of increasing returns on the doses of variable factors.

After differentiating the causes of diminishing and increasing returns, Sraffa wonders how diminishing returns in production turn out to be so similar to diminishing utility in consumption? His answer to this question is that both of them are rooted in the same human nature—diminishing returns in production is not a technical factor but rather a rational human arrangement of successive production programs in a similar way as diminishing utility is a rational human arrangement of successive consumption programs. Now, we already know that if the fixed factor can be reduced in size without cost then the producer would combine the doses of capital and labor with land in optimum proportion until the limit of fixed land is reached. After that every additional dose of labor and capital requires a non-optimum combination of the three factors. Sraffa argues that this arrangement of successive decline of marginal and average output is made by the producer because it is in his advantage to choose successive techniques in this way. For example, after arriving at the optimum combination for the total land, if the farmer has additional capital to invest, he will have various different uses for it (given the substitution possibilities) and from those various uses the farmer would choose the use that gives him the maximum output. If the farmer has still more capital to invest, he will again have various uses of this capital and he will again choose the use that gives him the maximum output but the additional output will be less than the previous addition simply because

[11] In his 'Lecture Notes of 1928–31' Sraffa acknowledges Turgot's (1768) 'Observation on the memoir by Monsieur de Saint-Péravy in favour of the indirect tax' for this idea.

the more productive use is associated with the previous combination, which is no longer available. The whole scheme is similar to Menger's description of the various uses of a consumption good arranged by the consumer in order of declining importance of needs. Thus the curve of diminishing returns, according to Sraffa, is simply a descriptive curve in the same sense as the arrangement of lands with declining fertility in the case of Ricardo's extensive rent, and not a functional curve as argued by Wicksteed (1914). This also explains, Sraffa argues, why Marshall's ([1890] 1949) argument that the order of fertility of land could change with increase in intensity of cultivation is incorrect. Marshall argues that in a given equilibrium situation when the marginal product of a dose of capital is equal on two pieces of land then the land with higher average fertility should be reckoned more fertile. However, with increases in the intensity of cultivation the average productivity of this piece of land may fall below the other piece and therefore become less fertile. Sraffa's argument shows that this cannot happen because the fertility of lands must be arranged by taking the optimum combinations of factors on each piece of land and therefore an increase in intensity of cultivation cannot change it.[12]

After determining the essential character of diminishing returns, 'in that diminishing returns derives from it being desirable and generally possible to arrange the efficiency of the doses of the factors of production and the different ways of using them in descending order—an order that is determined exactly' (*ibid.*, p. 340), Sraffa takes up the case of its use in Marshall's derivation of the supply curve of a particular good. Marshall argues that one can consider the whole industry as a single firm that employs the constant factor. In this case, the marginal revenue product

[12] It should be noted that Sraffa later realized that the order of fertility of land cannot be arranged independently of the rate of profits or wages. For example, if two plots of lands, not of the same size, are so chosen that they produce identical products in equal quantities but use different techniques, that is, a different combination of capital-goods, then a change in the rate of profits (r) would change the relative prices of the capital-goods used on the two plots of land in such a complicated manner that within certain ranges of r one set of capital-goods may be the cheaper one while for some other ranges of r the other set of capital-goods may become the cheaper one. In this case, since fertility of land can be determined only on the basis of the values of the output against the values of the total capital invested per unit of land, the relative fertilities of the two lands may switch with changes in the rate of profits (see D3/12/25: 1–2, dated 13 November 1942).

curve of the firm would also represent the supply curve of the industry. This procedure amounts to assuming that the industry supply curve can be derived by horizontally adding the marginal revenue product curves of all the firms in the industry, which is analogous to deriving the market demand curve of a good by horizontally adding the individual demand curves. Sraffa's objection to this is a simple one: although it may be true that a factor of production is fixed for the industry as a whole, it is not fixed for any individual firm in the industry and a firm may be free to increase, to an extent, the use of this factor and its output while lowering its private cost of production due to economies of scale, without impacting on the price of the factor. Although this is possible for a firm it is not possible for all the firms at the same time; and therefore,'the sum of a series of individual curves of this kind is absurd, since each one of them is valid only on condition that the production of the other individuals remain unchanged' (*ibid.*, p. 343). Thus the upward sloping Marshallian supply curve can only be drawn under the condition that the number of firms is fixed and their share in the constant factor is fixed too. This, of course, is too restrictive a condition to be found in a freely competitive environment. In the case of a factor being fixed for a small group of products then an intensive use of the factor by one industry would equally affect the cost conditions of all the goods in the group because the condition of equilibrium requires that the marginal value product of the constant factor must be equal for all the goods. Thus this violates the *ceteris paribus* assumption. Again, in the case of a fixed factor that is used by a large number of products, a small increase in the use of that factor by one industry[13] should not affect the cost conditions of the other goods, but then it will not affect the cost condition of the good in consideration either, so it will be produced under the constant cost condition.

In the case of increasing returns or decreasing costs, Sraffa at the outset distinguishes two sets of possible causes for this phenomenon. The first set contains two causes: the first one is the case of being able to utilize better methods of production due to greater scope for the division of labor within the firm due to an increase in the size of the firm. Thus the

[13] It should be noted that a large increase in output by any industry would always destroy the *ceteris paribus* condition. Thus Marshallian supply curves can only be contemplated for small changes in supply in the neighborhood of the equilibrium point.

marginal cost falls, causing the average cost to fall along with it. In this case, although the scale of the firm changes, the proportion in which the factors are combined may remain the same. The other cause happens to be the falling overhead costs. If the total overhead cost is fixed, or at least does not rise in proportion to the rise in output, then this would lead to a fall in the average cost, leaving the marginal cost untouched. Both of these causes, however, must be ruled out in the Marshallian context, because these causes of increasing returns would lead to the firm that takes the lead in increasing its output turning into a monopolist, which violates the assumption of a competitive market.

The one cause that could be applicable to the Marshallian case is given by the instance of economies of scale that is external to the firms but internal to the industry. This refers to the case in which changes in the size of the industry affect the cost conditions of individual firms. Thus equilibrium of the individual firms at their lowest U-shaped cost curves is conditional to the total output of the industry—if new firms come in then the cost conditions of all the firms in the industry change and for every new level of industrial output a new equilibrium for the firms would be established. By plotting industrial output on the horizontal axis and the corresponding minimum average costs of firms (assuming all firms have the same cost conditions) one can draw an industry supply curve, which would be downward sloping. However, this supply curve is not the marginal cost curve but rather the average cost curve of the industry and its marginal cost will always be below it. Yet again, such situations are almost non-existent in the real world. Most of the external economies due to 'general progress of industrial environment' or 'improvement of means of communications and transportation' and so on affect other industries in the same manner, thus destroying the assumption of 'particular equilibrium'. It is almost unheard of that a small increase in the output of an industry could create such external economies of scale that it would rebound back on its cost by lowering it, but leave other industries untouched.

In the case of constant returns, Sraffa argues that economists who take the variability of costs as the general case have a tendency to attribute constant returns to the balance of forces between the causes of decreasing and increasing returns, and they suppose that such circumstances could only be rare. Sraffa, on the other hand, thinks that he has now shown that the circumstances that could give rise to either decreasing or increasing returns within a Marshallian framework are so remote that it is more meaningful to simply assume that these forces are absent and therefore constant returns prevail, as was the position of Ricardo.[14]

After establishing the fact that the conditions required for the Marshallian theory of price to be coherent are almost non-existent, Sraffa, in his better-known 1926 paper, goes on to argue that there are two alternative routes that one could follow. One route is to abandon the notion of 'particular' equilibrium and follow the well-known route of general or 'simultaneous' equilibrium under the competitive conditions established by Walras and Pareto. He rejects this line on the grounds that '[its] complexity, however, prevents it from bearing fruit, at least in the present state of our knowledge, which does not permit of even much simpler schemata being applied to the study of real condition' (1926, p. 541). The other possible route, which Sraffa follows in this paper, is to keep the idea of 'particular' equilibrium and jettison the condition of free competition.

In the 1926 paper Sraffa proposes to define an industry as made up of several small firms that produce *almost* identical or *slightly* differentiated goods such that the consumers can identify the producer. The consumers are supposed to have a certain amount of loyalty towards one firm or the other in the sense that they are willing to pay something extra for the product of their favorite firm as opposed to its competitors'. Therefore,

[14] Sraffa's paper was also an intervention in the controversy between Clapham (1922) and Pigou (1922), in which Clapham argues that in reality it is hard to characterize any industry as a 'decreasing', 'constant' or 'increasing' returns industry. Pigou's defence is that this is due to a lack of adequate statistical research work rather than the weakness of the theoretical criteria of classifying industries. Sraffa's intervention clearly sides with Clapham. In this context, he goes on to add that the theoretical criteria for classifying industries in one of three boxes are rather arbitrary. For example, if one defines an industry very broadly as 'agricultural' then there is a good chance that some factors could be found to be fixed for this industry and therefore it will be classified as a 'diminishing returns' industry. However, if an industry is narrowly defined as 'tomato' then there is a good chance that no factor could be found to be fixed for this industry and therefore it will be classified as an 'increasing returns' industry. Similarly, an industry could be characterized as a 'diminishing returns' industry if one takes a short-run point of view, but the same industry could be characterized as an 'increasing returns' industry if one takes a long-run point of view.

each firm faces a downward sloping demand curve for its product, similar to that of a monopolist.

Now, if we start with the situation that all firms sell at prices equal to their average cost then it is in the interest of a firm to raise its price, because by doing so it can make some positive profit. (Sraffa apparently assumes that the downward sloping demand curve of the firm cuts through the U-shaped average cost curve of the firm.) Since this is the case with all the firms, they all will in turn raise their prices.[15] Thus as prices rise for all the firms, the individual firm wins back the customers that it had lost to its rivals due to the relative price rise, but still all the firms lose some customers who fall out of the market due to a general price rise. Thus, contrary to Edgeworth's (1925) contention, this process would reach a limit because the market for every firm shrinks with every rise in price and therefore a point will be reached when any further increase in price by a firm would amount to a larger fall in total revenue due to shrinkage of its market than the fall in its total cost.[16] Sraffa acknowledges that this equilibrium of the industry may not be at a single price because the cost conditions as well as consumers' loyalties may not be identical for all the firms. In the case of these conditions being identical, however, Sraffa contends that in this case a uniform equilibrium price will be reached, which would be identical to the solution for a single monopoly case.[17]

---

[15] Sraffa, however, acknowledges that a general rise in price may affect the demand and supply conditions of a firm in such a way that it could be advantageous for a firm to cut its price rather than raise it. But he discounts this possibility on the grounds that 'it involves great elasticity in the demand for the products of an individual business and rapidly diminishing costs for it—that is to say, a state of things the almost inevitable and speedy result of which is complete monopolisation, and which, therefore, is not likely to be found in a trade operated normally by a number of independent firms' (pp. 547–8). Secondly, when there are possibilities of increasing profits by either raising or lowering the price, the forces (including psychological and sociological ones) operating on the side of raising prices are usually stronger than the forces operating on lowering prices.

[16] Sraffa does not contemplates the entrance of new firms in the market mainly on the grounds of high entrance cost and low profit margin in such monopolistic markets.

[17] In his fellowship dissertation written between October 1928 and December 1929, Richard Kahn—a student and friend of Sraffa—criticizes Sraffa's conclusion. He argues that under 'polypoly' or oligopoly conditions the equilibrium price must be below the monopoly price solution (see Marcuzzo 2001 for details). Dardi (2001) has argued that Sraffa's conclusion was not necessarily wrong, although it needed explicit assumptions regarding the players' strategies in an infinitely repeated game.

This paper spawned a literature on 'imperfect' or 'monopolistic' competition and brought Sraffa into international reckoning as a rising star.[18] Interestingly, Sraffa did not take any further interest in this line of research. Cristina Marcuzzo (2001) argues that Sraffa later realized that advertising expenses that a firm must incur to coax away a customer from another firm cannot be included in its cost curve, because the advertising expenditure depends on the price at which the firm wants to sell its goods. It is therefore designed to affect the demand, which makes demand dependent on the firm's cost. Thus in such monopolistic markets he cannot keep the firm's demand curves independent of their supply curves, as he had done in his paper.

Marco Dardi (2001), in his incisive comment on Marcuzzo (2001), argues that it was not the problem of entanglement of demand with supply as such that necessarily caused Sraffa to abandon this line of research. According to Dardi, the problem of advertising cost revealed to Sraffa that there was no way of *minimizing* the subjective or psychological aspect of the agents in analyzing the market phenomena. Now, as we shall see, the idea of taking psychology out of economic theory became important to Sraffa. However, I have found no evidence that lends support to Dardi's interpretation that this was already happening in 1926. As I have mentioned above, in his 1925 paper Sraffa explicitly acknowledges that '[t]he "demand function" is based on an elementary and natural hypothesis, that of decreasing utility' and in his 1926 paper he gives no allusion to a movement away from this position—both the Marshallian demand curves and the firm's profit maximizing behavior remain the building blocks of the model. As a matter of fact, the 1926 paper may be an attempt to rescue the partial or 'particular' equilibrium analysis from the problem of entangling demand with supply under the assumption of perfect competition. Furthermore, the idea of minimizing the subjective element or, as Dardi puts it, 'only a small part from subjective, utilitarian or other sorts of motivation' (2001, p. 134) does not make sense. How does one *measure* the 'smallness' of this subjective part? As we shall see,

[18] Commenting on Sraffa's 1926 paper, Schumpeter (1954, p. 1047, fn. 54) goes on to add, 'But the main ideas, critical and constructive, had appeared a year before: "Sulle relazioni fracosto e quantita prodotta," *Annali di Economia*, 1925, which shows Sraffa's starting points and the nature of his brilliantly original performance much better than does the English article.'

with Sraffa it is quite clear: either human psychology enters or it does not enter—one cannot lock up a prisoner and leave the back door open at the same time.

Dardi, however, may be correct to the extent that during the controversy with Kahn and Shove (see Marcuzzo 2001) in the late 1920s and early 1930s, Sraffa came to the conclusion that there was no future for this line of enquiry for him because of the psychological factor that could not be removed from the analysis. But then we are running ahead of our story. At this stage, we should note that Sraffa remains completely within the orthodox thinking in his 1926 paper. The law of demand is beyond question, the role of increasing and decreasing returns is not repudiated, and the notions of causation and equilibrium are still the central aspects of the theoretical construct: 'What is important is to ascertain how the various forces at work can be grouped in the most homogeneous manner, so that the influence of each of them on the equilibrium resulting from their opposition may be more readily estimated' (p. 544).

The Turning Point

We find a significant movement away from Sraffa's position of 1925–26 in the first rough draft of his lectures on the modern theory of value that he was preparing to deliver at Cambridge. This was written in the summer of 1927, titled in Sraffa's hand, 'Notes: London, Summer 1927 (Physical real cost etc.)'. This is a hand-written long draft of about 70 pages with a few pages now missing. On my inspection, it appears to have been written in a few successive sittings over a brief period of time. Here he first draws a distinction between the old classical theory of value and the modern one. According to Sraffa, the two theories of value are fundamentally different (and not just because one assumes constant returns and the other does not within a partial equilibrium framework); and this is because they are designed to answer different questions.

Sraffa argues that classical economics was mainly interested in the question of national wealth, that is,'how to increase the national wealth' (D3/12/3:13) or the question of distribution of aggregate income to various factors, that is, 'how to change its distribution, or how to justify the present distribution' (*ibid.*). These are obvious references to Adam Smith and David Ricardo. He argues that in this context classical economists were mainly concerned with aggregate income and only secondarily concerned with the question of relative values of individual commodities. This leads them to answer questions such as: how to measure wealth? or what is the *ultimate cause* of value? Given these questions, one could argue that the answers— 'labor is the ultimate measure of value' or 'labor is the ultimate cause of value'—were satisfactory because they were able to explain why the wealth of a nation could increase by putting more 'productive' labor to work as opposed to 'unproductive' labor or, in the case of Ricardo, why the rate of profit must fall and rent rise if the labor time required to produce 'corn' (where 'corn' represents all the commodities in aggregate) rises. On the other hand, these explanations were not particularly successful in explaining the price ratios of the individual commodities produced.

One methodological point Sraffa seems to underline in this context is that such theories are rooted in the notion of 'ultimate' or 'essential' cause as opposed to 'mechanical cause':

> If we are inquiring into the general problem of the causes of value, it is no use for us to argue that the value of bread is determined by the price of corn and by the money wages of bakers, that the price of corn is determined by the money wages of labourers and by the price of agricultural implements, that the money wages of labourers depend upon the prices of food stuffs, and so on ad infinitum—this would be a perfectly futile way of reasoning in a circle. On this general problem we must find some ultimate standard, independent from the variables we are considering, such {as}utility or disutility or labour (D3/12/3: 17). {There is a large ? drawn in pencil in the margin against the last sentence. Since the note is written in ink, the pencil mark clearly shows a later reaction. I shall come back to this interesting marginal 'question mark' in the course of our discussion.}

The modern theory, on the other hand, according to Sraffa, is designed to answer such questions as: why are carrots 2d./kilo? To answer such questions the modern theory (for which the main reference is Marshall) has developed a mechanism which rests on the notions of equilibrium and mechanical causation. This distinction, Sraffa argues, shows the movement of economic theory from philosophical to technical, which he thinks has been the usual course of development of sciences. Furthermore, he contends that the primary questions that interested classical economists were highly political, and therefore ideological, in nature; whereas the movement from philosophical to technical represented a similar mutation of political economy from political to apolitical. This, Sraffa thinks, was one major reason why the modern theory almost immediately received wide acceptance, whereas its precursors had fallen flat. According to Sraffa, the politics of the Ricardian theory was turning out to be highly uncomfortable for the powers that be, because it was lending support to socialist ideas, including Marx's, and so a politically neutered economics was most welcome:

> But it is a fact that while classical economists were inquiring into the 'prime cause' and the 'ultimate cause' of value, the modern attitude is largely to ignore those questions: not that they have been solved, nor that they have been proved to be insoluble (although some assumptions of this sort lies more or less vaguely in the back of the mind of many economists) but simply they are ignored, and the main system of modern economic thought proceeds to analyse the ways in which change takes place, without being hindered by the fact that little is known of the ultimate causes of change.
>
> Two sets of causes have contributed to bring about this change. In the first place the general progress of economics as a science, with its consequent shifting from the consideration of broad philosophical questions to the technical analysis of the mechanism through which economic equilibrium is reached. In the second place, the change in the practical issues which have confronted the economists; the influence of the latter on theories which are supposed to be abstract and without any practical application is interesting.
>
> The labour theory of value was devised by Ricardo as a stick to beat landlords (rent does not enter into cost of production). But later, having been adopted by Marx to beat the capitalists, it was necessary for defenders of the present system to devise a new theory. The utility theory of value. (D3/12/3: 13–15)

Sraffa thinks that the main defects of modern economics, however, stem from its inability to completely break from classical economics. For example, it imports the concepts of diminishing and increasing returns from classical economics, which the classicists had devised for their analysis of aggregate production and distribution, and applies it to a completely different context of resource allocation and relative price determination. Furthermore, the classical notion of 'ultimate cause' still lingers on in the debates on 'whether cost, or utility, or both (and which {is} predominant) determine value' (D3/12/3: 5). As we have seen, the 1925 paper extensively deals with the above-mentioned first defect and it is again taken up in the final draft of the lectures written in 1928. In this brief sketch, however, Sraffa concentrates on the question: could modern economics also claim to rest on the notion of 'ultimate cause'?

The marginal utility of a thing must be measured by the utility of the alternatives forgone. For example, the marginal utility of the first slice of bread may be infinite to me but still I would not pay all my money for it as long as potatoes were available for a few cents. But such marginal utilities could be measured only under the partial equilibrium framework in which the marginal utility of money can be taken as fixed and so the money price of the alternative forgone could be considered as the measure of the marginal utility of the commodity bought. But this requires equilibrium in all other markets and so prices of all other goods to be fixed. This sort of measure of marginal utility is, by definition, dependent on the prices of other commodities and therefore can in no sense be considered the 'ultimate' cause or standard of value: 'if we accepted this sort of utility as an ultimate standard we would reason in a circle, explaining the utility of A with the utility of B, the utility of B with the utility of C, etc: worse than that, as of course the utility of B (being the rejected alternative, on the given scale of prices) being smaller than the utility of A, that of C smaller than that of B, etc., we would ultimately by successive degradations reach a commodity whose utility is practically zero, and this, through the chain of equivalences, would be equal to utility of A!' (D3/12/3:19).[19] The same argument follows for the measure of real cost as marginal disutility of work is measured in terms of alternatives to

[19] It should be noted that Sraffa's position on Marshallian demand has also significantly changed since the publication of the 1925–26 papers. In this piece he favors the idea of demand curves as empirical curves and attacks the explanation of demand curves as caused by 'utility' behind it. Soon after (see D3/12/7: 68) he also comes to the conclusion that the idea of constancy of marginal utility of money in the Marshallian framework implies that all demand curves are shaped like rectangular hyperbolas, that is, they have unit elasticity throughout.

which the labor could be put. The root of the problem lies in the availability of substitutes.

At this stage, Sraffa also examines the classical notion of 'labor' as the ultimate cause or the standard of value. Now 'labor' can be interpreted in two ways: (i) as the psychological or subjective disutility experienced by the worker or (ii) as a real and objective cost. The first interpretation of 'labor' cannot stand the test, as explained above, because the marginal disutility of labor must be measured by the value of the substitute not produced. But the second definition does not fare any better either. One way to 'objectivize' labor would be to reduce it to real items of consumption (or subsistence) of the worker. But if there are substitutes available for consumption (or the worker can consume various combinations of the same goods) then again there is no way of reducing 'labor' to some ultimate cause or standard. This leads Sraffa to comment:

> It should be remarked that if this difficulty (of no substitutes) were overcome and an absolutely necessary commodity found, the difficulty of reducing to a common measure the various things entering into real cost would solve by itself. (D3/12/3: 44)

After this, Sraffa moves on to a consideration of atomistic methodology within the partial equilibrium framework. He traces a continuous weakening of atomism within this tradition. He points out that the concepts of utility and disutility, which are rooted in the individual's psychology, are increasingly giving way to collective entities that are supposed to determine the individual. For example, as explained above, an individual's marginal utility from one good is dependent on the prices of all other goods, that is, the consumption of the collective. Similarly, Marshall's 'external economies' and Pigou's 'negative externalities' have made it clear that the market supply curves cannot be drawn by simply horizontally adding the individual supply curves—the individual supply curves are determined by the collective curve:

> In the individualist scheme it is the individual curve that entirely determines the collective: in the social, it is all the other way round, the collective determines the individual (certainly the individual cannot determine the

collective, as to all collective purposes it is only a point, that of equality of marg{inal}& average costs) or at least they are interdependent. The old scheme was of building up the collective from the individuals: the new is of deduce the individual from the collective.

Thus utility and disutility, as quantities that have their origin (are located) in the psychology (conscience) of the individual are being practically (gradually) expelled from the field of the determination of the value of single commodities. As to utility, it can no more be regarded as a function of the amount of one commodity possessed by the individual: it strictly depends upon amount collectively consumed. The individual utility curve is no more the cause of the collective demand curve; they mutually affect each other, but the influence of individual utility is the least important, nearly negligible. In fact, the collective curve has always been much more dependent upon inequality of income than differences in utility: the 'social' development has further restricted its influence. (Unless a new, absurd, conception of 'social utility' is invented!). As to supply curves, the more precise definition of the conditions appropriate to particular equilibria, has already entirely divorced them from disutility. When production of one article is varied, it is not a [corresponding] variation in marginal disutility for any individual that causes a change in supply price (V. Edgeworth's definition of ultimate standard of value): it is money costs that change, and they change in individual firms, not because their individual production changes (although it may change) but because the collective has changed. (D3/12/3: 55–57)

This, however, does not mean that the methodology of atomism and the idea of utility/disutility as the ultimate cause of value can be completely discarded. They may exist within a general equilibrium framework. For example, within the partial equilibrium framework the prices of factors of production must be taken as fixed from outside because, if a change in the quantity supplied of a product causes prices of factors to change then it in turn would affect the demand for the commodity and therefore, the demand for the commodity cannot be taken as independent from its supply. But in a general equilibrium framework, it could be argued that the prices of the factors of production are ultimately determined by utility/disutility of individuals and therefore, prices of commodities are ultimately, however indirectly, determined by the utility/ disutility of individuals.

In this context, Sraffa raises the problem of measurement of utility. Within the partial equilibrium framework, money could be used to measure utility; but in a general equilibrium framework this measure is not available to us. Sraffa thinks that within the general equilibrium framework we have no measure by which to apprehend utility: 'we have no direct way of apprehending it {utility}, of learning its existence: we have got its notion from an absolute hedonistic psychology, and on the collapse of the latter, we have simply kept it standing as an explanatory hypothesis, the explanation of demand price' (D3/12/3: 67). This leads him to conclude that 'Pareto himself (though personally not giving up the belief in utility) has found it necessary to make his general system independent of utility and base it on empirical indifference (i.e. demand) curves' (*ibid.*: 68). Thus Sraffa wonders whether the general equilibrium framework could be legitimately used to get rid of the notion of 'ultimate standard' altogether: 'It {Pareto's doctrine} surely is mainly concerned with the mechanism through which equilibrium is reached, and is not in quest of an ultimate standard. But on the other hand, could it be denied that it may legitimately be used in challenging the existence of any such standard?' (*ibid.*: 24).[20]

As we shall see in the next chapter, soon after writing this incomplete sketch, Sraffa moves on to explore the possibility of determining the 'cost' based theory of value by abandoning the quest for the 'ultimate cause' or

---

[20] At this stage, Sraffa seems to think that the General Equilibrium explanation of the theory of distribution is essentially correct but too complicated for practical use: 'We know that the ultimate forces which regulate the division of product of industry between factors are the same that regulate the price of hats (drawback: we are apt but forget them: use of Pareto's general equilibrium): but we also recognise that the frictions, the obstacles through which those forces have to work is {*sic*} so great, that their effect, when they reach what we may call the capillary blood-vessels of the economic body their action is so much different in degree as almost to be a difference in kind from what their action is in the main streams. The hypothesis {*sic*} the explanation of demand price on which the analysis of price fixing is based are fundamentally different from those of distribution. Certain subtle features which are essential act upon the first, may be neglected when considering the broad lines of the general equilibrium: while the dominating elements of the latter may be regarded as not affected by (and therefore not reacting) the microscopic changes of the latter' (D3/12/3: 20).

the 'ultimate standard' of value, which explains the marginal question mark in pencil in the quotation (D3/12/3: 17) on p. 42.

Garegnani (2005) has also characterized this note of Sraffa's as a 'turning point' in his theoretical position. Our readings of this note, however, differ substantially. Garegnani reads it as a swing of a pendulum in Sraffa's thinking within a single note: according to him, Sraffa begins with a rejection of the classical position of an 'ultimate cause' of value as 'primitive' in favor of Marshallian 'mechanical causation' as 'scientific' development and then comes back to an appreciation of the classical 'ultimate cause'. Garegnani, however, fails to notice that Sraffa had come to the conclusion that Pareto has succeeded in abandoning the quest for the 'ultimate cause' by basing the modern theory of value and also distribution on empirical demand rather than utility-based demand. Sraffa therefore, instead of returning to the notion of 'ultimate cause', is rather opening a new agenda for himself to see if a similar result could be achieved for the cost-based classical theory of value by taking only the empirical 'physical real costs' into account.

3

A New Beginning

The First and Second Equations

In the Notes titled 'Winter 1927–28', Sraffa begins to work out his 'equations'. It was quite easy for him to see that in a subsistence economy or the economy with 'no surplus', the relative prices of commodities could be directly determined by the given physical input–output data:

$$\left.\begin{aligned} A &= a_1 + b_1 + c_1 \\ B &= a_2 + b_2 + c_2 \\ C &= a_3 + b_3 + c_3 \end{aligned}\right\} \quad \text{where} \quad \begin{aligned} A &= \sum a \\ B &= \sum b \\ C &= \sum c \end{aligned}$$

> These are homogeneous linear equations. They have infinite sets of solutions, but the solutions of the each set are proportional. These proportions are univoche {unique}.
>
> These proportions we call ratios of Absolute values. They are purely numerical relations between the things A, B, … They are not necessarily the ratios in which the exchange will actually take place in any community in which the quantities of things respectively used in production (i.e. consumed) and produced satisfy those equations: such actual ratios

A. Sinha, *A Revolution in Economic Theory*,
DOI 10.1007/978-3-319-30616-2_3

of exchange are also conditioned by such things as legal institutions, etc. which vary in different organisations of society and which are 'arbitrary', i.e., irrelevant, from present point of view. (D3/12/5: 2)

Clearly, these 'equations' appear odd because the relative prices do not explicitly appear in the equations. Since Garegnani (2005) interprets Sraffa's equations as a search for the 'ultimate cause' of prices, he goes on to interpret these equations as: 'A way of representing "physical real cost"—what is *physically necessary* for the commodity's production—more direct than the "necessary commodity" has been found, and the attempt to achieve a "reduction" to such a commodity is apparently abandoned' (p. 467). Garegnani seems to forget that the search was for the 'ultimate cause' *of prices* and not 'commodity's production'. The fact that in Sraffa's equations the prices are implicit will become clear when we come to his equations with surplus. It would suffice here to note that, when Sraffa showed his first equations to Frank Ramsey,[1] he advised Sraffa thus:

1) Equations with surplus: Exact solutions can be found for up to 4 equations. Approximate solutions can probably be found for any number of equations.
2) It can probably be proved that, whatever the number of equations only *one* set of solutions is significant.
3) Equations without surplus: each quantity must be expressed by *two* letters, one being the number of units, the other the unit {*sic*, must mean price} of the commodity. Otherwise, if I use only one letter, this would stand for heterogeneous things and the sum would be meaningless. (D3/12/2: 28, dated 26 June 1928)

It is quite clear that Sraffa well understood the nature of the solution of a simultaneous equation system, where, of course, no arrow of causation

[1] Frank Ramsey was a brilliant mathematician-philosopher and a close friend of both Sraffa and Wittgenstein. He unfortunately died at the very young age of 26 in 1930.

can be drawn from the left hand side of the equations to the right hand side of the equations as one can do with the technique of production.[2]

These 'absolute values' are of course derived from objective data alone and their justification lies in the fact that exchange according to these values restores the initial position, if production is to go on. Sraffa calls these exchange relations 'absolute values' and considers them as 'natural' relations among commodities, given the equations. At this stage Sraffa thinks that the actual exchange ratios of commodities may differ from these 'natural relations', because they could be affected (or distorted?) by various social organizations. However, leaving aside such 'arbitrary' effects on the actual exchange ratios, the ratios given by the solution of the equations were 'natural'. Could this also be argued for an economy that produced a surplus as well? This is a fundamental question that occupies Sraffa, on and off, for a long period.

Sraffa's first attempt at this stage— 'winter 1927–28'—is to construct a system with 'equal proportional surplus'. In this construct, it is assumed that 'all [industries] increase in the same proportion'. In effect what is assumed is that the aggregate of every input used in the system as a whole increases by the same proportion as outputs—much later such a system will be called the 'Standard system'. But it was clear to Sraffa that a solution of his equation system with a surplus would also require the condition of an equal rate of profits for each industry, otherwise the number of unknowns will be greater than the number of independent equations. But his first problem was how this could be justified. It is important that the reader should be made aware of Sraffa's thinking on this issue at this stage in detail:

Equations with Proportional Surplus

{...}

[2] Kurz (2012) argues that Sraffa's equations are like chemical equations such as $2H_2O = 2H_2 + O_2$. In this case the equation can be interpreted either as an arrow (→), representing chemical reaction, or as an equation (=), representing the balancing of the number of elements of each type on both sides of the equation. As Kurz puts it: 'the mass of two molecules of water is equal to the mass of the two molecules of hydrogen plus the mass of one molecule of oxygen' (p. 1548). The problem with this analogy, however, is that in the case of chemical equations the so-called 'mass of hydrogen and oxygen' are known and not determined by the equation. However, in Sraffa's equations the counterpart of the 'mass of hydrogen and oxygen', that is, the values of a, b and c are unknowns and the 'solution' of the system of equations is supposed to determine those values. In this case the equations cannot be interpreted in terms of arrows, as 'a', 'b' and 'c' appear both as inputs and outputs in the system.

How to 'justify' or explain the equal percentage added to initial stock of each industry. This assumes tacitly a sort of 'equality' that has not been postulated.

Besides, thus, the 'absolute values' have no more the appeal to commonsense of restoring the initial position—which is required if production has to go on.

However, they restore initial stock with equal percentages added: so that there is no impulse to transfer resources to industries which get greater surplus: this result can be obtained without postulating demand, but simply assuming self interest in the entrepreneurs. If they did not get equal percentages, they would move to other industries. And since we assume that this is the distribution of resources that is 'wanted' some 'force' will act (*tendency* to changes in prices) so as to restore that distribution; and in order to get this result that 'force' will have to cause an equalisation of profits (through a tendency of some prices to rise, and others to fall)

- It must be clearly realised however that thus we are allowing to come back through the window the 'inducements' we had excluded from the door. These absolute values *with* surplus are no more what is necessary to *enable* to produce A, but what is necessary to *induce* to produce A: as appears also from the fact that these prices (with surplus) can only be paid *after* (though contracted before) the crop, while costs to enable must of course be paid *before* production begins.
- This must be made clear through an intermediate case, e.g. in which all surplus is taxed away by the state: this would be again the no-surplus case and would exhibit the true absolute costs –
- Then the with surplus case ought to be treated taking into consideration those inducements which are 'necessary' for 'equalisation', i.e., given the surplus this must be in equal proportions in all industries.
- It ought then to be shown that these ratios of values with surplus are identical with those of no surplus (i.e. if all surplus were taxed away; or, if these equations are a transformation of (1), if there had been no surplus)—But is this true? and can it be proved?... (D3/12/6: 10–11)

Before analyzing this remarkable report of an early breakthrough by Sraffa, let us first confirm whether his last proposition is true or not.

Let us take an economy that has produced a 'proportional surplus':

$$\begin{array}{l} 120\text{t.iron} + 160\text{t.coal} + 80\text{qr. wheat} \rightarrow 240\text{t.iron} \\ 40\text{t.iron} + 100\text{t.coal} + 120\text{qr. wheat} \rightarrow 360\text{t.coal} \\ 40\text{t.iron} + 40\text{t.coal} + 200\text{qr.wheat} \rightarrow 480\text{qr.wheat} \\ \hline 200\text{t.iron} + 300\text{t. coal} + 400\text{qr. wheat} \rightarrow 240\text{t.iron} + 360\text{t.coal} + 480\text{qr.wheat} \end{array} \qquad \text{(I)}$$

Suppose that all of the surplus is taken away by the state through taxes. Then we are left with:

$$\begin{array}{l} 120\text{t.iron} + 160\text{t.coal} + 80\text{qr.wheat} \rightarrow 200\text{t.iron} \\ 40\text{t.iron} + 100\text{t.coal} + 120\text{qr.wheat} \rightarrow 300\text{t.coal} \\ 40\text{t.iron} + 40\text{t.coal} + 200\text{qr.wheat} \rightarrow 400\text{qr.wheat} \\ \hline 200\text{t.iron} + 300\text{t.coal} + 400\text{qr.wheat} \rightarrow 200\text{t.iron} + 300\text{t.coal} + 400\text{qr.wheat} \end{array} \qquad \text{(II)}$$

This is a subsistence or no-surplus economy. We can convert this physical system into its value form, such as:

$$\begin{array}{l} 120P_i + 160P_c + 80P_w = 200P_i \\ 40P_i + 100P_c + 120P_w = 300P_c \\ 40P_i + 40P_c + 200P_w = 400P_w \\ \hline 200P_i + 300P_c + 400P_w = 200P_i + 300P_c + 400P_w \end{array} \qquad \text{(II}')$$

The solution of the relative price ratios of the equation system **II′** such as P_i/P_w and P_c/P_w are completely and uniquely determined. Now if the state distributes the surplus to each industry at the same rate as the community as a whole has produced the surplus, then the system would turn into:

$$
\begin{aligned}
&(120P_i + 160P_c + 80P_w)1.2 = 240P_i \\
&(40P_i + 100P_c + 120P_w)1.2 = 360P_c \\
&(40P_i + 40P_c + 200P_w)1.2 = 480P_w \\
\hline
&(200P_i + 300P_c + 400P_w)1.2 = 240P_i + 360P_c + 480P_w
\end{aligned}
\qquad \text{(III}'\text{)}
$$

The point to note is that, in a system with 'proportional surplus', the rate of surplus produced by the system as a whole could be determined in physical terms, which in our system I is given by 20%. Hence the rate of profits that could be equally distributed to each industry was already known. As is apparent, the equation system **II′** and the equation system **III′** are identical. Hence the price solution determined by the subsistence economy **II′** remains undisturbed in the economy with proportional surpluses. This is a remarkable discovery—similar to Ricardo's discovery that in the case of equal direct to indirect labor ratios of industries the labor theory of value remains intact even when positive profit as a new income category emerges. In this case the price ratios of the subsistence or no-surplus economy remain undisturbed even when surplus emerges. Even though we do not have a proof worked out by Sraffa in this note, it is not improbable that Sraffa could have simply thought through it without putting it on paper because the proof is so simple.

The question for Sraffa at this stage is how to justify an equal rate of profits for each industry. His first justification, more or less, is the classical gravitation mechanism, although he emphasizes that all he needs to assume is that the equal rate of profits for each industry is only a 'necessary inducement' for entrepreneurs not to transfer their working capital to other industries. This he thinks can be argued without 'postulating demand', and hence equilibrium of demand and supply. As we can see from our analysis, this can be achieved through the *deus ex machina* of the state distributing the surplus in equal proportion to each industry. In the absence of that, 'market-forces' of the classical kind will have to be postulated, which requires that the equal rate of profits must be related to the distribution of resources that is 'wanted', that is, that equilibrium of demand and supply must be assumed.

The other problem is how to get rid of 'inducement'. Even in the case where the 'necessary inducement' is not 'harmful', in the sense that it does not affect the prices of the subsistence economy, it does bring in a *subjective* notion that was excluded from the consideration of 'cost'. There is also incongruity of time between the two notions of 'cost' and 'inducement': 'cost' must be incurred *before* production begins whereas 'inducement' can only be paid *after* the production is over (even if it is contracted before).

Another problem is that in general the surplus is not produced in 'equal proportion':

> If the surplus is in quality in the same proportions as the initial stocks, i.e. +10% wheat, +10% coal, etc., the first step is easy. But if, as it will be in general true, the community chooses to have its surplus in different proportions, this will not hold. If the surplus in wheat is 15%, in coal 5%, etc., it will be meaningless to say that the surplus *of the* wheat *industry* is 15%, etc. *before* we have determined values: in fact, that 15% is the excess of the product *of the w. industry* over the initial stock possessed *by the community*; *not* the excess of the produce *in wheat* over the initial stock of *varied things* initially held by the industry—these two quantities being incommensurable before we have determined values.
>
> But since we have (in the no surplus system) a spare equation, we can use it to determine, simultaneously with values, the ratio that total surplus bears to total initial stocks of the community. (D3/12/6: 17)

The last paragraph is remarkable. Here Sraffa argues that even when the physical surplus of the system is not in the same proportion to its aggregate inputs, one could still determine the rate of surplus production for the system as a whole, that is, the ratio of the total surplus to the total capital. This he achieves by simply adding the value ratio of total surplus to total capital as an unknown and applying that as the rate of profits to the individual industries; that is, by assuming that each industry receives the average rate of profit of the system. Once surplus is admitted, the third equation of the no-surplus system becomes free (in the no-surplus system the third equation can be derived from the other two, given that total inputs of each commodity must be equal to total output of each commodity) and thus adding one unknown— the average rate of profits—to the system leaves the system with the same number of independent equations as the number of unknowns. This leads Sraffa to conclude that a solution for the unknowns exists,[3] although he is aware that the system of equations is not homogeneous or linear:

[Suppose we put the equations thus

$$A + A_s = (5a_1 + 6b_1 + 3c_1)(1 + R) / R$$
$$B + B_s = (4a_2 + 2b_2 + 6c_2)(1 + 1 / R)$$
$$C + C_s = (1a_3 + 2b_3 + 3c_3)(1 + 1 / R)$$

(or rather, to avoid intricacy, put $(1 + 1/R) = r$)

Now, these are still homogeneous equations and give us only ratios between unknowns: this is satisfactory for values, but is it for R? It will give us the ratios between R and our apparent unknowns, a,b,... Now these are only 'one unit of measure of each commodity' (1 bushel of wheat, one ton of coal etc.). If the equations will give us the ratio $a/r = 10/11$, since we know that a is really 1 bushel, we shall know that $r = 1.1$, i.e. rate of surplus is 10%.

If this were unsatisfactory, we could put the equations in a form which shows explicitly that our real unknowns are values, and rate of surplus—

---

[3] An impact of this could be seen in his final lecture notes of 1928–31. Here Sraffa argues:'I should like to notice that between these two notions of real cost {i.e., objective & subjective} it is not much a question of one of them being right and the other wrong, as of one being relevant for dealing with one set of questions, and other for an entirely different sort of questions. I think that the classical notion of costs, as quantities of things used up in production, is the most important from the point of view of the theory of value; in the determination of the price of a pair of boots I think that the amount of leather and of labour time employed in its production have much more to do than the inner feelings of the shoemaker and whether he enjoys his work or finds it unpleasant. But of course in such questions as that of measuring that (chiefly interest Marshall, such as) that of measuring maximum satisfaction, and finding means of increasing it, these objective quantities becomes {*sic*} irrelevant, and the amount of sacrifice has only to be taken into account'. (D2/4: 24–25)

Contrast this to the 'Summer 1927' draft in which the distinction between the classical and the modern theories of value is drawn on the ground that the classists were interested in questions of growth and distribution and not in what determines the relative prices of commodities, as the modern economists are. The rest of the lectures of 1928–31, however, do not have anything significantly different from the 1925, 1926 articles and the 'Summer 1927' notes.

This may be done thus. Suppose we want to know all the values in terms of B, or any other one. Call $V_{a/b}$ the value of A in terms of B, etc. We have

$$V_{a/b}\left(A + A_s\right) = \left(V_{a/b}\, a_1 + b_1 + V_{c/b} c_1\right) r$$
$$B + B_s = \left(V_{a/b}\, a_2 + b_2 + V_{c/b}\, c_2\right) r$$
$$V_{c/b}\left(C + C_s\right) = \left(V_{a/b}\, a_3 + b_3 + V_{c/b} c_3\right) r$$

The unknowns as $V_{a/b}$, $V_{c/b}$, r, same numbers as equations. We can divide right and left by r, and so the equations are *not* homogeneous [they are not even linear, as there are multiples between unknowns] (having each the known quantity b) and their solutions perfectly determined.] (D3/12/6: 17–18)

The first part of this extract proves that when Sraffa wrote his equations in terms of physical quantities without multiplying them with their prices, he was simply keeping those prices implicit. The second part of the extract shows that, at this stage, Sraffa was convinced that the condition of equality of the number of unknowns and the number of independent equations was sufficient to ensure that a positive solution for prices existed, even when the system of equations was non-linear. It is, however, not clear whether, at this time, Sraffa was aware that this solution for values would not be the same as the solution of the subsistence economy generated by simply removing all the surplus from the system, as was the case with the proportional surplus system. This is because in this case the equations of the subsistence economy and the surplus economy are not the same, even when the surplus values are distributed equally among the individual industries as a percentage of their capital investment. But it seems Sraffa intuitively felt that this must be the case, as in a note written a little later than 28 November 1927 he writes:

Physical costs & value

When I say that the value of a product is 'determined' by the physical volume of commodities used up in its production, it should *not* be understood that it is determined by the value of those commodities. This would be a vicious circle, because—by what then is determined their value? Besides it would be wrong because the value of the product is equal to the value of the factors *plus* the surplus produced.

What I say is simply that the numerical proportions between amount of factors and amount of product *is*, by definition, the absolute value of the product. (D3/12/11: 101)

Only in 1944 Sraffa would discover that a proportional surplus system is embedded in any surplus system, which could be discovered by simply chipping away the unnecessary parts. However, he does not pursue this matter here.

Difference and Change

Sraffa now comes back to the question of returns to scale:

The question is sure to be asked: what about variable returns?

The reply is that these equations cannot possibly answer as to how or why prices change. They only explain why, at a given moment (?) prices of different things bear to one another the proportions which they do. They explain variation (difference) between individual commodities at one time, not variations of one commodity at different times.

No system of equations, whether it considers variable returns or not, could tell this if time does not enter as a variable. {…}

The real point is that it is believed that Marshall's curves provide 'forces' which, in case the price falls below or above AB {the equilibrium price} by 'chance' will restore it to AB.

Now I am not assuming any forces: I simply say that, if the values will in reality be as given by the equations certain conditions will be satisfied: if not they will not be satisfied. In this case, profits will bear different proportions to capital in different industries. Since this happens to a considerable extent in reality, this means that the values in the markets will be different from those in the equations. {…}

I am afraid it will be difficult to make it clear that we are considering what has actually happened in the markets, and not what might have happened had things been different. It will therefore be useful to explain that the reader may assume that constant returns prevail. Because, in the

> assumption of free competition, incr{easing} & dim{inishing} costs are impossible. Exclude internal economies and overhead costs. Then, through external economies, size of industry affects costs: but size of industry as a whole, not size of any one given industry. Therefore, transferring capital from one branch of industry to the other does not affect external economies, and therefore not cost. Dim{inishing} ret{urns} in agriculture: land common to all agricultural products: if I transfer land and capital from wheat to potatoes there are no diminishing returns. Finally if I transfer cap{ital} from industry to agriculture, costs increase in industry because of less ext{ernal} econ{nomies}, they increase in agriculture because of dim{inishing} ret{urns}.
>
> Therefore I cannot make a simple statement of the sort that is implied in a supply curve: 'if output increases 10%, cost falls 2%'. It cannot be unconditional: the result depends upon how the demand increases, i.e. *whence* is the transference of cap{ital.} and lab{our} made. Entirely different results will take place if the increase in the demand for bicycles is due to a smaller demand of guns or of wine. And total demand, since it is simply the other name of total supply, is fixed.
>
> MAN FROM THE MOON
>
> The significance of the equations is simply this: that if a man fell from the moon on the earth, and noted the amount of things consumed in each factory and the amount produced by each factory during a year he could deduce at which values the commodities must be sold, if the rate of interest must be uniform and the process of production repeated. In short, the equations show that the conditions of exchange are entirely determined by the conditions of production. (D3/12/7: 65–67) {The title 'man from the moon' is clearly a later addition in pencil, the rest of the note is written in pen.}

Let us take stock of this long quotation. The very first question suggests that constant returns have been implicitly assumed (?) and he needs to answer why variable returns are set aside. The explanation is that his equations cannot answer such questions as how or why prices change. In other words, the question of variable returns becomes relevant only for questions relating to 'change in price'. His equations, however, are designed to answer why, 'at a given moment (?)' relative prices of commodities are what they are. But does his system of equations do that? The answer is 'no', because he requires equal rate of profits, which would *apparently* hold only when the system is in equilibrium, and, in general, that is not the case at any given moment. Hence the question mark in the parentheses after 'at a given moment'. This leads him to argue that the answers to questions relating to changes in prices postulate certain mechanical 'forces' that explain the movement of prices such as Marshall's demand and supply curves. He, on the other hand, does not assume any 'forces' operating behind his equations. Thus if prices 'in reality' happen to coincide with the prices determined by his equations then it can be concluded that 'certain conditions will be satisfied' and if prices turn out to be different from the prices determined by his equations then those conditions will not be satisfied and the rate of profits will not be equal. But this is not much of anything. Since reality is seldom in equilibrium, what meaning could be attached to his equations? On the one hand, he wants to hold on to the fact that his equations describe an empirical fact and that no counterfactuals are allowed in his equations; but, on the other hand, the solution of his equations apparently do not relate to the empirical fact. This leads him to concede that 'the reader may assume that constant returns prevail'. Then he reverts back to the case of 'constant cost' as the only acceptable assumption within a partial equilibrium framework. That this is not a satisfactory position for him to be in is clear from the last sentence of the short paragraph under the title 'Man from the Moon'. Here he says, 'In short, the equations show that the conditions of exchange are entirely determined by the conditions of production'. This is a position he would like to maintain—there is a double straight line drawn in pencil on the left margin of this paragraph, implying the great importance attached to it by Sraffa—but he has not been able to establish it yet as his conditional 'if the rate of interest must be uniform' suggests. Up till now the uniformity of the rate of interest/profits is explained on the basis of the equilibrium of demand and supply, which, of course, lies outside the 'conditions of production' described by the equations.

After a few pages Sraffa reverts back to this problem once again:

Difference	v.	Change
(Simultaneous)		(Succession in time)

The general confusion in all theories of value (except Marx probably) must be explained by the failure to distinguish between two entirely distinct types of questions and the universal attempt of solving them both by one single theory.

The two questions are:[+]

1) What determines the [*difference* in the ?] values at which various commodities are exchanged in a given market on a given instant?
2) What determines the *changes* in the values of commodities at different times? (e.g. of *one* commodity)

[f.n. + Perhaps the two questions are better enunciated thus

1) difference in value of two commodity at one time
2) changes in value of one commodity at two times (value in terms of commodities in general: whence Ricardo's troubles for finding an 'unchanging measure of value', which in the first question is not involved.]

From this formulation it would appear that the distinction turns upon time entering or not in the account. But this is not the fundamental difference: e.g. the inquiry into the causes of differences of value in different countries at the same time [e.g. Ricardo, Works, p. 12] come under the *second* class, although no lapse of time is involved.

The fundamental difference is that different conditions are assumed in the two cases. The conditions assumed in the first case are:

a) all the units of one commodity sell at the same value on the market
b) all workers of the same grade receive the same wage
c) all capitals receive the same rate of interest

{…}

In the second question the conditions are entirely different: so much different that the object of the inquiry are the changes in those very magnitudes which in the first case were supposed to be uniform all over the place (we cannot even say that they were assumed to be uniform in time: since they referred to a simultaneous situations, time changes could not be taken into consideration, not even in order to exclude them) i.e. the value of one commodity.

Therefore it is possible that the two problems have to be solved in different ways: and that of two opposite general theories of value, one may be true in respect of one question and the other in respect of the second. E.g. it is certain that the rate of interest [or the (amount) level of wages] cannot, in the first problem, determine differences in values of commodities, since they are assumed to be equal for all commodities: and a uniform quantity cannot determine differences. The solution will have to be found in some other quantity which is different in the case of different commodities. But in the second problem there is no a priori impossibility for changes in the rate of interest or level of wages to determine changes in values.

The first problem gives rise to a geometrical theory, the second to a mechanical one. The first is so much timeless that it cannot even be called statical. It does not represent an ideal stationary state in which it is assumed that no change takes place: but it represents a situation at one instant of time, that is to say something indistinguishable from the real state of things in such a short period of time that no visible movement takes place. Its object is, as it were, the photograph of a market place: and its problem is to determine why cabbages bear a label '6d. per lb.' and herrings '8d. a pair'. The first problem must be solved by the theory of value. The second, I think, can only be solved by the theory of industrial fluctuations.

All the old confusion between cause and measure of value is connected with the mixing up of the two questions. Marshall's theory of value, with its increasing and diminishing costs and marginal utility, scissors, pillars and forces, can only be understood as an attempt to solve the first question in terms of the second. All his machinery of supply and demand does not help us at all it {*sic*} the first question: but it seems to be directed to answer questions such as 'what will happen to price if a tariff be imposed?' 'or a bounty or tax? or change in tastes? or invention?' The point is—can such questions be answered in a general way, i.e., assuming the 'initial' movement to be entirely arbitrary? Or is it not necessary to know how it has arisen?

{…}

Essentially, in solving the first problem 'changes in the productiveness of labour in any one industry' cannot be used to explain differences in values of different commodities: incr{easing} & dim{inishing} returns have nothing to do with this problem, since in the given conditions labour has produced what it has produced, and it is irrelevant to speculate what it would have produced had conditions been different: this may only be used as between different periods (i.e. comparing the values under different conditions). Comparing two different times we may say 'boots have risen in value because they have risen in cost, and they have risen in costs because less are pro-

> duced': but at one and the same time, one and the same quantity of boots is produced (or brought to market)—how can it be relevant to insuring what would have happened if the given conditions had been different? (D3/12/7: 115–119)

This piece goes over a similar set of arguments that the theory of value does not admit counterfactual reasoning, because it is concerned with a given *ex post* fact ('labour has produced what it has produced'), 'at one instant of time'. Hence, the question of returns to scale is irrelevant for this problem, because returns to scale have meaning only in the case of changes in output. In these two long quotations, Sraffa is clearly trying to draw a methodological distinction between the two types of *problematiques*: the problem of *determination* of relative prices at one moment of time is a *non-causal* problem—it is concerned with the question of *how* commodities relate to one another; whereas the problem of *change* in the price of a commodity over a period of time seeks an answer in terms of a discovery of the *cause* of that change. Thus, Sraffa's apt metaphorical distinction between the two *problematiques* as one being *geometrical*, since in geometry there is no causation only logical relations, and the other being *mechanical*, since in mechanics forces cause change. In this context, Sraffa goes on to add that the causal answers, however, are generally of uncertain variety. For example, given the Marshallian demand and supply apparatus one cannot predict how prices would change even when one knows how much the demand curve has shifted because the slope of the supply curve is unknown. It depends on the source of the shift in the demand of the product; for example, a rise in demand for wheat due to a fall in the demand for potatoes, where no extensive margin of land comes into play, will have a very different consequence for the price of wheat from a rise in the demand for wheat due to a fall in demand for some industrial goods, where an extensive margin of land comes into play. This knocks down the idea of a 'supply function'. But when it comes to the determination of relative prices, all one needs to know is what exists—simply the conditions of its existence. In the case of price determination, Sraffa, however, contends that the given conditions at a time include an 'equal rate of interest', which is justified on the Jevonsian ground of the 'law of indifference', that is, no arbitrage possibilities. At this stage Sraffa seems to use the term 'rate of interest' in place of 'rate of profits'. However, in the classical tradition, the 'rate of interest' and the 'rate of profits' are not treated as identical concepts. Although it could be argued that the risk adjusted interest payments on borrowed capital can be taken to be 'uniform' at any moment of time on the grounds of the 'law of indifference', it does not necessarily imply that the rate of profits must also be uniform as well. Industrial rates of profits, in the classical theory, are determined by 'market prices', which in turn are determined by the quantity supplied and the quantity demanded at the moment. Thus Sraffa's prices would, in general, still not correspond to the prices of the empirical situation given at the moment.

To Induce or Not to Induce?

Soon after this, Sraffa comes back to the question of 'necessary inducement', as his inability to do away with this subjective notion was obviously bothering him:

> The assumption (in the 2nd equations) that rate of interest (surplus) is equal in different industries is much too rationalistic: it assumes that the capitalists are 'perfect economic men', who *move* their capital accordingly. It may be (partly?) eliminated by these considerations: When the value of a product is 'too high' it gets more interest than the others: it is not necessary to assume that capital 'moves' to it 'in consequence of the incentive': on the contrary, the rise in value itself *is* an increase of capital in that industry—these are in fact two expressions of one thing. If we assume the capitalists to keep no accounts, and to consume just what they are used to, the capital in that industry would increase as surely as if the{y} had the most up to date system of cost accounting for calculating their profits. The fact that in a later stage they keep accounts and 'move capital', simply hastens what is already a mechanical fact ('simply hastens' from the present point of view; it also creates a new phenomenon, trade cycle)

> All the movements of capital from one industry to the other in consequence of changes in demand (?), which increases in one direction and decreases in the other, must be explained in this way. The capitalists keep no accounts and go on consuming as usual: thus, automatically, in the industries which are making excessive profits, capital accumulates and the supply of the product increases: in those which are making smaller profits the capital is being eaten up and the supply of the products falls. (D3/12/9: 9)

Clearly this does not solve any problem even 'partly', as an assumption that capitalists do not behave as 'perfect economic men' is still an assumption about the behavior of the subject. What the above quotation highlights is the desperation Sraffa was experiencing because of the requirement of equal rate of profits in his 2nd equations and having to rely on two ideas for its explanation, that is, some notions of *subjectivity* and *change*, that he wanted to banish from his theoretical frame. After several pages, we find Sraffa coming back to this problem yet again, this time from an entirely new angle:

> The question asked of the theory of value is the following: Given (from experience) the prices of all commodities at one moment, find a set of conditions that will make these prices appear to be necessary. This means, given the unknowns, find the equations (i.e. the constants): we therefore have given, and know, the 'unknowns', and are looking for the constants.
>
> But this is the general question, the problem of finding the theory of value: when it is solved once and for all, the particular questions asked are the reverse, i.e.: given the constant equations, if the value of one of the constants is varied, how are the resultant prices determined? But of course this is only a matter of calculation. (D3/12/9: 65)

The problem Sraffa was facing is as follows. He starts off with empirically given production equations that produce a surplus. He realizes that he cannot solve for the prices that must prevail unless an extra condition that the rate of profits must be uniform across industries is imposed. But then, he thinks, the solution for the unknown prices is not necessarily the prices that must prevail under the given empirical conditions from which the equations are drawn. Furthermore, these prices can be justified as meaningful only if the subjective notion of 'inducement' and constant returns to scale are introduced as part of the explanation—something that he did not want to take on board. In the above quotation, Sraffa attempts to go from the opposite direction—in a way to set up a reverse problem. The idea is that empirically at any moment a set of prices exist. Now there must be certain conditions that make those prices appear. What are those conditions? A discovery of those conditions, which must empirically exist, would be the solution of the problem. *In this case it is clearly stated that a solution to the problem of value is to discover the conditions that give rise to empirical prices and not some 'ideal' or 'equilibrium' prices.* The last paragraph of the above quotation reinforces the previous position that a theory of relative prices is geometrical rather than mechanical in nature. In mechanics a change in the supposed *cause* of price may or may not have a certain outcome. It may depend on various other factors that may not be part of the given condition; for example, whether the rise in demand for wheat is due to a fall in the demand for potatoes or the demand for boots, or, for that matter, whether all other variables remain constant during the period of change. But when it comes to geometrical relations, there can be no doubt that in a Euclidian triangle if one angle changes by 10 degrees then the other two angles together must change by 10 degrees in the opposite direction—it is a logical relation and hence 'only a matter of calculation'.

In other notes of the same period we find Sraffa coming back to this problem once again. This time he thinks that the case could be made on the ground of efficiency:

> What is the significance of the numerical relation found between the different commodities? Why should it represent its exchange value?
>
> We assume that the initial resources were distributed so as to give the maximum produce. {…} Therefore, at the end of the process the goods have to be redistributed in the same proportion as they were initially. This redistribution will take place through exchanges (barter) between the producers of A, of B, etc.

> Now it should be possible to prove that the ratios resulting from the solutions of the equation{s} are the only ratios of exchange that lead to that result. (D3/12/11: 89)

If the initial distribution was 'efficient' then the redistribution must be such that the initial distribution is restored. This, of course, is the case with no-surplus systems . But in the case of with-surplus systems, it is possible only if the surplus is produced in the same proportion as the aggregate of inputs used in the system. This, of course, is the 'proportional surplus' system that we have seen above, and in this case the price ratios of this system are equal to the 'absolute values'. The point to note is that the efficiency criterion implies that the rate of profits in this system must be uniform, as only then can the system revert back to the same distribution through exchange as it started with. In other words, the efficiency criterion shows the maximum rate of growth the system can physically attain. This is an interesting property; in some sense it shows that there is no entropy production when the system is 'efficient'. However, if we grant some consumption for the capitalist class then, as long as the consumption bundle is not made up of all the goods in the same proportion, there must be some entropy production. The problem is that in the real world there is almost always some entropy production and Sraffa needs to have a solution for such a system.

Efficient and Final Cause

This is as far as Sraffa got on this problem during his first stage of research in the period from late 1927 to 1931. Along with the problem of determining value on the basis of 'physical real costs' of production, Sraffa also continues a parallel discourse on the subject of 'physical real costs' in the history of economic thought. In a note of the period 'End of Nov. 1927', titled 'Degeneration of cost and value', Sraffa wrote:

> A{dam} Smith & Ricardo & Marx indeed began to corrupt the old idea of cost—from food to labour. But their notion was still near enough to be in many cases equivalent.

> The decomposition went on at a terrific speed from 1820 to 1870: Senior's abstinence and Mill's mess of the whole thing, Cairnes brought it to the final stage 'sacrifice' (…)
>
> Simultaneously a much bigger step was taken in the process of shifting the basis of value from physical to psychical processes: Jevons, Menger, Walras. … (D3/12/4: 2(1))

A few pages later, in a note titled 'Evolution of concept of cost', we find Sraffa yet again writing:

> It was only Petty & the Physiocrats who had the right notion of cost as 'the loaf of bread'. Then somebody started measuring it in labour, as every day's labour requires the same amount of food.
>
> Then they proceeded to regard cost as actually an amount of labour. The{n} A. Smith interpreted labour as the 'the toil and trouble' which is the 'real cost' (Ricardo, p. 10, 15n) and the 'hardship'.
>
> Then this was by Ricardo brought back to labour, but not far back enough, and Marx went only as back as Ricardo.
>
> Then Senior invented Abstinence. And Cairnes unified all the costs (work, abstinence & risk) as sacrifice.
>
> Now Davenport, Cassell, Henderson, have carried it a step further, the last step in the wrong direction. (D3/12/4: 4)

Sraffa then distinguishes between the 'efficient causes' and 'final causes' as the line of separation between the classical notion of 'cost' from the modern notion of 'cost':

> Carrots, Efficient & final causes
>
> 'Efficient causes' are facts of the past that act on the present: 'final causes' are facts of the future that act on the present. The existence of the latter is at best dubious and they are better called 'illusions'. The classical P{olitical} E{conomy} dealt only with the first sort of causes, i.e. of 'material things' that have existed in the past. Modern economics deals with the second class, i.e. hopes for the future, such as utility, abstinence, disutility, etc.; these things, it must be noticed, refer only to the foreseeing of *future acts*. … Thus, P.E. was a science of things, Economics is a science of illusions.
>
> Example—carrots are necessary if we want a donkey to work. But there are two sorts of carrots. Those which we *must have given* to it *before* in order

to *enable* it to work (otherwise it would be dead) and those you must *show* to it and *promise* to it in order to *induce* it to work.

There is a great difference between the two: The first is a definite number or weight of real carrots, determined by physiological conditions, and—since they have been actually consumed, it has been possible to weigh them and to know exactly to the ounce their quantity: no tricks can be plaid {*sic*} about them.

The others are different. They need'nt {*sic*} even be real carrots—it may be a mashed paper carrot, rubbed against real carrots to take up the smell, which we simply show to the donkey, or it may be a stick, or it may be that at the end of its working day we fulfil our promise and give it its evening ration of carrots. But I suggest that we don't do this because we are honest or because we don't want to damage our credit with the donkey, but simply because we want to enable it to work tomorrow.

Now economics deals with mashed paper carrots and whips, P.E. deals with real carrots. (D3/12/10: 61(1-3))

Several pages later, the theme is repeated:

Physical Costs

Another *very* important difference between physical costs, and psychic costs (besides enabling and inducing—rather deriving from it) is that the former have to be paid (i.e., *borne* by somebody) *before* the beginning of production, since they must 'enable', and they have actually to be destroyed in the course of production; the latter have to be paid (or *distributed*) *after* production has been made, they are simply a way of distributing the surplus, and this cannot be distributed before it exists, i.e. at the end of the period; if it has to induce only, at the beginning it is sufficient a promise, and at the end there is only legal obligation to fulfil it, but no material physical necessity, as in the case of enabling.

Now the past cost can be a cause, but how can the future be a cause? (D3/12/10: 97)

Yet again, all this must make it abundantly clear that the idea of 'inducement' as an explanation for the condition of 'uniform rate of profits' in the equations of 'physical real costs' must be causing a serious problem for Sraffa.

We also, in this context, begin to see an attempt to disassociate the classical notion of 'cost' from the notion of 'ultimate cause' of value:

> The old conception of cost and value was designed to solve this fundamental problem: what is the relation, if any, between the importance to the community (R's absolute value){,} *not* value in use{,} of a commodity and its price (exchange value). They assumed that there was a relation of some sort between the two, and they expressed this mysterious relation by such words as 'cause' or 'measure'—but obviously they did not mean what is their appropriate sense (analyse). (De Quencey, traditional confusion perpetuated by Böhm-B, Edgg., Clark)
>
> The modern conception is derived from the erroneous belief that the classics were literally looking for the 'causes' of value, and not its relation with importance, i.e. its 'meaning'—{…}. (D3/12/4: 5(1))

A few pages down, in a note written on 26 November 1927 and titled 'Metaphysics', he comes back to this point once again:

> All the inquiry about value has always been (and still is and probably always will be) a purely metaphysical quest. When the old economists asked for the 'causes' or the 'measure' of value, they really were looking—as in fact we are, under the illusion of our equations 'determining' value—for the 'nature' of value (It is not an accident, as Cannan, elsewhere, says that the word is in A. Smith's title) in the same metaphysical sense in which we look for the nature of 'matter' or of 'mind'. In fact, we want to 'explain' in terms of familiar words or notions (i.e. to which we are used) the 'new' thing that we meet: but when we have got used to them (as now economists have with prices) we take them for granted and require no further explanation. The explanation has simply to be 'satisfactory' that is provide the accommodation suited for our mental habits, and prove restful to the mind—cool down the fever of quest and sate the thirst for explanation. (D3/12/4: 16)

The Modern Scientific Outlook

Before going any further, I should point out that around the same period Sraffa had read Heinrich Hertz's *Principles of Mechanics*, in which Hertz emphasizes the fact that the question of the 'nature' of anything such as 'force' or 'electricity' or for that matter 'gold' or 'velocity' do not reside in the 'thing' itself. They stand for 'a large number of relations with other terms and it is only when some contradictions begin to emerge between those relations that the question about the 'nature' of something begins to be asked. Thus the solution to the problem of the 'nature' of something is not a solution of the problem as such, since no such thing as the 'nature' of something exists. Its solution lies in removing those contradictions that have arisen between the relations with other terms—in other words, the solution lies in *dissolving* the problem rather than 'solving' it. The idea of interconnectedness of things was also emphasized by Percy Bridgman in his *Logic of Modern Physics*. Bridgman asked the question: 'What is the possible meaning of the statement that the diameter of an electron is 10^{-13} cm?' He argues that this particular notion of length is intricately linked to certain field equations of thermodynamics and thus these space coordinates cannot be given an independent meaning apart from the equations. He further goes on to state: 'what we have suggested might be regarded as the cardinal and most general principle of all physics, the principle of essential connectivity, which states that differences between two systems must be associated with other differences' (p. 158). There is no doubt that Sraffa had found these ideas of Hertz and Bridgman highly interesting, as he had taken copious notes from the two books in this period. I should further add that Sraffa was a keen reader of Henri Poincaré, who had also emphasized the importance of relations in mathematics and physics: 'Mathematicians do not study objects, but the relations between objects; to them it is a matter of indifference if these objects are replaced by others, provided that the relations do not change. Matter does not engage their attention, they are interested by form alone' ([1902] 1952, p. 20).[4] And again in the case of electric current in physics, Poincaré goes on to state: 'They teach us now, as they did then, that there is such and such a relation between this thing and that; only, the something which we then called *motion*, we now call *electric current*. But these are merely names

[4] This sentiment is echoed much later by Schrodinger in the context of physics in *Science and Humanism*—a book that Sraffa read closely in 1943—'But when you come to the ultimate particles constituting matter, there seems to be no point in thinking of them again as consisting of some material. They are, as it were, *pure shape*, nothing but shape; what turns up again and again in successive observations is this shape, not an individual speck of material' (Schrodinger, E. 1952, 2nd ed., p. 21; original emphasis).

of the images we substituted for the real objects which Nature will hide forever from our eyes. The true relations between these real objects are the only reality we can attain, and the sole condition is that the same relations shall exist between these objects as between the images we are forced to put in their place. If the relations are known to us, what does it matter if we think it convenient to replace one image by another?' (p. 161; original emphasis). This perhaps is the context in which we should put Sraffa's new attempt to interpret the problem of value in the classical tradition as a problem of 'meaning'.

Sraffa then contemplates how to begin either his book or his lectures titled 'Principio' {Principle, Start}:

> I shall begin by giving a short 'estratto' {extract} of what I believe is the essence of the classical theories of value, i.e. of those which include W. Petty, Cantillon, Physiocrats, A. Smith, Ricardo & Marx. This is not the theory of any one of them, but an extract of what I think is common to them. I state it of course, not in their own words, but in modern terminology, and it will be useful when we proceed to examine their theories to understand their portata {scope, reach, range, carrying capacity, delivery capacity} from the point of view of our present inquiry. It will be a sort of 'frame', a machine, into which to fit their own statements in a homogeneous pattern, so as to be able to find what is common in them and what is the difference with the later theories. … (D3/12/4: 12)

This distinction between two theories of value—one based on *objective* notion of cost and the other based on the *subjective* notion of cost, is further developed in his final lecture notes of 1928–31.

Along with this, there also runs a theme on pure methodology. On the question of 'cause' there are several notes. Here I present just a few short excerpts that relate directly to the current theme:

> Interdependence is equivalent to causality as opposed to causation: it holds between categories; but between particulars only causation (one direction) can exist. Its limiting case is identity.
>
> Cause required only when there is a deviation from what is normal, or uniform, or constant. That is to say, it is required only to explain change or difference. {…}

> If from the measure of a group of quantities (A) I can deduce the measure of another group of quantities (B), the first determines the second in the sense of causa cognoscendi. In this case there is a causal connection (causa essendi) between the two sets of quantities. Thus the theory reproduces as a logical relation between two concepts, or as an arithmetical relation between two numbers, the concrete, causal relation between the two facts.

> The causal relation between A and B includes, as a limiting case, identity. If they are different in time, it says nothing as to one being the cause of the other, or viseversa {*sic*}, in any particular case to which it is applicable. And, of course, between concepts, or abstract categories there are logical, but not causal relations. (D1/9: 4–10)

We have already mentioned Hertz and Bridgman and their ideas of 'relations' as opposed to 'causations' in modern physics. As a matter of fact, Sraffa was extremely interested in the ideas of modern physics, particularly quantum mechanics. In 1929, Sraffa read A.S. Eddington's *The Nature of the Physical World*. This book is heavily annotated by Sraffa. Apparently, after reading his book, Sraffa went to see Eddington. In his appointment diary there is an entry on 13 November 1929: '8 1/2 Eddington'. The nature of heavy annotation and this meeting suggests to me that this book had made a significant impact on him—actually there is one more entry for Eddington in his appointment diary on 27 November 1944 at 2.15. Since Eddington died on 22 November 1944, this appointment was obviously for his memorial service, which reinforces my contention that Eddington had some impact on Sraffa.

In his lucidly written book of lectures for non-physicists, Eddington distinguishes between 'primary' physics and 'secondary' physics. He argues that the 'laws' of primary physics are completely deterministic: every cause is related to its effect and every effect is related to its cause, but this relationship is binary, that is, there is no 'time's arrow' between these relationships. In other words, there is no possibility of 'action', as any action that purports to 'change' the future course of events must simultaneously 'change' all the past course of events. For the purpose of clarity in exposition he calls such causes without time's arrow the relationship of 'causality' and distinguishes them from what he calls 'causation', where time's arrow exists and a relationship of cause to effect is a one-way avenue (Sraffa seems to follow Eddington's terminology in his notes.) He argues that the idea of time's arrow can only be established by invoking the second law of thermodynamics, which is a part of 'secondary' physics. However, in the theories of 'secondary' physics, to which quantum mechanics also belongs, the classical notion of causation breaks down because of the famous 'principle of uncertainty'. In this context he highlights the fact that, as opposed to classical physics, the theories of thermodynamics and quantum mechanics are completely holistic theories that do not split their objects into parts: 'It provided an alternative standpoint in which the centre of interest is shifted from the entities reached by the customary analysis (atoms, electric potentials, etc.) to qualities possessed by the system as a whole, which cannot be split up and located—a little bit here, and a little bit there' (Eddington 1927, p. 103).

We have already mentioned Sraffa's attempt to distinguish his theory of value as 'geometrical' or non-causal in opposition to the orthodox 'mechanical' or causal theory of value. In this context, it is interesting to note Eddington's remark: 'We found that it was impossible to confine geometry to space alone, and we had to let it expand a little. It has expanded with a vengeance and taken a big slice out of mechanics. There is no stopping it, and bit by bit geometry has now swallowed up the whole of mechanics. It has also made some tentative nibbles at electromagnetism. An ideal shines in front of us, far ahead perhaps but irresistibly, that the whole of our knowledge of the physical world may be unified into a single science which will perhaps be expressed in terms of geometrical or quasi-geometrical conceptions' (p. 136) {the underlined part represents two parallel straight lines drawn by Sraffa in the margin of the book—indicating high importance accorded to the statement}.

Apparently in 1931 Sraffa read Max Planck's *The Universe in the Light of Modern Physics*. This book is also heavily annotated. Here Max Planck goes over the same ground as Eddington. He highlights the fact that in classical physics it was held that the only kind of causality a system of physics could operate with was one in which all the events of the physical world were explained as taking place locally in independent and infinitesimal spaces. Against such a standpoint, Planck argues that: 'In modern mechanics matters are wholly different. According to modern mechanics, merely local relations are no more sufficient for the formulations of the law of motion than would be the microscopic investigation of different parts of a picture in order to make clear its meaning. On the contrary, it is impossible to obtain an adequate version of the laws for which we are looking, unless the physical system is regarded as a *whole*' (1931, pp. 25–6; original emphasis). He further argues that '[a]ccording to modern mechanics, each individual particle of the system, in a certain sense, at any one time, exists simultaneously in every part of the space occupied by the system. … According to this view the revolution of an electron around the nucleus is not so much like the movement of a planet around the sun as like the rotation of a symmetrical ring upon its centre, so that the ring as a whole retains the same position in space; thus there is no physical meaning in referring to the local position of the electron at any instant' (*ibid.*, pp. 26 and 32).

We have already mentioned Bridgeman's *The Logic of Modern Physics* in relation to the interconnectivity of a physical system. In the same book, Bridgeman argues that any physical concept is inseparable from the operation of its measurement:

> To find the length of an object, we have to perform certain physical operations. The concept of length is therefore fixed when the operations by which length is measured are fixed: that is, the concept of length involves as much as and nothing more than the set of operations by which length is determined. In general, we mean by any concept nothing more than a set of operations; *the concept is synonymous with the corresponding set of operation.* (1927, p. 5; original emphasis)

Much before Bridgeman, Poincaré had also stated that '[t]he important thing is not to know what force is, but how to measure it. Everything which does not teach us how to measure it is as useless to the mechanician as, for instance, the subjective idea of heat and cold to the student of heat' (1952, p. 106). During the same period, Sraffa had also read an article by H.S. Allen, titled 'The Quantum Theory' published in *Nature* (*Supplement*), 8 December 1928, from which Sraffa had excerpted:

> Heisenberg put forward the demand that only such quantities as are observable should be represented in the mathematical formulation of atomic theory.... This led to the development of the matrix mechanics, every term in a matrix corresponds to something which is, at least ideally, observable. (Allen 1928, p. 891)

An echo of all this can be found in a long note that Sraffa wrote in October 1929:

> The quantities involved in econ. Theory may be classed in 3 groups:
>
> 1) Those which cannot possibly be measured, because they are not defined in terms of the method of measuring them, e.g. marg. utility and sacrifice. (No definition at all is given for measuring them in the case of several individuals: in the case of one individual they are defined as being proportional to certain quantities, i.e. prices, but this is, as Cairnes says, 'merely giving a name to the unknown causes of price'.) Such quantities must be *excluded altogether*: at the most, they may be used as a fictitious device for solving problems, but must not appear either in the premises nor {*sic*} in the conclusions.
> 2) At the opposite extreme there are quantities which can be, and in fact are, statistically measured. These quantities have an objective, independent existence at every or some instants of the natural (i.e. not interfered with by the experimenter) process of production and distribution; they can therefore be measured physically, with the ordinary instruments for measuring number, weight, time, etc. Such are quantities of various materials used or produced, of land, quantities of labour(?), lengths of period(?), etc. These are the *only* quantities which must enter as constants in economic theory, i.e. which can be assumed to be 'known' or 'given'.
>
>   (The 'extensive' theory of rent, and the labour theory of value only assume this kind of knowledge)
> 3) Finally, there is the class of quantities, which form the basis of Marshall's theory (or, rather, of Pareto's), such as demand and supply curves, marginal productivities, (i.e. rate of growth of total) indifference curves, etc. Here the constant quantities have no names—they are the param-

eters of curves. The several quantities represented by these curves do not exist at any one moment, nor during any period of the recurrent steady process of production or consumption. They are alternatives, only *one* of which can exist in any one position of equilibrium, all the others being thereby excluded (even the one does not really exist if there is no change, since it is the rate of growth of a quantity, i.e. marginal product: it can be inferred from price, but so can marginal utility, which under (1) we have agreed does not exist). Therefore, they cannot be found by merely observing the process or state of things, and measuring the quantities seen. They can only be found by means of *experiments*—and these quantities in effect are always defined in terms of such experiments (successive doses applied to land; alternatives offered to the consumer; etc.)

These experiments cannot be carried out (and never have been, as a matter of fact) for various reasons: 1) the practical difficulties, 2) the lack of definition of the conditions to be required, which are always summed up in the absurd 'other things being equal'.

But even apart from these difficulties, which might conceivably be overcome, there remains something about these experiments which is very curious: they are generally regarded as acceptable, as if they were calculated to reproduce under controlled conditions, so as to be able to measure them, facts which actually happen 'in nature' all the time but cannot directly be pinned down for observation. But the experiments have an entirely different significance: they actually *produce* facts which would otherwise not happen at all; if the experimenter did not step in first to produce them, and then to ascertain them, they would remain in the state of 'unknown possibilities', which amounts to the deepest inexistence. Let us look more closely into this matter. We are given a pair of D & S curves for a commodity. Supposed to be ascertained experimentally: {the note breaks down at this point. However, there is a note by Sraffa on a small piece of paper inserted by Pierangelo Garegnani as p. 4, which is reproduced below}. (D3/12/13: 2–5)

Inexistent possibilities. Fantastic character of D & S curves. Also of productivity curves. But not of different lands.

Still there is some reality in Pr{oductivity} curves. Because, after all, the only explanation (cause) of a thing being what it is, is that, 'if it were different, absurd consequences would follow'.

The mistake is to assume *direct* knowledge of these (inexistent) consequences.

Changes (possible) must *only* be predicted from (actual) *differences*. Extensive and intensive {the note breaks down}.

Point (1) and (2) are straightforward. In point (1) Sraffa is using Bridgeman's and Heisenberg's criterion that anything that cannot be ideally observed or operationally measured cannot be considered a 'cause' in a scientific theory. The idea that individual marginal utility can be measured by its effect is rejected on the ground that it is only a roundabout way of accepting that the cause is unknown. However, it should be noted that in point (1) the claimed relationship between 'marginal utility' and 'prices' is of a direct causal nature such as $MU_x/MU_y \rightarrow p_x/p_y$, that is, the causal relation is between two 'states'—a mental or 'subjective' state of an agent is supposed to bring about an 'objective' state of his or her willingness to exchange x for y in a determinate ratio.

Point (2) confirms that only those variables that can be observed and measured in their natural state of appearance can be taken as 'givens' or 'constants' of a scientific theory and that labor theory of value and Ricardo's theory of extensive rent are built on only such variables. It should, however, be noted that Sraffa does not refer to these 'givens' or 'constants' as 'cause'.

Point (3) separates the notions of direct relation of causation such as $MU_x/MU_y \rightarrow p_x/p_y$, from functional relations such as $p \,.\, q = c$, say a demand function with unitary elasticity, which states that price multiplied by quantity demanded of the commodity remains constant. Even though one can claim that in a functional relation such as $p \,.\, q = c$, the price is an independent variable and the quantity is the dependent variable, it is still not correct to state that $p \rightarrow q$. This is because in this case neither p nor q in itself represents either 'subjective' or 'objective' states. It is their product at any moment that represents a state. The function gets its 'causal' sense from the notion of *change*, the relationship purports to show how a change in p must cause a determinate change in q. Sraffa's point is that at any moment only one point on the curve (or a state) can exist and all the other points on the curve, by definition, cannot exist—they are simply an hypothesis about possible states that cannot actualize once one of the possible states has actualized. He further goes on to add that if the system is in equilibrium and thus the point is recurrent over a period of time then one may not be able to claim that it actualizes even a point on such a curve as the curve has existence only in relation to change and in the absence of change its existence must remain unknown. Further on, he reinforces the idea made in point (1) that inference of a cause from its effect is not a legitimate way of establishing a hypothesis based on causation.[5]

Can the 'truth' of the hypothesis be established or at least tested by experimentation? Before we get to that, let us notice that our hypothesis that a change in p causes a determinate change in q of the demand function requires certain assumptions, which suggests that *all* possible causes that could also affect q must remain constant when p changes. Otherwise, it can easily be imagined that a simultaneous change in income with the change in p could counter-balance its effect and leave q constant. This requires a complete knowledge of all the relevant variables that could affect q. Since it is not possible to know *all* the relevant variables that could affect q, one usually resorts to the gambit of '*ceteris paribus*'. But this is 'absurd', in nature as well as in a controlled experiment. But leaving aside the practical difficulties in performing such experiments, Sraffa asserts that, even if successful experiments could be conducted to produce those changes as hypothesized by the functional relations, they would not confirm the original hypothesis because the experimenter interferes with these outcomes and without that interference such changes would not result in the natural course. This sounds very much like Heisenberg's uncertainty principle where the very act of observation of an electron must 'displace' it and therefore produce a fact that was not there before. Sraffa's precise reasoning behind this assertion is, of course, not known to us because the note breaks down at the crucial moment. However, from his other musings I surmise that his reasoning might be that human beings learn from past experience and therefore continuously change. Hence a repeated exercise on a human agent in a controlled experiment is creating a new agent and thereby creating his or her response that would never otherwise exist in nature where the agent is not introduced to the

[5] See von Wright (1974) for details on the notion of causation in a functional relation.

stimulus on a repeated basis. Further, on the small slip of paper Sraffa goes on to question the belief in *complete determinism* on which the functional relations are founded: 'The mistake is to assume *direct* knowledge of these (inexistent) consequences'. All this shows the proximity of Sraffa's thinking to quantum physics, which claims that there is no particular state of reality prior to its observation or measurement.

Did Sraffa Abandon the Modern Scientific Outlook?

Kurz and Salvadori (2005) partially quote from a long note of Sraffa's, written on 22 August 1931 and titled 'Surplus Product', to argue that '[i]n it Sraffa expounded why his science conceptualisation of objectivism had to be abandoned and what other conceptualisation was to be put in its place' (pp. 87–88). Below I shall argue that their conclusion is unwarranted and reflects a misunderstanding of Sraffa's scientific position.

As I mentioned in the 'Prologue', the classical 'cost' based theory of value was unable to resolve the problem of the contradiction between the notions of 'cost' and 'surplus'. If surplus is accounted for as 'cost' then the 'surplus' must disappear, but as long as it is not accounted for as 'cost', we have no satisfactory explanation for its existence. In this note, Sraffa picks up this problem and acknowledges that the problem is dialectical in nature. Here Sraffa divides the history of economics into two approaches to understanding the concept of 'surplus product': one approach defines surplus by explicitly taking an observer's standpoint and the other tries to understand it on purely 'objective' basis:

> The study of the 'surplus product' is the true object of economics; the great difficulty of the matter is that this object either vanishes or remains unexplained. It is a typical problem to be handled dialectically.
>
> This notion is connected with that of 'necessity'; & 'necessity' has only a definite meaning from a given point of view, which must be explicitly stated, & then adhered consistently.
>
> The surplus product goes all to expenses which are not 'necessary' for producing a given commodity.

What is necessary are the given circumstances, i.e. the known ones (whether natural or social), of a given subject: the surplus is what belongs (remains) to the subject himself. It must be mentioned at once that the boundary between the subject and his surroundings is by no means clearly defined, the subject himself may be doubtful as to where he himself ends and his circumstances begin. E.g. when one takes the classless human standpoint, he should regard all wages, rents, and profits as surplus; but then always (e.g. Ricardo, & Marshall) it is recognised that a part of wages are necessary for production, i.e. a worker is in part looked upon as a natural circumstance, an animal to be fed, & in part as a subject who participates in the distribution of the surplus (see especially Marshall's confusion as to the surplus which he says would not have to be distributed in a slave economy).

Therefore, according to what an economist selects as the 'subject' of his economy (usually identifying himself with it), the 'surplus' will be different.

The standpoint of capitalist society itself, is that of the ruling class, & therefore the surplus is composed of rent, interest, & profit: Marx is the only economist who take explicitly & consistently this point of view, – & also Ricardo (spec. in Notes to Malthus) but not consistently.

Marshall, who tries to take a classless human standpoint, regards all men as responsible subjects, & therefore all human consumption (he includes savings: this question of the inclusion of savings in income is also a question of who is the 'subject'), i.e. wages, interest & rent as parts of the surplus (which he calls the national dividend).

[The question of 'inducement', & the special position of rent in Ricardo & Marshall require special discussion. They contain perhaps an element of only the entrepreneur being the subject.]

Keynes, who takes the standpoint of the company director, regards only the entrepreneur's (who is responsible for production) 'profits' specially defined as surplus, all the factors having to be induced or paid according to contract (he goes as far as to regard past contracts of the company as part of the given circumstances).

[A history of all the recent conceptions of surplus, including consumers' surplus, must be given and discussed here]. (D3/12/7: 161(1–3))

The first approach is adopted, either consciously or unconsciously, by many economic theories such as the classical, Marshallian and Keynesian.

In this approach the surplus product is defined in opposition to necessity, where necessity is the 'given conditions' over which the subject has no control. Hence the surplus is defined from a subject's point of view or standpoint. This does not mean that the 'surplus' is a subjective notion. It simply means that 'surplus' exists only in relation to an observer, and therefore with the change of the standpoint of the observer the 'surplus' itself changes. Sraffa argues that it is the various positions of the subject's standpoints that reveal the different understandings of the notion of surplus in those various theories. This conforms with the position of quantum physics that there is no particular state of reality prior to its observation or measurement.

But from a purely objective or deterministic scientific point of view, which removes the subject from the picture, the surplus must also disappear. In this context, Sraffa alludes to three different ways in which economic theories have dealt with the problem. One approach is to find sufficient cause for every economic category that exists and hence eliminate the notion of 'surplus'. This could be an allusion to the marginal productivity theory of distribution of both Austrian and neoclassical varieties, in which all the income categories such as wages, profits and rent are explained on the basis of the marginal productivities of the respective factors, and therefore the notion of 'surplus' disappears. This approach is by nature conservative because it looks for a reason for all that exists.

Sraffa then goes on to argue that in nature nothing is eternal—what exists must at some stage die or pass into non-existence. So, could it be that 'surplus' has no explanation because the reason for it has disappeared? Sraffa thinks this is the problem for the revolutionary side of economics, which tries to resolve the problem by changing the facts on the ground so that what exists is made adequate to its reason. This could be an allusion to Marx's 11th thesis on Feuerbach: 'The philosophers have only interpreted the world, in various ways; the point is to change it' (Marx and Engels 1969, p. 15). These are the two aspects of the dialectical contradiction that exists in the problem itself:

> Finally, if one attempts to take an entirely objective point of view, the very conception of a surplus melts away. For if we take this natural science point

of view, we must start by assuming that for every effect there must be a sufficient cause, that the causes are identical with their effects, & that there can be nothing in the effect which was not in the causes: in our case, there can be no product for which there has not been an equivalent cost, and all costs (= expenses) must be necessary to produce it.

The conception of 'necessity' has to be extended to everything that happens, & thus vanishes. Every share distributed must be so for a reason, therefore it is necessary; how can there be a surplus left, unless we assume some sort of indeterminacy? This can be assumed from some subjective standpoint, where something is taken as known & given to him, but something is left unknown & dependent upon his will or his action. But from a purely objective point of view, all must be object of knowledge, & nothing can be indeterminate.

This is the general difficulty: the surplus is the object of the inquiry, but as soon as it is explained, a cause is found for it, and it ceases to be a surplus. This sounds as if the object of the inquiry had been defined as 'the unknown', but if the inquiry is successful it becomes known, & the object of the inquiry ceases to exist!

One solution might be this. The science of economics must find a cause, a reason, for every actual fact; thus it justifies the existence of the fact. Thus science (indeed, every science) is by essence conservative. –But for everything there are also reasons why it should not exist, so much so that at one time it must die, & indeed some things are going out of existence all the time; or else, simply, there are no more reasons for its existence. Thus there is work for economics in finding out these contradictions (existence against reason) or lack of reason. But these are simply other names for the failures of economics! –Thus it would appear that the true economic science can only study the conservative side (aspect) of things; and the revolutionary side is the object of study of the inadequate & contradictory economics. The revolutionary economics can only be completed by practice, which solves the contradictions & changes the facts making them adequate to their reasons. (D3/12/7: 161(3–4))

Yet again, the inherent relationship of the concept of 'surplus' with the *subject's* standpoint is reinforced. Here Sraffa's allusion to the concept of the 'indeterminacy' of quantum mechanics is quite telling. Sraffa, however, alludes to a third way of resolving the conundrum, and that is to critique the above application of the principle of 'sufficient reason'. He argues that a cause may be related to several effects and not just to one, and similarly an effect may be related to several causes. Thus, even though in a unified universe of deterministic science it is a tautology to state that 'all effects are contained in all causes', once an 'economic field' is defined it divides the universe into 'inside' and 'outside'. Thus the cause of an effect observed inside the 'economic field' may lie outside the field, and the effect that is observed inside the field may be a cause to some effect outside the field. Therefore, a 'surplus product' may be explained as caused by something that lies outside the economic field, and the effect of the distribution of surplus may lie outside the economic field again. Given that in a unified universe 'all effects are contained in all causes', if the cause of an effect inside the field lies outside, then there must be something in the field that has effects that leak out of the field. Sraffa alludes to Physiocrats for having such an explanation for surplus:

> Another solution however lies in criticizing the above application of the principle of sufficient reason.
>
> Any given effect is entirely contained in its causes (but these causes may contain something else besides that effect; i.e. they have other effects as well).
>
> Any given cause is entirely contained in its effects (But these effects contain more than it, i.e., they have also other causes)
>
> The two above statements cannot be rolled into one, except in the form 'all effects are contained in all causes': this is meaningless, & at any rate tautological, for 'all effects' would be merely another name for 'all causes' (if they meant anything at all).
>
> Thus there must be a leak at one end or other: the 'closed system' is in communication with the world. When we have defined our 'economic field', there are still outside causes which operate in it; & its effects go beyond the boundary. This must happen in any concrete case.
>
> Consider, e.g., the so-called 'natural causes' of rent.
>
> The surplus may be the effect of the outside causes; & the effects of the distribution of the surplus may lie outside. (When the surplus is connected only in one of these two ways with the outside, there may be disagreements

as to whether it is a surplus or not; e.g., saved income, which is connected with the outside only as an effect.) (D3/12/7: 161(5))

Now, here is how Kurz and Salvadori interpret Sraffa's above note:

Was there a way out of the impasse? Sraffa in fact saw two such ways. We turn immediately to the second alternative which he adopted:

> Another solution however lies in criticizing the above application of the principle of sufficient reason.
>
> Any given effect is entirely contained in its causes (but these causes may contain something else besides that effect; i.e. they have other effects as well).
>
> Any given cause is entirely contained in its effects (But these effects contain more than it, i.e., they have also other causes)
>
> The two above statements cannot be rolled into one, except in the form 'all effects are contained in all causes': this is meaningless, + at any rate tautological, for 'all effects' would be merely another name for 'all causes' (if they meant anything at all).
>
> *Thus there must be a leak at one end or other: the 'closed system' is in communication with the world.*
>
> *When we have defined our 'economic field', there are still outside causes which operate in it; & its effects go beyond the boundary.* This must happen in any concrete case. …
>
> *The surplus may be the effect of the outside causes*; & the effects of the distribution of the surplus may lie outside. (D3/12/7: 161 (3–5); emphasis added by Kurz and Salvadori)

The existence of a surplus is thus explicitly taken to reflect some 'outside causes' in operation. What are henceforth studied by Sraffa in terms of the equations of production are some of the effects of these causes, but not the causes themselves. (Kurz and Salvadori 2005, p. 87)

Now from the analysis of the complete note, it is clear that Kurz and Salvadori's conclusion that the third way (in their understanding, the second way) of resolving the contradiction inherent in the concept of 'surplus' was what Sraffa 'adopted' is unwarranted. Sraffa is simply listing the various ways in which the concept of 'surplus' is dealt with in the literature—the third way is the Physiocratic way. Had they not assumed beforehand that Sraffa's theory could not have been built on any other ground than the ground of causation, they would have not concluded that Sraffa's characterization of this standpoint as 'Consider, e.g., the so-called "natural causes" of rent' to be so entirely irrelevant to the point that it had to be altogether omitted from their quotation. Furthermore, had they not abruptly truncated the quotation just before the last sentence in the parenthesis and allowed Sraffa to complete the parenthetical remark, they would have realized that it was equally unwarranted to conclude that '[w]hat are henceforth studied by Sraffa in terms of the equations of production are some of the effects of these causes, but not the causes themselves'. Since Sraffa makes it clear in the parenthesis that, if one takes account of only the effect in the economic field of the cause from outside and not the leak from the field to the outside, then it can be disputed that the cause of the effect lies outside the economic field. The idea that outside the field leaks into inside but inside does not leak into outside would contradict the tautology of the deterministic science that 'all causes are contained in all effects'.

As a matter of fact, Sraffa never adopted the deterministic scientific point of view—he remained committed to the quantum physics point of view of indeterminacy. As we shall see, Sraffa adopted, what he calls in the note, 'the classless human standpoint', where wages, profits and rent are all treated as 'surplus'. Sraffa also shows the awareness throughout of the fact that it is not clear where the subject ends and his given circumstances begins, as he repeatedly shows, including in his published book, his discomfort in treating all the wages as surplus, since he maintained that the bare subsistence of the worker should be treated as necessity (that is, a part of the given circumstances) but then he had no conceptual means of drawing a clear line between the necessity and the surplus parts of the given wages.

The importance Sraffa accorded to the knowledge of 'natural sciences' is evident in his letter to Tatiana Schucht (Gramsci's sister in law, who copied the letter and sent it to Gramsci), which he wrote just one day after penning the note on 'Surplus Product', dated 23 August 1931:

Nino {Antonio Gramsci}[6] will receive, shortly I hope, a book which certainly will interest him: "Science at the crossroads" {Most likely the 'Papers Presented to the International Congress of the History of Science and Technology, held in London from June 29th to July 3rd, 1931' edited by Bukharin}. Maybe this will stimulate him to read other books on scientific topics. It is curious that in the cultural background of any learned Italian there is a hole: ignorance of natural sciences. Croce is an extreme instance, although typical. Philosophers believe that, when they prove that scientists would not pass an examination in philosophy, they have accomplished their own task. In this way natural sciences have been left in the hands of positivists, with the results we all know. Nowadays some scientists, in England at least, seem to have abandoned positivism to follow a sort of approximate mysticism. De Ruggiero has illustrated some of these tendencies in some articles in 'Critica': but these articles are, as far as physicists are concerned, very badly researched and written. You could ask Nino if he wishes to receive first-hand information and some books: maybe he would like to start from the beginning and read some old authors in the field.[7]

---

[6] Sraffa came to know Gramsci in 1919 and they quickly formed a close friendship that lasted till Gramsci's death in 1937. During the early years of 1919–20 Sraffa, under the leadership of Gramsci and his other socialist collaborators, was actively involved in the publication of the socialist journal, *L'Ordine Nuovo*. Sraffa was also highly instrumental in keeping Gramsci's intellectual interest alive during his time in prison and life under Fascist police surveillance from 1926 to his death in 1937 by opening an account at the *Sperling e Kupfer* bookstore in Milan for Gramsci to order any books he wanted, and also directly sending him interesting books from time to time. He was also instrumental in preserving Gramsci's 'Prison Notebooks'. (See Naldi (2000) for more details on Sraffa's relationship with Gramsci and the top leadership of the Italian Communist Party.)

[7] I am thankful to Nerio Naldi for providing me with this letter and, in his own characteristic humble words, 'a very approximate translation' of the original from Italian. Sraffa's letters to Tatiana Schucht are kept in Rome in the archives of Fondazione Istituto Gramsci, in 'Carte Tatiana Schucht, Corrispondenza'; this letter has also been published in P. Sraffa, *Lettere a Tania per Gramsci*, edited by V. Gerratana, Roma, Editori Riuniti, 1991, pp.21–4. The original in Italian is: 'Nino riceverà, spero tra non molto un libro che certo lo interesserà intitolato "Science at the crossroads". Forse lo invoglierà a leggere degli altri libri di argomento scientifico. È un fatto curioso come nella cultura di tutti gli Italiani che hanno una cultura vi sia un gran buco: l'ignoranza delle scienze naturali. Croce è un caso estremo, ma tipico. I filosofi credono che, quando han provato che gli scienziati sarebbero degni di esser vergognosamente bocciati in filosofia, il loro compito sia finito. E così le scienze naturali sono rimaste affidate alle cure dei positivisti, con gli effetti ben noti. In questi tempi alcuni scienziati, almeno in Inghilterra, sembrano aver lasciato il positivismo per darsi ad una specie di grossolano misticismo. Il De Ruggiero ha dato conto di alcune di queste tendenze in una serie di articoli nella Critica: ma questi articoli sono, per quel che riguarda i fisici, assai male informati e tendenziosi e mancano di ogni senso di proporzione. Potreste chiedere a Nino se desidera informarsi di prima mano, e ricevere un certo numero di libri: forse vorrebbe rifarsi ab ovo, e ricevere anche dei vecchi scrittori scientifici.'

4

The First Interlude

On Keynes's initiative, Sraffa was appointed the editor of the Royal Economic Society's project of publishing the works and correspondence of David Ricardo in 1930, and in September 1931 Sraffa's three-year teaching contract at Cambridge University ended. After this, Sraffa stopped lecturing and apparently turned all his attention to the Ricardo project. Strangely enough, at this juncture, there is almost a complete break in Sraffa's notes for a full decade. Apart from several drafts of his review of Hayek's *Prices and Production*, his reply to Hayek's response and one small note on language (perhaps written in early 1932), we have almost nothing in his files until 1942, and not much on Ricardo either.[1] Is it plausible that Sraffa, who was at the verge of a significant theoretical breakthrough at this time, could have simply shelved the whole project for a decade in such a way that he did not even allow himself to have any thoughts about it? Interestingly, in the 'Preface' to his book, Sraffa reports: 'While the central propositions had taken shape in the late 1920's, particular points, such as the Standard commodity, joint prod-

[1] There are a few drafts written in 1941 of a lecture on Italian economic problems that was delivered to a study group of British military officers by invitation, and some lecture notes, mostly written in 1942 but some in 1941, on industry for lectures delivered during 1941–43. None of these notes contain anything of interest for our purpose, however.

A. Sinha, *A Revolution in Economic Theory*,
DOI 10.1007/978-3-319-30616-2_4

ucts and fixed capital, were worked out in the 'thirties and early 'forties' (Sraffa 1960, p. vi). So, where are the notes from the 1930s? The matter becomes more mysterious when we find a re-occurrence of the same phenomenon after 1944, soon after the Mill–Ricardo papers were found and Sraffa had to redirect his attention to the Ricardo project once again. More interestingly, this time we do not find even a draft of his famous 'Introduction' to Ricardo's *Principles* in his files—all we have is the galley proof of the 'Introduction', although we have an earlier proof of the 'Acknowledgement', where one can see a couple of names deleted. Thus there is no doubt that important papers are missing from the Sraffa files at the Wren Library. Could it be possible that Sraffa put most of his intellectual notes from the two decades of work mainly on Ricardo in separate files, which somehow got lost or purposely destroyed by Sraffa? The suspicion of intentional destruction becomes stronger when we find that many files relating to the Ricardo project that contain mostly non-intellectual materials such as Sraffa's correspondence with others regarding Ricardo's papers or his life and so on are preserved. Be that as it may. We have to work with what we have.

The Friendship Between Sraffa and Wittgenstein

The first period of interlude is also very important because it was this period that witnessed intense discussions and exchanges of ideas between Sraffa and Ludwig Wittgenstein. Wittgenstein had come back to Cambridge in 1929. Soon after, he met Sraffa and they struck up a friendship—a relationship that was intellectually intense and at times highly stressful to both. Sraffa's first entry in his appointment diary for a meeting with Wittgenstein is listed as 4:30 pm on 17 February (Sunday) 1929 and the last one on 9 March 1946, although among the extant letters we have the last letter from Wittgenstein to Sraffa dated 24 October 1950—six months before Wittgenstein died. So the relationship continued till the end of Wittgenstein's life. During this period they met regularly, at times interrupted by their sojourns abroad or for other reasons such as Sraffa's internment for three months from 4 July to 9 October 1940 on the Isle of

Man for being a citizen of an enemy country, or Wittgenstein's voluntary work during the war as a hospital aide at Guy's Hospital (first as a porter and then as a pharmacist's assistant) for more than six months during 1941–42. At times these discussions were augmented by written notes and letters. [2]

The intellectual relationship between Sraffa and Wittgenstein remained extremely intense and difficult throughout. On 19 January 1934, Wittgenstein wrote to Sraffa: 'Now you know that the conversations which we had in recent times (meaning roughly the last 6 or 9 months) were always a very great strain for me; and I'm sure for you too. This in itself wouldn't matter but I think it is clear that, for the present at any rate, we have given each other all that we can give. I have learnt an enormous amount from you in the conversations we had during the past 2 or 3 years; but I can't say that I have learnt much from you in our last conversations. Not that I've learnt all you can teach! But I have learnt most of what at present can be assimilated by me. That's why our last conversations haven't been profitable. Now this, I think, is no ground for never meeting again; but it is the reason why, until I feel more powerful, I avoid having a conversation with you.' Interestingly however, there was at least one conversation between 19 January and 31 January, as we have a letter to Sraffa from Wittgenstein dated 31 January 1934 in which Wittgenstein refers to our 'last conversation'. We will come back to the intellectual content of this letter later. On the topic of the nature of their relationship, however, we find Wittgenstein yet again complaining: 'I think that your fault in a discussion is this: YOU ARE NOT HELPFUL! I am like a man inviting you to tea to my room; but my room is hardly furnished, one has to sit on boxes and the teacups stand on the floor and the cups have no handles, etc etc. I hustle about fetching anything I can think of to make it possible that we should have tea together. *You* stand about with a sulky face; say that you cann't{*sic*} sit down on a box, and cann't hold a cup without a handle, and generally make things dif-

[2] All the known extant exchanges between Wittgenstein and Sraffa (except for one letter by W to S written in 1935, which was bought by an anonymous buyer at the Berlin auction house Stargart on 22 March 2006) are now published in McGuinness 2008. I follow McGuinness's practice of maintaining the authors' idiosyncratic spellings and *italics* for single underline, small capitals for double underlines and normal capitals for thrice underline.

ficult.—At least that's how it seems to me.' Again in a note to Sraffa written on 21 February 1934, Wittgenstein wrote: 'I think that writing down my arguments might possibly be the only way of making it worthwhile expressing them at all. –For correct or incorrect I believe they are in *most* cases worth hearing and properly considering & the mere fact that I know they are wasted on you when I just *say* them fills me with a kind of despair while I'm stating them. It's like trying *hard* to fill a barrel which has no bottom.' Sraffa, on his part, felt that Wittgenstein had a tendency to saunter from one point to another, which were apparently unconnected. He responded by saying that 'I am much too slow for that, and cannot find the hidden connection. Also I cannot be content with hints or allusions (or things that cannot be laid down black or white), I must have it all thrashed out. But there is no use laying down conditions to which anyhow we could not stick; if in practice it works out in a way that is intolerable to either of us, then we shall give it up.' By 1941 the relationship had deteriorated considerably. In a letter dated 8 January 1941, Wittgenstein wrote to Sraffa that a 'deep discussion' had become impossible with him because he had 'gone *soft*'—'Its symptom is that you are unable now to stand decently *strong contradiction*, the contradiction of someone, I mean, who mistrusts your reasoning … you used to take contradiction as medicine; and by contradiction I don't mean the expression of polite disagreement but a *challenge*! You did not always take it graciously (but who would?) but you used not when contradicted to kick with forelegs and hindlegs like some animals.' Finally, in another letter to Sraffa dated 23 August 1949, Wittgenstein wrote: 'In order to understand why it's impossible, or almost impossible, for certain people to understand each other, one has to think *not* of the few occasions on which they meet, but of the differences of their *whole lives*; and there can be nothing more different than your interests and mine, and your movements of thought and mine. Only by a real tour de force it was possible for us to talk to each other years ago when we were younger. And if I may compare you to a mine in which I worked to get some precious ore, I must say that my labour was *extremely* hard; though also that what I got out of it was well worth the labour. But later, when we no longer could give each other anything (which does *not* mean that each of us had got all the other had), it was natural that only an almost complete lack of understanding should remain; and, at least on my part, for a long time a wish that an understanding should again be possible.'

Such were the intensity of those exchanges that Wittgenstein refers to them in 1945 in the 'Preface' to his *Philosophical Investigations* as the 'stimulus' for the 'most consequential ideas' of the book:

> For since beginning to occupy myself with philosophy again, sixteen years ago, I have been forced to recognize grave mistakes in what I wrote in the first book. I was helped to realize these mistakes—to a degree which I myself am hardly able to estimate—by the criticism which my ideas encountered from Frank Ramsey, with whom I discussed them in innumerable conversations during the last two years of his life. Even more than to this—always certain and forcible—criticism I am indebted to that which a teacher of this university, Mr. P. Sraffa, for many years unceasingly practised on my thoughts. I am indebted to *this* stimulus for the most consequential ideas of this book. (p. viii).

Unfortunately not much of intellectual value of these exchanges has survived, except for a few letters and notes for discussions. However, the importance of them cannot be underestimated. Here we have one of the greatest philosophers of his time crediting Sraffa with making him realize that he had made grave mistakes in his earlier classic, the *Tractatus Logico-Philosophicus*, and that his criticisms provided the 'stimulus' for the 'most consequential ideas' of his second classic, the *Philosophical Investigations*. In his 'Biographical Sketch' of Wittgenstein, Von Wright reports that '[Wittgenstein] said that his discussion with Sraffa finally made him feel like a tree from which all branches had been cut' (1955, p. 539).

One way to speculate about the nature of Sraffa's influence on Wittgenstein's later philosophy would be to look for the decisive shifts in his thinking from the *Tractatus* to the *Investigations*. This would give us some indication of what might be the 'grave' mistakes of the *Tractatus* that Sraffa could be indicating. We should, however, keep in mind that these discussions were on a variety of topics (e.g. on 18 February 1931, Wittgenstein wrote to Sraffa, 'I want to talk with you about vivisection, I think it is closely related to the things we are talking about') and perhaps never on the *Tractatus* directly, although Sraffa had read *Tractatus* and had made several annotations in the early part of the book. We should also keep in mind that in 1935, 13 July to be precise, Wittgenstein had come to the conclusion that Sraffa was exposing some fundamental problems with his thinking, but he was not sure whether Sraffa's finger was pointing to the right spot. As he wrote to Sraffa: 'I said to you today that I would write to you sometime, but in fact I think that it wouldn't be quite natural for me to write to you; unless one day I see clearly that you were right in the essential points of our conversations, or, if I should ever see clearly that you were wrong. All I can now say is this: that there is *something* fundamentally wrong with me. –if a layman with healthy eyes looks at a bad portrait he sees that it is bad and will often tell you straightaway *what* is wrong in it, in his opinion; he will insist, say, that the nose is too long. The painter can then safely take it from him that the portrait is bad; but he would as a rule be ill advised to shorten the nose. For it is one thing to see that a picture is bad, and an entirely different thing to see where the fault lies.—Thus, when you look into me you see that here is something wrong—and I agree—but whether in showing what is wrong you point to the right spot is very doubtful, –and perhaps not really relevant, as it is *my* job anyway to do something to put it right. Let us hope that this shall really be done and that one day I shall feel allright [*sic*]'. Keeping such caveats in mind, we now turn to Wittgenstein's two books to locate Sraffa's possible pointers.

The Philosophy of *Tractatus*[3]

In the *Tractatus Logico-Philosophicus* Wittgenstein took the position that the philosophical questions or rather confusions arise because of the lack of understanding of what language *can do*. His task was to draw the limit of language and he thought that this could be achieved by an investigation of the foundations of logic because logic covers all necessary truths.[4] The fundamental question he poses to himself is: *Where from* does a proposition get its meaning or sense? His answer to this question boils down to this: Any proposition can be analyzed or broken down into *elementary* propositions. An elementary proposition represents one 'fact'.

[3] This and the next section rely heavily on Sinha 2009.

[4] See David Pears (1969, 1985) for the development of this thesis.

All elementary propositions are *logically independent* of each other. An elementary proposition is made of a string of words. Words are names of simple 'objects' or things, whose form is to combine with other simple objects in a determinate order.[5] The order in which simple objects can combine with other simple objects is the structure of the 'state of affairs'. The structure of the state of affairs exhausts all the logical possibilities of the possible state of affairs. A fact is a realization of a state of affairs out of all possible states of affairs. Thus the structure of a fact must be the structure of the state of affairs. Now, for an elementary proposition to represent a fact, it must mirror the structure of the fact that it depicts, similar to a pictorial representation of facts. As McGuinness (2002) explains: 'A picture which represents that a is to the left of b by putting 'a' to the left of 'b' has as its form of depiction 'that x is to the left of y' and is a spatial picture, and has spatial form in common with reality. On the other hand, a picture which represents that a loves b by putting 'a' to the left of 'b' has its form of depiction 'that x stands in relation to y' and is a logical picture, having logical form common with reality. It will be clear that a spatial form of depiction is one kind of, and thus presupposes, a logical form of depiction' (p. 72). However, as a picture cannot depict its pictorial form but can only display it, the logical form cannot be said in language through propositions—it can only be shown. Thus on the basis of the above analysis, we can conclude that a factual proposition derives its meaning or sense from the reality which it depicts and the *essence* of reality is the *logical form*, a form that language must share with reality to get its sense. The criteria for distinguishing sense from nonsense are clear. Any proposition that entails logical contradictions or fails to give meaning to a sign in the proposition is non-sense.[6] The *logical independence* of

[5] The simple 'objects' are not necessarily the things to which proper names are attached in our day to day life. For example, a statement that 'Excalibur, a proper name, has a sharp blade' makes sense even if Excalibur is broken into pieces. Thus in this case the sentence 'Excalibur has a sharp blade' makes sense even when there is a word in it to which nothing corresponds. Thus, for this sentence to have sense, Excalibur must disappear when it is analyzed and its place is taken by the words that name simples. Thus, simple 'objects' are the logical necessity of Wittgenstein's theory, even though he is unable to give concrete examples of his 'objects' or 'things. (See Wittgenstein 1953).

[6] Thus the *Tractatus* argues that language has severe limitations. Only factual propositions can be sensible as only factual propositions can have 'things' correlated with words. More important aspects of life such as ethics, aesthetics, mystic and spiritual fall in the realm of silence: 'what we cannot speak about we must pass over in silence' (p. 89).

one possible state of affair from another implies that no causal connection can be drawn between two successive states of affairs in reality, as Wittgenstein states: 'superstition is nothing but belief in the causal network' (Wittgenstein [1922] 1974, 5.1361, p. 47). Yet, it appears, there is some kind of a notion of causation hidden behind the Tractarian explanation of meaning. The words of the elementary propositions are supposed to invoke or bring forth images of real 'things' and their combination in a possible 'logical form' gives 'sense' to the proposition. Thus it is a mental process of remembering or picturing the real that seems to give or *cause* the meaning of the words and the proposition.

The Nature of the Break

Wittgenstein, in the *Philosophical Investigations*, begins with a subtle attack on the idea that 'Every word has a meaning. This meaning is correlated with the word. It is the object for which the word stands' (2[e]). With careful construction of extremely simple languages, which he calls 'language games', he shows that the words do not get their 'meaning' by reminding us of some mental images of things. He argues that the meaning of a word is its *use*. As Oswald Hanfling (1984) writes: 'The meaning will consist in the work the word is doing in a given context, and not in a corresponding entity' (p. 49). Such contexts are like games with their rules known to the players. The meaning of a word is neither attached to the things it names (a word is like a tool that can be used for many purposes) nor derived from the subjectivity of its user. The rules of the game are *objective* and are known to all the players who use words in a particular language game. Thus learning a language is akin to getting *training* in how to play a game—'"language game" is meant to bring into prominence the fact that *speaking* of language is part of an activity, or of a form of life' (Wittgenstein 1953, 11[e]).

As mentioned above (f.n. 4), in the *Tractatus* Wittgenstein is unable to give examples of 'objects'. It is taken as a logical necessity of the theory.[7]

[7] 'To Norman Malcolm, who in later years asked what he [Wittgenstein] would have regarded as an example of an object, Wittgenstein replied that his thought at the time of the *Tractatus* had been

In *Philosophical Investigations*, however, he points out that the *Tractarian* dictum that 'a word has no meaning if nothing corresponds to it' uses the word 'meaning' illicitly if it is used to signify the thing that 'corresponds' to that word. The first casualty of this is the disintegration of the concept of simple 'objects' that was the basic building block of his atomistic theory of meaning. After discussing several examples, he concludes that:

> We use the word 'composite' (and therefore the word 'simple') in an enormous number of different and differently related ways. (Is the colour of a square on a chessboard simple, or does it consist of pure white and pure yellow? And is white simple, or does it consist of the colours of the rainbow?—Is this length of 2 cm. simple, or does it consist of two parts, each 1 cm long? But why not of one bit 3 cm. long, and one bit 1 cm. long measured in the opposite direction?)
>
> To the *Philosophical* question: 'Is the visual image of this tree composite, and what are its component parts?' the correct answer is: 'That depends on what you understand by "composite".' (And that is, of course, not an answer but a rejection of the question.) (pp. 22[e]–23[e]).

Along with the collapse of the atomistic theory of meaning of the *Tractatus*, the *essentialism* of his previous theory also falls by the wayside as Wittgenstein recognizes that in general the meaning of words cannot be strictly defined. It varies from one context of its use to another and these contexts, which he calls language games, are not reducible to any common denominator such as 'logical form' but rather only resemble one another like the faces of individuals in a family. Thus the *essence* of language does not lie outside of the language in the so-called *real*—that is, the meaning of words or propositions cannot look for support outside of language. A proposition is not a *pictorial representation* of the real world or facts. Thus Wittgenstein's theory of meaning makes a decisive and dramatic shift from an *abstract causal* theory based on *logical necessity* to an *anthropocentric description* of language.

"that he was a *logician*; and that it was not his business, as a logician, to try to decide whether this thing or that was a simple thing or a complex thing, that being a purely *empirical* matter!"' (Hanfling 1984, 13).

It is important to note that Wittgenstein himself credited Sraffa for this crucial move in his philosophy. Monk (1991) reports that once Wittgenstein told his student Rush Rhees that 'the most important thing he gained from talking to Sraffa was an "anthropological" way of looking at philosophical problems' (pp. 260–61).This point needs some elaboration. As we have seen, the logical analysis of *Tractatus* is a search for the *hidden* essence of language and the world. It provides us with a logical analysis (or an abstract theory) that brings to us the hidden essence of language, which is its logical form. Whereas, in the *Investigations*, we are told to 'look and see' (31[e]) how language is actually used. As Pears (1969) writes, 'the source of the mysterious character of language is no longer its deep essence: it is everywhere, and it is on the surface" (p. 32). To quote Wittgenstein:

> [w]e may not advance any kind of theory... We must do away with *explanation*, and description alone must take its place... The problems are solved, not by giving new information, but by arranging what we have always known. (1953, 47[e])

The point of the 'anthropological way' is an appeal to move away from search for *essence*, that is, from questions raised in the general context to the questions raised in the context of particular cases. Philosophical questions such as 'what is meaning?', 'what is knowledge?' and so on cut the words 'meaning', 'knowledge' and so on from the stream of life. Whether these questions are sensible depends upon concrete circumstances in which such questions could be asked:

> When philosophers use a word—'knowledge', 'being', 'object', 'I', 'proposition', 'name'—and try to grasp the *essence* of the thing, one must always ask oneself: is the word ever actually used in this way in the language-game which is its original home?—
>
> What *we* do is to bring words back from their metaphysical to their everyday use. (Wittgenstein 1953, 48[e])

But once such questions are placed in concrete circumstances where they could legitimately arise, the philosophical problems dissolve:

> If we are using the word 'to know' as it is normally used (and how else are we to use it?), then other people very often know when I am in pain. (Wittgenstein 1953, 89[e])

David Pears (1969, 1985) has argued that one of the fundamental concerns of both the *Tractatus* and the *Investigations* was to draw a line between sense and non-sense. In the *Tractatus* Wittgenstein drew an outer limit of language, which pushed all other propositions except the factual propositions to the other side of the limit. In the *Investigations*, however, there is no single outer limit of language but several internal limits are drawn. The 'language games' represent those internal limits. A word may have sense within a particular language game but an attempt to drag it from one language game to another produces non-sense. For example, words such as God or Soul may have well-understood meanings in a religious language game but produce non-sense in a scientific language game. Similarly the general philosophical problem of looking for a substance corresponding to a substantive such as Hume's problem of 'sensations' is caused by forgetting the internal boundaries of the language games. In other words, philosophical problems arise when we forget what language *does*. As Wittgenstein once remarked, 'philosophical problems arise when language *goes on holiday*' (1978, 19[e]). In a nutshell, we find Wittgenstein moving from the problem of *what language can do* to the description of *what language does*.

The Nature of Sraffa's Influence on Wittgenstein

Now let us come back to the few extant notes and letters of Sraffa and Wittgenstein that relate to the intellectual exchanges between them. Most of them are from the year 1934, notably the year of the lectures contained in the *Brown Book* of Wittgenstein. However, we begin with a note on 'Language' written by Sraffa in early 1932, presumably for a future discussion with Wittgenstein and most likely a part of an ongoing discussion:

> If the rule of language can be constructed only by observation, there never can be any nonsense said. This identifies the cause & the meaning of a word.
>
> The language of birds, as well as the language of metaphysians can be interpreted consistently in this way.
>
> It is only a matter of finding the occasion on which they say a thing, just as one finds the occasion on which they sneeze.
>
> And if nonsense is 'a mere noise' it certainly must happen, as sneeze, when there is cause: how can this be distinguished from its meaning?
>
> We should give up the generalities & take particular cases, from which we started. Take conditional propositions: when are they nonsense, & when are they not?
>
> 'If I were king' is nonsense, for either I, or the job, would have to be entirely different. I know exactly what the reasons are that make this unthinkable: & I see that the modifications required to make it thinkable would be so great, that I would not recognise myself so transformed, nobody would say that the job, as adapted to my present self, is that of a king.
>
> 'If I were a lecturer' has sense. For I was last year, & I don't think I have changed much since, nor has the job. The difference is small. Or rather I cannot see it: I don't know exactly in what I have changed since last year. There is nothing repugnant to me in the idea.
>
> But does this simply depend on my knowledge? (For a difference is big or small, according to whether I see it clearly or not). If I knew enough they would all be nonsense.
>
> Then of course there are the propositions where 'if' stands for 'when': i.e., the name stands for a class, & the proposition is true (or thinkable, as supra) for one member at least of the class. (D3/12/71, also quoted in Sinha 2006)

The question is how to distinguish 'sense' from 'non-sense'. Sraffa's first point is that understanding the rules of a language by mere observation of the occasions when participants of a language speak identifies the meaning of a word with the *cause* of its occurrence. But in this way one can never distinguish when something 'sensible' or 'nonsensical' has been spoken because there is always some cause for 'nonsensical' expressions as there is always some cause for a sneeze. Sraffa seems to suggest that the criterion or the rule for distinguishing sense from non-sense cannot be determined in such generalized contexts. One needs to take up particular examples of certain expressions and see on what criterion we judge such expressions either as sensible or nonsensical. The example he takes is the case of conditional counterfactual expressions, as it seems this was the case under discussion: '[w]e should give up the generalities & take particular cases, from which we started'.

This point that rules of language cannot be constructed by simple observation was apparently not accepted in its entirety by Wittgenstein. In *Philosophical Investigations* he writes:

> Or a rule is employed neither in the teaching nor in the game itself; nor is it set down in a list of rules. One learns the game by watching how others play. But we say that it is played according to such-and-such rules because an observer can read these rules off from the practice of the game—like a natural law governing the play.—But how does the observer distinguish in this case between players' mistakes and correct play? –There are characteristic signs of it in the players' behaviour. Think of the behaviour characteristic of correcting a slip of the tongue. It would be possible to recognize that someone was doing so even without knowing his language. (27[e]).

It should, however, be noted that Wittgenstein's point seems to be not about the *causal* theory of meaning. As a matter of fact, his point seems to be that the grammar of language is completely implicated in our practice of language, including the mistakes that we make, and can be discovered by mere observation as the laws of physics can be discovered by observation. The argument that the 'mistakes' or 'non-sense' can also be identified by observation takes away Sraffa's main concern that it identifies 'meaning' of a word with the cause of its occurrence. In fact, in his copy of the *Philosophical Investigations*, Sraffa puts a double straight line in the margin of the line, '—like a natural law governing the play' and a single straight line running from the beginning of the quotation to that point; apparently showing his full agreement with the quotation, particularly the idea of the grammar of a language being completely implicated in the practice of the language as a 'natural law' governing the play.

Sraffa then takes up a conditional proposition such as 'if I were king' and judges it to be 'non-sense'. But, of course, this is not a full sentence.

The full sentence has the structure: 'if I were king then …'. Now, let's say we complete the sentence with 'if I were king then I *would wear the crown*'. There appears to be nothing unthinkable or nonsensical about that. But then this is not a typically counterfactual conditional sentence. 'Wearing the crown' is simply a description of what it is to be king. In such cases one can easily change 'if' to 'when' without changing the meaning of the sentence, e.g., 'if I were king then I would wear the crown' can also be expressed as 'when I will be king then I will wear the crown'. Here 'I' stands for any man who, when he will be king, then he will wear the crown. But Sraffa is mainly concerned with a counterfactual conditional such as 'if I were king then *I would sign the peace treaty*'. Here the consequent is an action of *a* king, which the king may or may not make. Sraffa's claim is that such a sentence is nonsensical. Not because anything is wrong with its 'logical form' but because it is nonsensical to speculate what Sraffa (in early 1932) would do if he were king. This is because the real Sraffa of 1932 cannot know what King Sraffa would think, feel or do as the circumstances of the real Sraffa are so greatly different from the circumstances of the king. Therefore, speculation of this sort is meaningless. But what about the antecedent of a counterfactual: '*if I were a lecturer* then I would criticize Marshall's theory of value in my lectures'? Sraffa says that this has 'sense' because he was a lecturer only last year and he knows that neither the job nor he has changed much since last year, or at least he cannot see any change. So, is it acceptable to make counterfactual reasoning at the margin of the real? Sraffa's answer turns out to be non-affirmative. He thinks that the idea of sensibleness of the antecedent 'if I were a lecturer' turns out to be based on his lack of knowledge of all the changes that have taken place in him as well as in the job of a lecturer since last year. If he knew them all then perhaps this would also be nonsensical.

The next item is a letter from Wittgenstein to Sraffa written on 31 January 1934:

> Dear Sraffa,
>
> The following are some remarks I've put down on the topic of our last conversation. I hope they won't be too disconnected and I hope that you'll read them to the end.

You said: 'The Austrians *can* do most of the things the Germans did'. I say: How do you know? What circumstances are you taking into account if you say they can? 'He *can* remove the wedding ring from his finger'. True, it is not too heavy and it doesn't stick to his finger. *But*: he may be ashamed of doing it; his wife may not allow it, etc.

You say: 'Learn from what has happened in Italy'. But what should I learn from them? I don't know exactly how things happened in Italy. So the only lesson I could draw from it is, that things one doesn't expect sometimes happen.

I ask: How will this man whose face I cann't [*sic*] imagine in a rage look like when he gets into a rage? And *can* he get into a rage? What shall I say when I see him in a rage? Not only 'ah, so he could get into a rage after all', but: 'so this is the *way he* can be in a rage; so this is how it connects up with former appearance.'

It is a fact that I can easily imagine some features turning angry (remember what I said about Germans in Bohemia) and not others. This of course does not mean that I deny that the latter can look angry too; but I am puzzled as to the *kind* of anger they are capable of. And perhaps I will make a conjecture about the sort of anger I imagine it to be.

You say to me: 'If a man is in a rage the muscles a, b, c of his face contract. This man (Austria) has the muscles a, b, c, so why shouldn't they contract. In fact if you Wittgenstein wish to know what he will look like in a rage just imagine him with these muscles contracted. What will Austria look like when it turns Nazi? There will be no socialist party, there won't be jewish judges, etc, etc, etc. That's what it'll look like.' I reply: This gives me no picture of a face; appart [*sic*] from the fact that I don't know enough about workings of things to know whether all these changes which you point out will *happen* together. For I understand what it means to say that the muscles a, b, c, will contract, but what will become of the many muscles etc. between them. Cann't the contraction of the one in this particular face prevent the contraction of the others? Do you know how in this particular face things interact?

You may say: Surely the only way to tell the future physiognomy is to know more and more exactly the contractions etc. of all (not only the main) muscles.

I say: I don't think this is the only way; there is another one, although the two ways meet. I may ask a *physiologist* what the face will be like, but also a *painter*. The two will give different answers (the painter by drawing

> the angry face) although if they both are correct they will agree. Of course I know that painters have to study anatomy. *I* want to know the painters [*sic*] answer, and I also want to know what the physiologist can tell me to check the painters [*sic*] answer.
>
> I am interested to know what phrases the Austrians will use when they'll have turned Nazi. Supposing their patriotism is only *talk* then I'm interested *in their future talk*.
>
> ...

The crucial difference between what Sraffa was supposedly arguing and what Wittgenstein is resisting is that Sraffa claims that Nazism has certain features or characteristics that would be repeated no matter which country turns Nazi. Wittgenstein is resisting this by maintaining that there is something called 'national character' or mentality of a people, which may not allow a country to turn Nazi in the first place or even if it turns Nazi, its Nazism may look very different because of its peculiar 'national character'. There is something *internal* or *qualitative* about a people or a person that an artist, a painter, can catch but a physiologist may not.[8]

After this there has been at least one conversation between Sraffa and Wittgenstein in which this letter must have been discussed, because in a letter to Sraffa dated 21 February1934, Wittgenstein refers to their conversation and admits his mistake. He argues that people usually associate a change in fashion with change in taste, i.e., a mental state (taste) first changes that *causes* fashion in turn to change. In other words, Wittgenstein argues: 'one presupposes a mental reservoir in which real causes of our actions are kept'. This way of reasoning, he thinks, is flawed and argues that his mistake in the previous letter was to presuppose that change in government was not related to any changes in the mental reservoir of primary causes: 'Now this connects up with our first question because one is tempted to think of such a reservoir, I.E. "the mentality of a people" and when one speaks of changes which the government of a country might undergo one imagines this thing, the mentality, not to alter'. So Wittgenstein realized that his mistake was to assume that

---

[8] Incidentally, in his copy of the *Tractatus*, in the margin of Wittgenstein's observation in 2.01231: 'In order to know an object, I must know not its external but all its internal qualities', Sraffa wrote: 'what does this mean{?}'.

there is something called 'national character' or mentality of a people that would remain constant when a country changes from being non-Nazi to being Nazi. This was unreasonable. This connects with Sraffa's point in the earlier note of 1932 that it is illegitimate to assume that the human character remains the same in a real and a counterfactual condition.

In a short note written on 4 March 1934, we find Sraffa responding to some note from Wittgenstein (the exact note is not known), in which the issue of human action and its relation to justification is raised:

> The error is to regard intuition as a provisional substitute for science: 'when you will produce a satisfactory science, I shall give up intuition'. –now the two things cannot be set against one another they are on entirely different planes. Intuitions are a way of acting, science one of knowing (Physician)
>
> Actions do not require a rational justification—they are *objects* of explanation.
>
> You try to rationalise intuition{s}—and say they are pisaller {*sic*, *pis-aller*—lesser evil} for science.

Let us suppose an instructor gives her pupil a mathematical series such as 2, 4, ., ., . and asks him to fill the three following dots. Suppose the pupil fills the dots by 6, 8, 10. Now, to the question: why did the pupil fill them by 6, 8, 10 and not by 8, 16, 32? The answer could be that the pupil *intuitively* saw the series to be adding 2 to the previous digit rather than doubling it. This answer is a *rationalization* of the action of the pupil. Such rationalizations have a causal structure. The act of the pupil of completing the series is logically independent of the pupil's 'intuition' or his 'state of mind' and it is the pupil's state of mind that is supposed to have *caused* him to write 6, 8, 10. Sraffa rejects the problem of 'rationalization' of human action as non-scientific. A scientific explanation of human action must not be built on the basis of the actor's 'state of mind', which cannot be observed.

In all these exchanges we see one constant theme, Sraffa is constantly attacking all explanations of human action based on psychology or mental state. All such explanations are built on the notion of 'reason' as the 'cause'. The lesson that Wittgenstein learns from these exchanges, which is apparent in both his *Brown Book* as well as *Philosophical Investigations*, is to abandon 'reason' as an explanation taut court, which also explains why his 'picture theory of meaning' of the *Tractatus* had also to be abandoned. For example, apparently directly responding to Sraffa's note discussed above, Wittgenstein in his *Brown Book* writes:

> It is no act of insight, intuition, which makes us use the rule as we do at the particular point of the series. It would be less confusing to call it an act of decision, though this too is misleading, for nothing like an act of decision must take place, but possibly just an act of writing or speaking. And the mistake which we here and in a thousand similar cases are inclined to make is labelled by the word 'to make' as we have used in the sentence 'it is no act of insight which makes us use the rule as we do', because there is an idea that 'something must make us' do what we do. And this again joins on to the confusion between cause and reason. We need have no reason to follow the rule as we do. The chain of reasons has an end. (1958, p. 143)

And in *Philosophical Investigations* Wittgenstein writes:

> Try not to think of understanding as a 'mental process' at all. –For *that* is the expression which confuses you. But ask yourself: in what sort of case, in what kind of circumstances, do we say, 'Now I know how to go on,' when, that is, the formula *has* occurred to me?—
>
> In the sense in which there are processes (including mental processes) which are characteristic of understanding, understanding is not a mental process. (61[e])

> Misleading parallel: psychology treats of processes in the psychical sphere, as does physics in the physical.
>
> Seeing, hearing, thinking, feeling, willing, are not the subject of psychology *in the same sense* as that in which the movements of bodies, the phenomena of electricity etc., are the subject of physics. You can see this from the fact that the physicist sees, hears, thinks about, and informs us of these phenomena, and the psychologist observes the *external reactions* (the behaviour) of the subject. (151[e]).

Further on, in Part II of the book, Wittgenstein, in his detailed discussion of the psychological problem presented by the 'duck-rabbit' image derived from Jastrow's *Facts and Fable in Psychology*, clearly lays out a position that, in my opinion, closely represents what Sraffa set out to do with the modern or the 'subjective' theory of value; that is, to provide an objective explanation of value that puts the subjective explanation out of reach:

> Imagine a physiological explanation of the experience. Let it be this: When we look at the figure, our eyes scan it repeatedly, always following a particular path. The path corresponds to a particular pattern of oscillation of the eyeballs in the act of looking. It is possible to jump from one such pattern to another and for the two to alternate. (Aspects A) Certain patterns of movements are physiologically impossible; hence, for example, I cannot see the schematic cube as two interpenetrating prisms. And so on. Let this be the explanation. –'Yes, that shews it is a kind of *seeing*.' –You have now introduced a new, a physiological, criterion for seeing. And this can screen the old problem from view, but not solve it. –The purpose of this paragraph however, was to bring before our view what happens when a physiological explanation is offered. The psychological concept hangs out of reach of this explanation. And this makes the nature of the problem clearer. (212[e])

5

'My Hypothesis'

Before the Hypothesis

At one point in 1928 Sraffa thought that the main purpose of his work was to develop a critique of the theory of marginal productivity of capital, as in a note titled 'Preface', he wrote:

> The object is to find the 'rational basis' of the theory of marg. prod. of cap. This is done by describing the process of accumulation in such a way that those features which give rise to the appearance of marg. theory are emphasised: in particular, the idea that what is 'saved' is transferred to accumulation; that of an increasing quantity of capital; & that of a marg. prod. It must also be shown in detail how the idea of an increasing quantity of capital arises (Bortkeiwicz). Link with Bentham's idea of quantity of capital (wage fund). (D3/12/7: 1)

The point to be noted is the strategy of the critique envisaged here. At this stage Sraffa wants to follow the reasoning of marginal productivity theory in order to find the problem with it. However, he had already come to the conclusion that Jevons's and Böhm-Bawerk's method of measuring capital by the 'period of production' was unsatisfactory. In general terms

A. Sinha, *A Revolution in Economic Theory*,
DOI 10.1007/978-3-319-30616-2_5

Sraffa reasoned that there is no way of determining either the 'beginning' or the 'end' of the production of a commodity:

> Different lengths of time
>
> The question, whether the values of the two commodities, produced with the same amount of *labour*, but during time of different length are equal, has no definite meaning. In effect, how can we say 'when' the production of a given unit of goods was begun? If it is a shirt, it is when the tailor, or when the weaver, or when the spinner began to work? or is it when the cotton was sown? or is it when the food for the cotton-growers was begun to produce? or is it when the food for the food-makers was begun? and what about the factories, the machines, etc.? The process of production of a thing has no real definite beginning—the inquiry leads us into infinite time backwards. (In the same way it can be proved that it has no end).
>
> Common sense will not help us in fixing this limit: we are looking for the objective ground of value, and not for what the producers or the accountants, or the economists regard as sensible.
>
> Of course, when the question is put as above in terms of labour, the obvious solution is: *risalire lamgo ciascuma delle remificasioni del processo produtivo fino a che s'incontra il lonoro, e li fermarsi* {tr: go back up each of the ramifications of productive process until labor is met, and then we stop}.[1]
>
> There are two difficulties: the first that we have no reason to attach such a peculiar importance to human labour (but that importance is already involved in the question itself!). The second that we shall always meet the difficulty of the machines constituting fixed capital. These machines may be old or new: obviously this cannot affect the value in the sense that the product of old machines will be charged with more interest than that of the new. But then, if years are not time, what have we to understand for length of time? The fact that on the old machines other units of product have already paid the interest for those years, does not change the fact that the process of producing the unit we are considering was begun many years before. E.g. in the case of the shirt, was its process (period) begun when the ship that carried the cotton from America was built? But then, of two shirts, one of which was carried in a new ship and the other in a 30 year old, is the latter much more valuable than the first?

[1] I am indebted to Riccardo Bellofiore for this translation.

(That this is a small part of the cost does not affect the theoretical problem: is time by itself an element determining value?) (D3/12/7: 27–28)

Sraffa then takes the next step of translating Böhm-Bawerk's method into his equation system. Here he discovers that the rational way of translating Böhm-Bawerk's method would be to take the 'dated labor approach'; that is, to collect wage advances and compound interests received only on wages by going back and back in the period of production until the commodity residue becomes so small that all the compound interests received on the commodity residue becomes negligible. This immediately brought to his notice that the commodity residue would become negligible relatively more quickly if wages were high than if wages were low. In other words: 'The length of the period of production is not a purely physical (objective) fact, which can be measured by a clock; and which is independent from the way in which, after it is completed, the product is going to be divided between workers and capitalists' (D3/12/7: 90, dated 8 July 1928). By 1931 this had led Sraffa to formulate the problem thus: '*Problem*: find formula which relates variations in wages to variation in the *rate* of interest.' (D3/12/7: 157, dated 13 February 1931).

Enter Marx

In 1942 Sraffa appears to pick up from where he had left off a decade earlier. In a note written on 2 July 1942 and titled 'Agenda (All equations: Measure of Capital)', he writes:

The first thing to be done is to use the system for application to particular problems.

The marginal product theory of capital crashes on the impossibility for it to define a quantity of capital before knowing 'the marginal product'.

On the other hand, these equations prove that for the problem of value it is not necessary to define such a quantity a priori—an inventory of physical quantities of materials used is sufficient: the value of capital is determined at the same time as the rate of interest.

> The question is: does this supply a method for evading or solving the difficulty of the marg{inal} prod{uct} theory? In any case, to do this, the equations must be adapted a) to show wages separately*, b) to allow for changes in product as a function of the quantity of materials used. This must be attempted.
>
> If the answer is *no*, then the reason for the failure of the marg. prod. theory must become apparent.
>
> In general, on this problem, it is important to explore how the 'value of total capital' changes with changes in the distribution between wages* & profits {...}
>
> It is clear that the only way in which we can speak of quantities of capital & their increase a priori is by measuring it by quantity of labour contained (not by wages, & to eliminate these the equations ought to be corrected).
>
> {...}
>
> *N.B. The equations imply that wages are known quantities: if they are treated as variables, the system is indeterminate. (D3/12/16: 41–42)

Thus Sraffa had already arrived at three conclusions before once again picking up the matter in 1942: (i) there is no *a priori* measure of capital independent of the rate of interest ('marginal product'), (ii) his system of equations has a solution that determines prices and the 'quantity of capital' simultaneously and (iii) 'capital' cannot be measured *a priori* by the reduction of it to wages over a period of time. The idea of measuring capital in terms of 'labour contained', however, is defended in a note titled 'Equations: Measure by Quantity of Labour (infinite series)' written on 7 August 1942:

> The objection is made: why labour? What are its magical or mystical virtues? Why not coal, or labour of horses, or any other quantity? Isn't the choice of labour purely arbitrary? –Answer is the *formal* reason why it is possible only with labour is that it is the only, among the physical quantities which enter into production, that does not vary with variations in the distribution between capital & labour. *All* the other possible ones must vary, since all must enter directly or indirectly into wages: in effect, to make the 'tracing back' process possible, the thing chosen must enter directly or indirectly into production of all commodities (thus luxuries are excluded); therefore also into the commodities composing wages, thus the quantity of it 'entering' into production decreases with a fall in wages. (D3/12/16: 13(1))

The first attempt is to measure capital by 'embodied labor' and is defended on the formal ground that it is the only element in production that remains constant when wages and the rate of profits vary, given that all the prices must be affected by changes in the rate of profits. Thus at this stage Sraffa begins to work with Marx's conceptual categories of constant capital, variable capital and surplus value, i.e. c, v, and s. In a note dated August 1942 and titled 'Model & Period of Production', Sraffa proposes that:

> What is demanded of a model is that it should show a constant (constant with respect to variations of *r*) ratio between quantity of capital & quantity of product. If this can be constructed, and proved to be general, a number of important 'consequences' follow. (D3/12/16: 14)

This becomes a central proposition for Sraffa and later on he refers to it as 'My Hypothesis'. Sraffa thinks that the consequences of this hypothesis would be to prove the marginal productivity theory wrong.

> Now the above ratio is proportional to the 'Period of Production' of Böhm-Bawerk & Wicksell. They were trying to prove that this period is constant with respect to variations of *r*.
>
> If they had succeeded, they would have implicitly proved that the consequences did follow. And it is very curious to find that all the efforts of B.B & W. were (unwittingly) directed to prove that the author of the consequences was right.
>
> The reason why B.-B., Wicksell & Co. fail to find an invariable measure of capital is their obsession with the marginal product theory of interest. For them a measure is satisfactory only if it suits the marg. prod. theory: naturally they fail to find *any* satisfactory. In the end W. confesses that the difficulties of a measure are "insuperable", but always clings to, & in fact never has any doubts about, the marg{inal} prod{uct}. It never occurs to him that it is the latter problem that is impossible & has to be given up. (D3/12/16: 14)

The consequences seem to be apparent. If the output–capital ratio is constant then it can be argued that there is a finite maximum rate of profits in the system. In other words, even if wages were zero the rate of profits would not exceed a finite maximum—this is a consequence of the fact that during the reduction process the commodity residue cannot be completely eliminated (that is, total capital cannot be reduced to only wage advances or variable capital) and therefore the reduction series is infinite rather than finite, as assumed by Böhm-Bawerk and Wicksell. The point Sraffa emphasizes is that, by reducing the commodity residue to a negligible amount, one can compute the period of production (given wages) correctly for all practical purposes but still the acknowledgement of infinite series (that is, commodity residue) or finite series (that is, commodity residue vanishes) makes all the difference in terms of the picture of the economic phenomenon, and it is the picture that is important. This is because the relationship between w and r worked out on the basis of finite series must turn out to be incorrect because its rate of profits reaches infinity when wages become zero:

> The error of Jevons-BB (omitting Commodity residue term) has much more far reaching consequences than the trifling ones that are made to appear above.
>
> For in the above, the relation of w and r in the Reduction equation is still as determined in the original equation. But since the original equation includes (implicitly) the Residue Term, the latter has not been effectively eliminated.
>
> But J-BB *start* from a *finite* series similar to the Reduction series, & know nothing of an original equation. Therefore they have no 'given' relation between w and r: they must deduce this from their finite series of pure labour terms. But the relation thus deduced must be very different from the one obtained from the original equation – in particular: a) there can be no maximum for r, and b) r *throughout its movement* (as w falls) cannot behave as if it approached a maximum.
>
> Therefore the effects of omitting Residue term are not shown only for values of r very near the maximum (as is implied in the previous pages) but throughout. (D3/12/26: 13, dated 29 November 1942)

The argument also applies to Marshall who uses the reverse process of reduction, that is, compounding to eliminate all variable capital:

> Now, Compounding, like Reduction, is purely a manipulation: and while neglecting negligible quantities does not affect calculation at ordinary values, it does completely transform the picture: but then the whole point of these schemes is to give a picture, not a quick method of calculation. (D3/12/26: 9, dated 25 November 1942)

This reminds us of the difference in the classical and quantum pictures of the universe in physics. The calculations of natural events done by using classical physics at the human level are practically the same as the calculations done by using the quantum theory, but their pictures of the universe are radically different and that is seen when one looks at the level which is ignored by the classical physics.

Sraffa begins his work on the proof of his hypothesis by first translating it into Marx's value categories:

> The requirement{s} of a *model* are:
>
> With annual (agricultural) production:
>
> That the ratio of Total Product (C + V + S) to Constant Capital should be constant with respect to variations in *r* (in distribution). Also that the ratio of Total Product to Constant & Variable Capital should be the same whether measured in value or in Price, at the ruling *r* [not as in first case, for any *r*, for variable changes with *r*]
>
> This is satisfied if the three groups have each the same organic composition, [whatever the prices & *r*] (D3/12/16: 15, dated 19 August 1942)

The first condition states that $(C+V+S)/C = [1 + (V+S)/C] = 1 + R$ (constant), with variation in the rate of profits (r). This is Sraffa's hypothesis stated in Marx's labor-value terms. The second condition states that $(C+V+S)/(C+V) = [1 + S/(C+V)]$ is the same for both value accounting and price accounting. The second condition amounts to the claim that Marx's average rate of profits in his transformation equations from values to prices of production given by $S/(C+V)$ is the valid rate of profits for price accounting. If this claim could be proved to be true then it implies that the price and labor-value accounting of total capital $(C+V)$ and the total gross output $(C+V+S)$ must be proportional to each other. Thus at wages equal to zero, the maximum rate of profits (R) must be the same for both value and price accounting. Could R remain constant in a price regime when wages are positive? The answer is yes! Let us say that the aggregate equation of a system of equations is given by:

$$\begin{aligned}&(p_a A_a + p_a A_b + \ldots + p_a A_n + p_b B_a + \ldots + p_n N_n)\\&(1+r) + wr(L_a + L_b + \ldots L_n) + w(L_a + L_b + \ldots L_n) =\\&(p_a A_t + p_b B_t + \ldots + p_n N_t).\end{aligned}$$

We put $(p_a A_t + p_b B_t + \ldots + p_n N_t) - (p_a A_a + p_a A_b + \ldots + p_a A_n + p_b B_a + \ldots + p_n N_n) = 1$. We need to prove that the ratio $(p_a A_t + p_b B_t + \ldots + p_n N_t)/(p_a A_a + p_a A_b + \ldots + p_a A_n + p_b B_a + \ldots + p_n N_n)$ is constant with changes in prices. If Marx's transformation of values to prices of production is correct, then $(p_a A_t + p_b B_t + \ldots + p_n N_t)$ is equal to $(C + V + S)$, which is a constant, say X. Thus we need to only prove that the non-wage capital $(p_a A_a + p_a A_b + \ldots + p_a A_n + p_b B_a + \ldots + p_n N_n)$, say K, is constant. We know that $K(1 + r) = X - wr(L_a + \ldots + L_n) - w(L_a + \ldots + L_n)$. We put $(L_a + \ldots + L_n) = 1$. Thus

$$\begin{aligned}&K(1+r) = X - w(r+1) \rightarrow K = \{X - w(1+r)\}/(1+r)\\&= X - w\{1 + S/(C+V)\}/\{1 + S/(C+V)\}\\&= \{X - w(C+V+S)/(C+V)\}/(C+V+S)/(C+V)\\&= \{X(C+V) - wX\}/X = (C+V-w)\end{aligned}$$

Now, since $(w + rw + rK) = 1$ and $(rw + rK) = S$, we have $w = (1 - S)$, which is equal to V. Hence $K = C$, a constant with respect to changes in prices. In the above demonstration we have not made clear in which commodity the prices are expressed. The reason for this is that the results of Marx's transformation, that is, total value of gross output in terms of prices $= (C + V + S)$ and total profits in terms of prices $= S$, imply that prices are measured against a commodity that is produced by the 'average organic composition of capital' of the system for which labor-value and price of production coincide and therefore against *only* this commodity may the deviations of prices of production from their values be measured.

This leads Sraffa to investigate the extent to which Marx's transformation of values to prices of production is correct or can be justified. The first case presented here appears to be of three sets of industries (as sectors) distinctly identified as producing goods that constitute constant capital, wage-goods and capitalists' consumption goods. (In all these examples Marx's simple reproduction schema is assumed, that is, all the surplus is supposed to be consumed by the capitalists—this keeps at bay the problem of realization of profits and therefore equilibrium.) In this case, Sraffa thinks that, if the average organic composition of capitals in all three sectors happen to be equal, then the *r*'s of the price system must turn out to be equal to $S/(C+V)$ for all three sectors on average, so changes in the wage–profit ratio will not affect the prices of the average of the three groups of commodities. Therefore, the hypothesis should hold. In the next file (D3/12/19, written on 31 August 1942) Sraffa goes on to argue that a commodity produced by any industry could end up being used as capital good or consumption good in a random fashion, and if the number of industries is large enough, then following the 'law of large numbers' it could be argued that the composition of goods falling under either non-wage capital, C, or consumption goods, i.e., $(V+S)$, would turn out to be the same. In that case, changes in the distribution of $(V+S)$ or wages and the rate of profits will not have any impact on the ratio between the aggregate non-wage capital and the net output. Thus R will remain constant. In this context, Sraffa moves away from the notion of wage as an inventory of goods to a share of net output. Interestingly, he argues that the problem at hand only requires the notion of paper transfer of the share in the net income between the two classes, that is, it concerns only the 'implication' of changes in the distribution of income and not the 'effect' of those changes because the analysis of the 'effect' would require an adjustment of the composition of net output if the consumption bundle of the workers differs from the consumption bundle of the capitalists:

> The reason for my confusion is that I forgot that w in these equations appears as a proportionate part of an aggregate of commods. and not (as in the previous equations) as a list of commodities. In other words I forgot that under the present standpoint of considering only implications &

> not effects, it is the *given* commodities that must be shared between V and S; their nature, or composition, cannot be changed by their passing from V to S – since this 'passing' is only a paper process. Later, however, when we come to consider the effects of changes in V and S, it will be necessary to make the assumption of constancy in composition of the average units of S and V respectively (or some equivalent assumption), to avoid that the mere shift from V to S causes a change in the nature of what is shifted. But here there is no such danger. (D3/12/19: 7, dated 3 September 1942)

Keeping with this important problem, I should point out that Sraffa revisits it repeatedly in 1943 when again he makes the point that '*r cannot* depend on how capitalists *spend* their income, in our conditions, since way of spending cannot affect prices.' (D3/12/33: 80(9), dated 12 March 1943). And again: 'That the workers & the capitalists consume commods. of different org. comp. (or even rot{ation} Per{iod}) cannot have any effect on *r*, provided the things produced are not changed with changes in *r* {...}. (Note that we exclude consideration of demand)'. (D3/12/33: 80(11), dated 13 March 1943)

This again reminds us that the condition of equal rate of profits in Sraffa's system is not related to the equilibrium condition of classical economics. His concern is only with the accounting of total income and its distribution at the aggregate level.

Now let us get back to the chronology of our story. Soon after, Sraffa began to probe the nature of changes in prices of individual commodities with respect to changes in the rate of profits or wages. Now, in the context of Marx's transformation of values to prices of production, the nature of the movement in prices of each commodity depends only on the inequality in their organic composition of capitals. A rise in wages would require more than what is received by a fall in the rate of profits of a relatively lower 'organic composition of capital' industry compared to a relatively higher 'organic composition' industry. Thus the transfer of income between the two classes cannot take place at the industry level. Therefore, prices of relatively lower 'organic composition of capital' industries must rise compared to relatively higher 'organic composition of capital' industries. What does this price mechanism do? Following Marx, Sraffa thinks that a rise in wages leads to a fall in profits of all industries, but all these deductions from profits go into a 'social pool' from which they are distributed uniformly per unit of labor across industries. It is this transfer of profits to wages for the system as a whole and not at the industry level that is achieved through the price mechanism. In this context, the size of the net income or $(V + S)$ remains constant throughout the movement of wages from 0 to 1. This suggests that the price of a commodity which falls in the 'middle' in terms of its organic composition of capital would have no tendency to change.

But if this reasoning were correct then it poses a serious problem for Sraffa's hypothesis. For example, if the organic composition of capital of the net revenue is different from the organic composition of capital of the non-wage capital (let us say the net revenue mainly consists of consumption goods which has relatively low organic composition of capital compared to non-wage capital), then a fall in r would imply that prices of non-wage capital must fall compared to prices of net revenue. This amounts to a negation of Sraffa's hypothesis, since R can no longer remain constant. This led Sraffa to think that both the net output and the non-wage capital must be thought of as one composite commodity produced with the 'average' organic composition of capital of the system. However, by 27 September 1942 Sraffa had realized that the ranking of industries by their organic composition of capitals, that is, c_i/v_i, may not remain constant as r varies from maximum to zero, since the price of the non-wage industrial capitals would change with changes in prices even though it is assumed that the prices of the net output and the aggregate non-wage capital remain constant:

> As soon as we classify commodities (capitals producing them) according to their composition into constant & variable, we notice that the constant part of a *particular* capital is itself variable; in fact we have only stipulated that it should be constant only in social capital as a whole, & have no complaint.

That is to say, we solve the Agr{icultural} equations {i.e., all equations with equal rotation period or annual or 'harvest' cycle} for r = 0 and attach to each equation an index $\frac{c}{v}$, such that *c* is equal to the sum of the commodities used in production in that industry, valued for r = 0, and v is the quantity of labour multiplied by an arbitrary wage (any w_0 will do provided we stick to it throughout).

We immediately notice that, for variations of *r*, this c is itself variable – though always less variable than v. (D3/12/21: 3, dated 27 September 1942)

Exit Marx: Enter Standard System

Soon after, Sraffa drops the organic composition of capital approach and, in a note written on 7 October 1942 and titled 'Change of *Standard of Prices: Average Commodity*', goes back to his aggregate equation and uses the idea that his 'hypothesis' must be true to develop his 'average commodity':

We add up all the *n* equations and obtain a general equation:

$$(A_a + A_b + \ldots + A_n + p_b B_a + \ldots\ldots + p_n N_n)(1+r) + (wL_a + wL_b + \ldots + wL_n)(1+r) = A_t + p_b B_t + \ldots + p_n N_t$$

We know that the value of the aggregate of commodities within the first bracket (constant capital) bears a constant ratio to the value of the commodities on the right hand side (social product); constant, that is to say, in relation to the variations of the particular prices as wages and profits change.

We can therefore replace both aggregates with two quantities of an imaginary a composite commodity, made up of the same commodities in the same proportions as the social product: we shall call it the Average Commodity [or General?] and denote it by the letter C. The *quantity* of C used in production (C_c) will have the same ratio to the *quantity* produced (C_t) as the *value* of the aggregate of commodities composing the social constant capital has to the *value* of the aggregate composing the social product. And the quantity of labour used will be equal to the total quantity of labour.

We thus get the *general* equation:

$$(C_c + wL_c)(1+r) = C_t$$

We add this as an n + 1th equation and take the Average Commodity C as the standard of prices. We also add one variable, since the commodity A, arbitrarily chosen as standard so far, must now have its price p_a. The only difference is that all the prices $p_a, p_b, \ldots, p_n$ as well as wages w are now expressed in terms of the average commodity C.

From the general equation we derive simple expressions for w in terms of r and r in terms of w, which are valid for society as a whole.

$$w = \frac{C_t - C_c(1+r)}{L_c(1+r)}$$

$$r = \frac{C_t}{C_c + wL_c} - 1 = \frac{C_t - C_c - wL_c}{C_c - wL_c} \quad \text{from which} \quad (1+r) = \frac{C_t}{C_c + wL_c}$$

Also the maximum to which r can rise (i.e. when w = 0) is:

$$r_{\max} = \frac{C_t - C_c}{C_c} = \frac{C_t}{C_c} - 1$$

therefore

$$(1 + r_{\max}) = \frac{C_t}{C_c}$$

(D3/12/24: 25–26)

As we have seen, one of the implications of Marx's transformation of values to prices of production is that the composition of the aggregate net output and aggregate non-wage capital must be the same. Sraffa had tried to legitimize this on the basis of 'law of large numbers' and the division of a commodity falling under either production or consumption goods being random. He apparently follows that reasoning here by adopting the notion of composite commodity for the aggregate of net output and non-wage capital. It should, however, be noted that if the hypothesis is that the ratio of the values of net output to non-wage capital, i.e., R, is constant with respect to changes in r and the consequent changes in prices then it only sets a constraint on price movements such that the value of the ratio R must remain constant. However, in the above passage Sraffa implies that the condition that R is constant can be replaced by an aggregate equation where the physical composition of output and non-wage capital are identical and thus they can be replaced by a composite commodity with their ratio being equal to $1 + R$. In this case the hypothesis will hold without putting any constraints on price movement.

In early 1943 Sraffa approached the problem from the other side. What are the implications of the 'hypothesis' being denied? This amounts to saying that variations in the rate of profits would be associated with variations in the measure of the quantity of capital (measured in terms of either the value of gross or net output = 1) or, in other words, the quantity of capital is a function of r. Thus, given the value of capital or R at any moment, both r and w would be simultaneously determined by the equations:

> *It follows immediately*, if our hypothesis is denied, that, given the 'quantity of capital' (the price of C_t in terms of C), *r and w* are directly determined by our equations, *without need of further information*.
>
> (The denial amounts to saying that $\frac{C_t}{C}$ is a function *of* r & w. Therefore, if the ratio $1 + R_0$ between C_t and C is given, we have an additional equation
>
> $$\left(A_a p_a + \ldots + K_k p_k\right)\left(1 + R\right) = Ap_a + \ldots + Kp_k$$
>
> Without any additional variable, & the system of (now) k equations with the old k variables is determined. (D3/12/33: 89, dated 2 January 1943) {Note that Sraffa's notation has changed from his previous example. In the current notation, Sraffa's previous 'general equation' would be given by $(C_t + wL_t)(1 + r) = C$, where C is normalized to 1}.

This line of reasoning is further pushed by early July 1943, where apparently Besicovitch's[2] advice has been sought on the question of whether a solution exists if *R* is not constant but known at one moment by 'observation'.

Curiosity: Hypothesis as Equation

Besicovitch

We can formulate the Hypo. as an additional equation to the system, thus

$$\left(\mathrm{A_a p_a} + \mathrm{B_a p_b} + \ldots + \mathrm{A_k p_a} + \ldots + \mathrm{K_k p_k}\right)\left(1 + \mathrm{R}\right) = Ap_\mathrm{a} + \ldots + Kp_\mathrm{k}$$

Where R is a constant (found, say, by observation like the other constants). This introduces a new equation, without adding to the variables. Thus, as we had *k* equations and *k + 1* variables (including *r* & *w*), the numbers are now equal.

Are the variables now determined?

We know that they are determined, if our hypothesis *is not* fulfilled. Because in that case to any one value of R there corresponds only one value of *r* & *w*.

And that they are not determined, if our hypothesis is fulfilled. For then the same value of R corresponds to any of the possible values of r and w.

That is to say, if the Hypo is *not* fulfilled, the new equation is an *independent* one. If the Hypo *is* fulfilled, the new equation could be deduced (derived) from the other equations, & is therefore *not independent.*

Whether the system is determinate, or not, cannot be said when it is expressed in letters. It is necessary to substitute, in each case, the actual numbers for the capital letters representing the constants: and then it can be found out by solving it. But in general terms no proof is possible either way. (D/3/12/34: 18, dated 2 July, 1943)

There are two aspects to this problem. First of all, if the 'given' *R* is the 'true' *R* then the system will not be able to solve for *p*'s and *w* and *r*, if Sraffa's hypothesis holds. This is because this *R* must be compatible with

---

[2] A.S. Besicovitch was a noted mathematician at Cambridge University and a friend of Sraffa who helped Sraffa enormously with his mathematical problems.

all the permissible values of w and r, so the system will not recognize any additional information from this additional equation. But if the system is able to solve for unique p's, w and r then obviously the 'given' R is compatible only with one set of solution and therefore the hypothesis would be proven false. Besicovitch seems to think that in general one cannot prove whether the system has a solution or not, it would depend on the specific values of the constants. But this is not good news for Sraffa because if the system has some possibility of a solution then Sraffa's hypothesis must be false.

The second aspect of the problem relates to the question: how can one know R? R cannot be taken as any arbitrary number because Sraffa's hypothesis relates to R as a *derived* result of the equation system. Sraffa suggests that R could be found out by 'observation' as other constants of the equations. But such 'observed' R is possible only on the basis of empirical or observed prices. Now, if the system of equations has a solution then the 'observed' R must be compatible with both the sets of prices, that is, the solution prices that are compatible with uniform rate of profits and wages as well as the empirical or observed prices. Therefore, if the set of empirical or observed prices is not identical to the set of solution-prices then this would itself make the possibility of a solution highly remote, if not non-existent. Thus the terms of the problem suggest that Sraffa maintains, as we have pointed out in Chap. 3, that 'observed' prices must be identical to the solution-prices associated with the uniform rate of profits and wages.

By September 1943, Besicovitch had provided Sraffa with a 'proof' that there are not one but n solutions of r and more than one can be positive. Sraffa's reaction to it was that the 'proof' was based on the assumption that his hypothesis did not hold. If his hypothesis is true then the aggregate equation is statistically made of one composite good and in that case it is obvious that there can be only one r with respect to a given w:

> Sept. 1943 *One* or n solutions of r?
>
> This (attached sheet) is an answer, by Besicowitch, to the above Q{uestion}.
>
> It proves that, in general, there are n solutions, & that several of them may be positive. It proves this, first, by assuming that each commodity uses

> only 'itself' as Const. Capital: though in different rates R: and then (at the end, extends it 'by continuity' to the general case.
>
> This example however, & its extension, assumes that the Hypothesis does not hold.
>
> It is agreed, however, that when the Hypothesis holds, there is only *one* solution for *r* (for every value of *w*): for, in that case, the whole system can be added up in the single equation $(C_t + L_t w)(1 + r) = C$ which, for any value of *w* has one value of *r* & one only. (D3/12/35: 37)

Up till now the hypothesis was presented in physical terms such that the aggregate equation could be represented by a composite commodity on both sides of the equation. However, by November 1943, Sraffa had decided to shift the hypothesis from physical to price terms. In a note written on 9 November 1943 and titled 'Constant Capital as Proportions instead of Inventory', Sraffa wrote:

> As at an earlier stage we passed from inventory wages to proportional wages, so now we must pass from inventory Constant Capital to proportional Constant Capital.
>
> The question is whether, as in the former case we by-passed the difficulty (of which Bortkeiwicz makes so much) of different organic composition of the capitals producing resp{ectively} articles of working class consumption and articles of capitalist class consumption, so now we can get over the difficulties of the different organic composition of the capitals producing resp{ectively} Constant Capital and consumption goods, (a difficulty which we have so far evaded by the Hypothesis).
>
> Note that, as the transition from inventory wages to *w* was connected with, made necessary by, and only intelligible as a result of, making wages into a *variable* (whereas inv{entory} wages we only considered as constant) so the transition in the case of Constant Capital must be related with making *it a variable*: and in particular a variable related to changes of *w* and *r*.
>
> Note also that we can at once introduce an element of proportionality into Constant Capital. For, in our system of equations, we can multiply both sides of any equation by an arbitrary number, leaving *all* the results unaffected; and we can multiply by different numbers different equations. –Thus, e.g., we can reduce each of our equations to represent the conditions of production, (not of the quantity actually produced in the system, but) of a single unit (ton, yard, etc.) of the product.

Ipso facto there disappear from the equations some absolute quantities which so far I have regarded as of fundamental importance. (D3/12/35: 26–27)

On 28 November 1943, Sraffa further investigates the implications of his altered or new hypothesis in a note titled '*Two meanings of R Hypothesis (implications of)*':

Given our system of equations; suppose it satisfies hypothesis.

Any equation can be multiplied (on both sides) by arbitrary numbers, leaving the system unchanged.

Now the Hypothesis says that, whatever value is given to w, the ratio of the aggregate price of the commodities on l.h.s. bears the same ratio (R) to the aggregate on r.h.s.

This applies to the whole—not to any one commodity. If I multiply, say, by 1000 the equation of a commodity near one of the extremes (one which, say, rises in price with rise of *w*), clearly the Hypothesis in this form will hold no longer. The aggregate of the transformed system's r.h.s. will now rise, with rise of w, as compared with l.h.s. […]

It would appear therefore that in the transformed system of equations R is no longer constant & therefore the Hypothesis does no longer apply.

Yet the essence of our Hypothesis must still be true. For the transformed system is equivalent to the original one, and therefore for any given value of *w*, the solution it yields for *r* must be the same as is yielded by the original system: in particular, for $w = 0$ it must give the same value for r as the original system gave, that is, R. And this is all we want from the Hypothesis.

Thus R_I(max *r*) is valid more generally than is R_{II}(ratio of commodities on two sides). Therefore it seems that the above formulation of our Hypothesis (in terms of constancy of ratio of comm$^{s.}$ on two sides) is sufficient, but not necessary: it assumes more than we require; it is too restrictive: It must therefore be cleaned up, and reduced to its essentials.

One form in which it might be expressed is: that $w(1 + r)$ must be a linear function of *r*. (This certainly would hold for the transformed system: its defect is that it seems purely formal—how can it be expressed in concrete terms? […]

N.B. The importance of this question is not its applicability to the arbitrarily transformed system. But the possibility of *extending* it (Hypo) from

> a strictly repetitive to a *non-repetitive system* (e.g. accumulating) where (as in transformed system) not all l.h. commodities reappear on r.h.s. (D3/12/35: 42)

Thus, given R_{II}, R_I will be satisfied by any equivalent equation set derived from the original set of equations. But this could be claimed for the solution of *R* when wages are equal to zero. Will the value of *R*, however, remain constant even when it is measured at varying prices when wages go from zero to their maximum? And this is what is needed by the hypothesis. Sraffa's example of multiplying one equation by 1000 whose price rise with rise in wages shows that this will not necessarily be true. Soon after Sraffa realized that for R_I to be true, the unit of measure for wages cannot be left to be arbitrarily chosen. However, if we start with R_{II} and take the unit of measure for wages to be the net output of R_{II} then at any level of wages from 0 to 1 the ratio of total profits to non-wage capital will be made of the composite commodity, no matter how prices move. But this ratio is simply a linear function of *r* that moves from *R* to zero as wages move from zero to one. Now, this relationship must also hold for all equivalent systems of R_{II} as long as the unit of measure for wages is taken to be the net output of the system R_{II}:

> A set of (proportional) equations to which it {Hypothesis} applies if you choose an appropriate unit for measuring *w*. (e.g., suppose we start from absolute equations, take the Social Revenue as unit and find that it (Hypo) does apply. Then *this* unit will give results according to the hypothesis *whatever* coefficients we give to the equations. You may give them such coefficients which, e.g. increase the org. comp. of final consumable products and decrease the org. comp. of means of production – so that the ratio of const. cap. to product *seems* to change with changes of *r*. Still, if you use *this* unit the hypothesis will apply. (D3/12/36: 62, dated 27 January 1944)

Hence, this is not an arbitrary *numéraire* but has some specific mathematical properties that qualify it to be the standard of measure for wages and prices of the system. What is the nature of this mathematical property? This remains to be seen.

Nevertheless, this shows that the hypothesis does not require the aggregates of non-wage inputs and outputs to appear as a composite commodity, and therefore the idea that the non-wage capital and the output must have identical organic compositions of capital for *R* to remain constant with variations in *w* or *r* is no longer needed. In other words, if the system takes out net output mostly in consumption goods with lower organic composition of capital compared to the organic composition of capital of non-wage capital, that should not in itself affect the hypothesis. This indirectly reveals that Marx's analysis of movements in prices based on organic composition of capitals alone is incorrect. But Sraffa uses this result to laud Marx by suggesting: 'That M. knew all this is shown by the (otherwise contradictory) implying "simple rule" in reduction of values to prices and S {surplus-value} to r {rate of profits}; while elsewhere denying that org{anic}Comp{osition} of cons{umption} goods & of means of prod{uction} are equal. Contrast nonsense of Tugan-B. & Bortkiewicz.' (D3/12/36: 67)

The most interesting and important point of the above quotation under discussion, however, is made in the 'N.B'. Here Sraffa makes the point that the advantage of shifting the hypothesis from R_{II} to R_I lies in the fact that the hypothesis could now be extended to even 'non-repetitive' systems. A 'non-repetitive' system is a 'snap-shot' of a system going through technical change in its process of accumulation. In this context some industries that produce machines or raw materials used in the old dyeing technique would be shrinking, that is, their outputs would be less in quantity than their use as capital. In such a case the 'surplus' or the net output of the system cannot be determined on a physical basis since the used-up capital cannot all be replaced item by item. Hence the hypothesis R_{II} can never apply to such situations. However, by suitably rescaling some of the industries such a system could be converted to a 'repetitive' system where it could be shown that R_I applies. The point to note is that application of R_I requires that the rate of profits in the system must be uniform. This flies in the face of the classical notion of gravitation since in the classical scheme an industry could shrink only if its rate of profits is lower than the natural rate—this is the only signal that causes the capitalists to decide to shrink the size of the industry. If the rate of profits is uniform across the industries then the system by definition is in equilibrium and there will be no tendency to move away from it. Hence, Sraffa's consideration of the case of non-repetitive system makes it clear that the condition of uniform rate of profits in his system of equations has nothing to do with the classical notion of equilibrium or the center of gravitation. The case of non-repetitive system, however, was so important to Sraffa that, in a note written on 30 December 1945, he referred to it as 'all real systems are such' (D3/12/17: 6). And in a note written in 1955, he wrote: 'But the economic systems of reality are not self-replacing. They are in a constant state of transition and obsolescence, due to changes both in the types of (kind of) commodities produced and in methods of their production …'(D3/12/75: 16).

Now that all real systems could be found to be non-repetitive systems, it was necessary to give up the idea that, from the law of large numbers, it could be justified that the aggregates of non-wage capital and outputs of any given system could be considered to be made up of a composite commodity. The problem now is to see how a non-repetitive system could be converted to its equivalent system that is repetitive and fulfils the hypothesis. Given that all prices are positive, a non-repetitive system can be converted to a repetitive system in any number of ways. Given that the number of commodities is large, all one needs to do is to rescale the system by increasing the weight of the shrinking industries in the system such that their total outputs become larger than their total use as capital. Sraffa thinks that one can always rescale any given system to one that fulfils the old hypothesis:

> Perhaps this can be said: given *any* set of n methods for producing n commods. (provided n is large) we can construct out of them a repetitive system such that the Hypo will apply to it. We certainly can make a pattern of goods composing the Soci{al} Rev{enue} that will have *any* chosen org{anic} Comp{osition} (we can include not only cons. goods, but also prod. goods, for 'saving', without disturbing repetitiveness). (D3/12/36: 66)

However, at this stage Sraffa thinks that it may not be necessary to work out how any given system could be converted to a Standard system in physical terms. He argues that one only needs to solve the equations for $r = 0$. This makes the equation system linear and gives us the labor-values of all the commodities. He thinks that he could now use these labor-values as prices to derive R of the system by putting $w = 0$ in the equations. Now the only problem to be solved remains how to construct the *numéraire* or the unit of account, which, as we have already seen, must be given by the value of the net output of the Standard system. So how can the construction of the Standard system be avoided?

But then, which unit do we use for *w* & p's? The Soc. Rev. of the transformed system (equivalent to the original, or real) which is repetitive *and* satisfies the Hypo.

But we need not go to the trouble of actually working it out. The knowledge of R and of the quantity of labour annually employed by society, suffice to construct it.

We write the equation defining the unit of wages & prices in terms only of w, r, R and L (and what about p's? sufficiently linked with w?)⇦ yes.

{…}

The correct unit is defined by

$$\left(\frac{1}{R}+Lw\right)(1+r)=1+\frac{1}{R}$$

and transferring $\frac{1}{R}$ to the l.h.s.

$$\frac{r}{R}+Lw(1+r)=1$$

which is the Standardised Social Revenue. L is annual quantity of social labour [might be made = 1 and dropped].

$\frac{1}{R}$ is the 'social period of production' and $\frac{1}{R}$ times the St. Soc. Revenue (=1) is the Constant Capital. $\frac{r}{R}$ is the aggregate profit on Constant Capital.

To obtain the linear relation we must assume wages paid out of the product, not advanced. The above becomes

$$\frac{r}{R}+Lw=1$$

N.B. This equation can only be established after the other equations have been solved for both extreme values of w, to find R. (D3/12/36: 67–69)

Soon after, however, Sraffa realizes that the determination of R on the basis of labor values (i.e., prices when $r=0$) may not be the correct R for any given system that is not in the Standard proportion, even though at $w=1$ the measure of the actual social revenue is equal to the measure of the Standard social revenue. This is because the measure of social revenue at $r=0$ is independent of R and only represents the total labor of the system, which is equal in both the systems. The requirement of the hypothesis, however, is that for any given system the value of R, that is, the value of net output-capital ratio, must remain constant when measured by all the different price solutions as r moves from 0 to R. But apparently the value of R changes when measured on the basis of changing prices as r moves from 0 to R. Hence the R measured when $w=1$ would apparently be different from the R of the system that is obtained by the solution of r when $w=0$. *Sraffa's contention is that such changes in R are only apparent and are purely due to the use of an arbitrary measuring yardstick for measuring prices and wages, which itself is affected by the movement of r from 0 to R*. As we have already seen, Sraffa has already satisfied himself that any given system, which may be a non-repetitive system, can be rescaled to a Standard system and in the Standard system it is clear that R must remain constant at any set of prices as long as the net Standard revenue is used as the measuring standard for wages and prices and, since the Standard system is nothing but an equivalent system to the 'original or actual' system, this mathematical property, which he has already derived to be $r=R(1-w)$, must also hold for the real system as long as the Standard net revenue is used as the standard of measure. The problem Sraffa is now trying to solve is whether he could find an indirect way of using the Standard net product as the unit of measure, that is, use the mathematical property of the Standard system, without having to work out the Standard system itself. But one needs the true value of R to use the property of the Standard system in lieu of the Standard net revenue as the measuring rod. Going via the labor-values was the first, but mistaken, move. The next move was to use Besicovitch's method of 'compound commodities':

> Besides, it is not absolutely necessary to solve for values, the actual equations, for the scheme. I could find the Stand. Soc. Rev. directly by transforming the Actual equations into it (by using B.'s method of compound commodities); & from that R can be found by solving for values {of} the transformed equations. (D3/12/36: 77)

This, however, once again brought Sraffa face to face with the problem of *n* possible values of *R*: 'B.'s Compound Commods. suggests that there are *n* possible Standard Systems, corresponding to one Actual, each of the S.S.'s with a different value of R' (D3/12/36: 81, dated 1 February 1944). This led Sraffa to look for a proof of the existence of a *unique* Standard system associated with the actual system.

We have already seen that, when the possibility of *n* values of *R* was brought to Sraffa's notice by Besicovitch in September 1943, Sraffa had responded that if his hypothesis holds then there can only be one *R*. This was based on the fact that the hypothesis assumed that the statistical aggregates of both total output and total non-wage capital of the actual system were made of one composite commodity. In the present case, we find that Sraffa goes back to the method of finding the Standard system. Since the Standard system is supposed to be derived by simply rescaling the individual equations of the actual system, the *R* of the Standard system is not a statistical average but rather an algebraic result derived by the algebraic manipulations of the actual equations. Thus *R* of the Standard system is the 'algebraic average' of the actual system as well:

> α) At *r max* the *ratio* (Old Hyp.) of Cap. to Rev. in *every* Actual System is *the same* as in Standard System
> β) But in Stand. Syst. the ratio is the same for Values and *any* possible prices. Does it follow that the same is true in any Actual System? [No].
> γ) The α holds because at r max the ratio is the same in *each* equation, and therefore in aggregate. In β it holds for the aggregate of Standard System, not necessarily for every equation in it.
>
> Yet the aggregate is *not a statistical* result, but an algebraic one. (D3/12/36: 79)

Although Besicovitch's proof of a unique Standard system came in September 1944 (D3/12/39: 42), Sraffa was not simply waiting for it. He was actively working out a solution for himself. On 1 February 1944 Sraffa goes back to his 'Old Hypothesis'. In this case, the actual system statistically happens to be a Standard system and in this case the value of *R*, given $w=0$, is determined by the physical ratio of net output to non-wage capital. So how could any other *R* be associated with this system since prices cannot affect this ratio, and if that is true for a statistically given Standard system then how could it not be true for a derived Standard system from an actual system that is not itself a Standard system?

> Suppose we start from an Actual System to which the Old Hypothesis applies: therefore it is a Standard System. I thought in such a system the solution was unique.
>
> But now, it can be transformed into any of the $n-1$ other equivalent Standard Systems. Each of these supplies a different unit, a different r, & a different set of solutions of p^s and w. And each is 'correct'. But in the Actual System the 'ratio' of l.h.s. to r.h.s. is constant with resp. to r, only in 'its own' Unit, and R; i.e. the 'ratio' which it gives when measured at 'Values.'
>
> So that it appears that even when the Old Hypo applies, the solution is not unique. But isn't there a contradiction in all this argument?
>
> A Standard System is one [we may say] in which *all* commods. occur in the same proportions on l.h.s. and r.h.s. Therefore in which *each* commod. on r.h.s. is 'itself on l.h.s. multiplied by a constant factor (R)'. In such a system at $w=0$ there can be only *one* value for r ; since it is determined by the quantity of each commod. in terms of itself, without reference to prices. How can we apply to such a system *another* value of R, derived from an equivalent Standard System? No tampering with prices can possibly satisfy this – not even negative prices. (D3/12/36: 82–83, dated 1 February 1944)

So even if Sraffa was satisfied that logically there must be a unique Standard system associated with the actual system, he still needed a solution for *R* because to prove that *R* remains constant with respect to changes in *r* or *w* he needed the Standard net output as his *numéraire*, and to get to that he thought that a solution for *R* was imperative:

> The finding of R, *before solving* (or even writing in final form) the equations is my main problem. The solution by Values is not valid in general, because, a) if I use the Actual Revenue as unit, I assume the Old Hypothesis, i.e. assume the thesis proved, b) I cannot use the Standard Revenue, because it is defined in terms of the number R.
>
> Thus (given an Actual System) finding R and finding the Standard System are the same thing (R *plus* the labour force are the St. System). (D3/12/36: 58, dated 1 February 1944).

During March–April 1944 Sraffa was again working intensely to reduce the problem to a system of linear equations so that a unique solution of R could be derived. In a long note written on 7 April 1944 (D3/12/37:75,(1–5)), Sraffa tried to solve for R by following the procedure described below:

Take a physical system given by:

$$
\begin{aligned}
&A_a + \ldots + K_a + L_a \rightarrow A \\
&\vdots \\
&A_k + \ldots + K_k + L_k \rightarrow K
\end{aligned}
$$

On the assumption that labor-values prevail, we can write:

$$
\begin{aligned}
&A - \left(A_a + \ldots + K_a\right) = R_a\left(A_a + \ldots + K_a\right) \\
&\vdots \\
&K - \left(A_k + \ldots + K_k\right) = R_k\left(A_k + \ldots + K_k\right) \\
&\rightarrow \\
&A = \left(R_a + 1\right)\left(A_a + \ldots + K_a\right) \\
&\vdots \\
&K = \left(R_k + 1\right)\left(A_k + \ldots + K_k\right),
\end{aligned}
$$

where R_a, … , R_k are the proportions given by the ratio of net output to total capital of respective industries or in other words, the organic composition of capital of respective industries measured by their labor-values. Now, if all industries should be able to take their net output in the same proportion as their inputs then:

$$q_a(R_a+1)(A_a+\ldots+K_a)=q_a(R_a+1)A_a+\ldots+q_k(R_k+1)A_k$$
$$\vdots$$
$$q_k(R_k+1)(A_k+\ldots+K_k)=q_a(R_a+1)K_a+\ldots+q_k(R_k+1)K_k,$$

where $q_a, \ldots, q_k$ represent the proportions of their total inputs in which respective industries are able to take their net output. Since one of the equations can be derived from k−1 equations, we add a constraint on the system by adding the equation: $L_a + \ldots + L_k = 1$. This is a linear system of k independent equations with k unknown q's. After solving for q's one can write the equation for the system with $w=0$ as:

$$(q_aA_a+\ldots+q_kA_k)(1+R)=q_aA$$
$$\vdots$$
$$(q_aK_a+\ldots+q_kK_k)(1+R)=q_kK$$

Given that q's are known, we can solve for R from any equation. But the problem with this solution is the same as the one that Sraffa had encountered earlier. The q's are determined on the basis of the prices prevailing when $w=1$ and there is no reason to think that they will be the same when $w=0$. However, this had taken Sraffa a long way in formulating his q-system, which is evidenced by §33, ch. IV of his book, where the same equations appear but R and q's are treated as unknowns in the system.

In September 1944 Besicovitch (D3/12/39: 42, dated 21 September 1944) finally provided Sraffa with a method that directly manipulates the physical system (without having to bring in prices at all) to convert any repetitive system to a Standard system, and also provided a mathematical proof that the Standard system so derived must be unique if all prices must be positive.

This makes it clear that Sraffa's search for a proof of the uniqueness of the Standard system was not due to his (and also Besicovitch's) apparent unawareness of the now well-known Perron-Frobenius theorem, as obliquely suggested by Kurz and Salvadori (2001), for example. As we have seen, since late 1927 Sraffa was never worried about a unique solution for his actual system, given uniform rate of profits. For him the condition of equality of the number of independent equations and the unknowns in the system was good enough to ensure a unique solution. The real problem for him was to prove the constancy of R with respect to changes in r and not just a unique solution of R given zero wages. He realized that the proof required a Standard commodity (that is, the Standard net output) as a particular *numéraire*, which has certain mathematical property that any arbitrary *numéraire* does not have. Sraffa does not seem to be ever in doubt that a Standard system exists. Therefore, the mathematical relation, $r = R(1 - w)$, based on the mathematical property of the Standard system and the Standard commodity was already derived before the way to arrive at the Standard system from the actual system was found. It was only when Besicovitch suggested that there can be n Standard systems and therefore n Standard commodities that Sraffa realized that he needed to prove that there can be only *one* Standard system that is compatible with all positive prices.

Gerkhe and Kurz (2006) claim that:

> Henceforth he [Sraffa] called the assumption that the value of social capital relative to that of social product does not change with a change in distribution 'My Hypothesis' or simply 'Hypothesis.' ... Sraffa eventually had to abandon the idea that any actual economic system could ever be expected to satisfy the hypothesis. He therefore had to construct an artificial system out of his equations that did so. This he accomplished in late January 1944 in terms of the device of the 'Standard commodity' and 'Standard system' (see the pages beginning with 61 in D3/12/36). (p. 109)

This is clearly a misunderstanding of Sraffa's 'Hypothesis'. And since Sraffa's 'Hypothesis' was so central to his entire project, it reveals a serious misunderstanding of Sraffa's project on their part. As we have shown above, Sraffa did finally prove his 'Hypothesis' to be correct and there is no case for their conclusion that 'Sraffa eventually had to abandon the idea that any actual economic system could ever be expected to satisfy the hypothesis'. If this was true then Sraffa's most consequential equation, $r = R(1 - w)$, would be meaningless. The equation is meaningful only if R remains constant when w varies from 0 to 1. But the constancy of R with respect to variations in either w or r is the 'Hypothesis'. Now, Sraffa's claim, both in the notes above discussed as well as the book (Sraffa 1960), about the truthfulness of this equation is not only for the so-called 'imaginary' Standard system but is for the 'real economic system of observation'. If it was true only for the 'imaginary' Standard system then it would have no analytical significance for any given real economy. The importance of the Standard system to Sraffa's argument is that it provides a unit of measure (the Standard commodity) that is unaffected by variations in wages or the rate of profits and therefore, once this measuring standard is used to measure the variations in wages and the prices, then it can be proved that R remains constant in the real system as well. In other words, the 'Hypothesis' is true for the real system as well.

This misunderstanding has also led Gerkhe and Kurz to incorrectly claim that 'Sraffa upon resuming his work on his book in the summer of 1942 adopted *for good* a share concept of wages in his third equations, with wages, w, expressed as a proportion of the net product ($1 \geq w \geq 0$).' (p. 107, emphasis added) (The same idea was also expressed in Kurz and Salvadori 2005.) Now, as we have shown above and will further discuss in Chap. 7, Sraffa does not hold on to a share wage concept 'for good'. He realized that, if the net output of the real system is used as the measuring standard, then there is no reason why this composite commodity itself will not be affected by the variations in wages. Therefore, if it is used as the standard of measure for wages and prices then it cannot be demonstrated that R remains fixed with respect to variations in wages or the rate of profits. This is why Sraffa had to abandon the share wage concept and adopt the Standard commodity as the standard of measure, because this composite commodity has the property of not being affected by variations in wages.

If it could be proved that R remains constant when wages are taken to be a share of the real net output then Sraffa's critique of marginal productivity theory would be complete. It would demonstrate that the size of capital remains fixed with respect to variations in the rate of profits; that is, the rate of profits is independent of the size of capital. Since Sraffa could not prove his 'Hypothesis' within a share wage concept, he had to move to a commodity money wage concept with 'money' strictly defined in terms of the Standard commodity. But in this case it cannot be proved that the size of capital remains constant with respect to variations in the rate of profits—all it proves is that both the value of the net output and the value of the capital change proportionately and hence their ratio remains constant. Therefore, Sraffa had to develop his analysis further to demonstrate that the relationship between variations in the size of capital and the rate of profits can be such that it violates the predictions of the marginal productivity theory (see Chapter VI of Sraffa 1960).

Followers of Garegnani have consistently shown their inability to understand the significance of Sraffa's Standard system and the Standard commodity for his theory. This has led to another misunderstanding that Sraffa's Standard commodity was actually designed to solve Ricardo's problem of the 'invariable measure of value', to which we will turn in the next chapter. But before proceeding any further, it may not be out of place here to point out my disagreement with a few other recent interpretations of this problem based on archival research.

De Vivo (2003) and Gilibert (2003, 2006) also think that Sraffa abandoned his 'hypothesis' rather quickly. They interpret his 'hypothesis' as a 'trick' to solve for prices:

> Sraffa appears to think, if the '*Hypothesis*' held, it was possible to proceed as follows: Making $r = 0$ determine prices (which would be equal to labours embodied); reckoning product and capital at these prices, determine the 'true' r, by means of the 'true' r determine the 'true' prices. Basically, Sraffa thought that by means of the '*hypothesis*' he could do what Marx had done in his 'transformation', i.e., use *given* prices (equal to embodied labours, i.e., the prices determined for $r = 0$) in order to determine the rate of profits, and in turn use this rate of profits to determine the prices. The validity of the '*hypothesis*' would have warranted the validity of this way of proceeding. At this stage Sraffa even thought that he had rehabilitated '*Old Moor*' (i.e., Karl Marx). (De Vivo 2003, p. 17)

Now we come to the 3rd equations, where the actual production levels are set equal to 1, i.e., $x = 1$:

$(1 + \mathrm{r})Ap + lw = \mathrm{p}$ The 'trick' used to solve these equations, according to the 'hypothesis', is the following:

(i) Solve the (linear) equations for relative prices p^* corresponding to $\mathrm{r} = 0$;

(ii) compute the maximum profit factor (equal to the surplus factor) using these prices: $(1 + R) = 1p^* / 1Ap^*$;

(iii) By setting $\boldsymbol{1l}$ and $\boldsymbol{1ApR}$ equal to 1, derive the fundamental relation $r = R(1 - w)$;

(iv) Compute actual prices corresponding to a certain level of w (or r);

(v) Note that prices p^* are proportional to labour contents and that therefore the rate of profit is equal to the ratio of Marxian surplus value to constant capital.

Afterwards, Sraffa realized that this hypothesis amounted to the very restrictive assumption of a rigid proportionality among the components of $\boldsymbol{1}$ and $\boldsymbol{1A}$, a true disaster for the model. (Gilibert 2003, pp. 39–40)

Now, in the light of the evidence produced in this chapter, this is clearly a misinterpretation. As we have seen above, Sraffa at one point did try to derive R by first deriving prices at $w = 1$ and then using those prices to find R but quickly realized that this was illegitimate. The point of finding R, however, was not to somehow simplify the problem of determining the prices or to show that Marx was right after all in transforming values to prices of production. The point was to find the specific *numéraire* that was needed to prove the 'hypothesis' on which his whole theory depended, which was to show that distribution of income or the net output in terms of wages and the rate of profits could be taken as 'given' from outside independently of prices—prices played the role of only accounting for the given distribution of income. The point of abandoning the 'hypothesis' because Sraffa realized that it amounted to a highly restrictive assumption also does not hold water because it is clear from the evidence produced in this chapter that Sraffa quite consciously made such an assumption in the beginning, so there is no case for the thesis that he abandoned it after 'realizing' that this was too restrictive.

Bellofiore (2008) follows de Vivo's and Gilibert's interpretation of Sraffa's 'hypothesis' but he misinterprets it:

The 'Hypo', as he calls it, will crucially drive his research for a few years, and will be reluctantly abandoned, leaving traces behind it. According to it, the 'surplus rate' (i.e., the physical ratio of the social product over the whole of the anticipated means of production) is put equal to the 'maxi-

> mum rate of profits' (i.e., the value of profits when wages = 0 over the value of anticipated capital; a ratio which may also be read as the value of the net product, or gross income, over the value of the means of production, or the non-wage capital advanced). The 'Hypo' asserts that, though income distribution may be influenced by prices, this ratio, on average, is constant. (p. 76)

I'm inclined to think that here the major problem perhaps is with the language. Contrary to Bellofiore's assertion, Sraffa's context does not allow prices to influence income distribution (unless Bellofiore thinks that the context of the 'Hypo' is the adjustment of 'market prices' to 'natural prices', which would be a serious conceptual error). In Sraffa's context, it is the variations in income distribution (i.e., r or w) that affect prices and the 'hypothesis' asserts that such price movements will not affect the ratio of the total values of net output to non-wage capital—thus the question of any kind of 'average' does not even arise here. In any case, it is not clear to me what Bellofiore could mean by the phrase, 'this ratio, on average, is constant'. Either the ratio remains constant with respect to variations in r or it does not. Bellofiore, however, further argues that:

> The Standard System allows to accurately measure the 'distortion' of prices from values, due to the circumstance that the 'net product' and the means of production are made of an aggregate of commodities in proportions which diverge from the weights they should have in the Standard system. (p. 81)

The meaning of this again is not clear. The prices in the Standard system are not equal to values—they will be exactly equal to what must prevail in the actual system—and the Standard commodity has no means by which to measure how much prices diverge from values. All this is, however, a prelude to Bellofiore's main thesis that:

> The long journey recorded in the Sraffa papers allows us to give a deeper meaning to the 'normalizations' written down in §10 and §12. As we know, in §12, national money income is taken as the standard of prices. In §10 direct labour of the society is also set equal to 1. Putting arbitrarily the 'monetary expression of labour time' also equal to 1, this is exactly the

> 'postulate' of the New Interpretation proposed by Duménil and Foley. The Italian economist actually met an argument to justify the idea that behind 'new value' in money there is nothing but 'living labor': the argument in chapter 7 of Marx's Capital. An argument Sraffa may well have had at the back of his mind when finishing his book. (p. 84)

Here §10 and §12 are references to Sraffa's normalizations of total labor to 1 and the value of total net output being equal to 1 (Sraffa 1960). Bellofiore's thesis has three fundamental problems however. First, in Sraffa's 2nd equations there is surplus production but labor does not show up in the equations, so to what could this surplus be attributed? Second, normalizations of two separate quantities to 1 by no means imply equating the two quantities. As a matter of fact, Sraffa's two normalizations have separate units and nowhere in Sraffa's book or the notes is the concept of 'monetary expression of labour time' introduced. But most importantly, the third problem is that the normalization of the value of net output of the actual system to 1 as introduced in §12 has, as mentioned above, a very brief life in Sraffa's book. Soon after Standard system is derived the normalization of §12 is abandoned and a new normalization adopted, which is equal to the value of the net output of the Standard system (see Sraffa 1960, §34, pp. 24–25). And there is no reason to think that the value of the net output of the actual system and the Standard system would be equal anywhere in the range of $r > 0$. Thus Bellofiore's fundamental premise for his thesis that Sraffa equates total labor with the value of the total net output of the actual system is false.

All this notwithstanding, Carter (2014) closely follows in the footsteps of Bellofiore in maintaining that Sraffa's two normalizations in §10 and §12 amount to equating total direct labor with the value of the total real net output. He argues this on the ground that Sraffa 'refers to both as "the national income" (§13, p. 12)' (Carter 2014, p. 7). Now, this is clearly a misunderstanding. Sraffa's reference in §13 is to the range of wages from 1 to 0 as fractions of 'national income'. Because the national income is normalized to 1 and is taken as the *numéraire* for prices and wages and the total labor is normalized to 1, the wage per unit of labor is nothing but a fraction of national income. But this does not mean that both the value of net output and total direct labor time (say 1 year of labor) can be equivalently referred to as 'national income'. From here on, a string of elementary mistakes follows. For example, Sraffa's 'repetitive system' is incorrectly interpreted as a system in Standard proportion with only 'basics' and his 'non-repetitive' system is incorrectly interpreted as a system that includes non-basics (p. 29). This naturally leads to a non-understanding of the role of the Standard system and the Standard commodity in Sraffa's notes, which is evidenced by Carter's use of the straight line relationship between r and w without bringing in the Standard commodity as the *numéraire*. Carter further goes on to claim, on the basis of a Sraffa's note D3/12/2: 20, which he 'conjectures' was written in 1945, that 'generally speaking cracking this nut of the feedback effect (the so-called "transformation of the inputs") would occupy Sraffa's thinking for many years, and it was precisely on this path that he was led to the concept of "stability" in the means of production, a notion which eventually blossomed into the Standard commodity and the Standard system' (p. 24). But this again is a clear misunderstanding. As we have seen in this chapter, the fully fledged mathematical construction of the Standard system and the Standard commodity including the proof of its uniqueness was already in Sraffa's possession in September 1944.

The main problem with most of the neo-Ricardian and the neo-Marxist interpretations of Sraffa's Standard system and the Standard commodity stems from the fact that they think this device was developed to solve either Ricardo's problem of the 'invariable measure of value' or Marx's problem of the 'transformation of values to prices of production'. But the truth of the matter is that the Standard system and the Standard commodity was developed to prove his own 'Hypothesis' and, as we shall see in the next two chapters, only after that did Sraffa attempt to reinterpret both Ricardo's problem of the 'invariable measure of value' and Marx's 'transformation problem' as a problem of finding an 'average commodity'.

This long digression from the main story was only to demonstrate how poorly Sraffa's central theoretical concept is understood in the Sraffian literature even today, more than fifty years after the publication of his book and more than twenty years after the opening of his archive.

Switch in Techniques

The fact that the foundations of Sraffa's critique of 'marginal product of capital' theory of interest rested on his proposition that R is constant with respect to changes in w or r becomes clear when we look at his notes on switch in techniques. It should be kept in mind that Sraffa had a habit of working on both a simplified model as well as more general and complicated cases simultaneously. For example, all through this period he kept working on the problem of fixed capital and depreciation and general joint-production cases, as well as the case of several rotation periods for various industries and so on. In this context, by June 1944 Sraffa relaxes the assumption of only one given technique and introduces the idea of several techniques being available and with it the possibility of switches in techniques with respect to changes in r or w. Sraffa thought this case to be important in the context of 'accumulation of capital'.[3] As Sraffa had already established that for any given technique the movement of w from 1 to 0 would make the price of any commodity move up and down in a complicated pattern against the Standard commodity as the unit of measure, and if the movements of prices were superimposed for two techniques then the two curves could cut each other several times. This led Sraffa to conclude that, since the relationship between w and r is a straight line in both the techniques, this could happen only if the two straight lines where superimposed on each other, otherwise they could cut only once. The conclusion Sraffa was trying to get at was that the existence of several techniques and the possibility of switches in techniques with respect to changes in w and r would not affect the conclusion that he had arrived at for one given technique. It was, as a matter of fact, Besicovitch, who pointed out to Sraffa that the two w–r curves of the two techniques would not coincide because, if he took their respective

[3] It should be noted that the direction of causation with respect to switches in techniques in the case of accumulation of capital is not the same as in the case of marginal productivity theory of interest. In the case of 'accumulation', a rise in wages due to accumulation of capital leads to a switch in favour of a more machine intensive technique, whereas in the case of marginal productivity theory, the increase in capital intensity leads to a rise in wages. Sraffa used the 'accumulation' case to make sense of Marx's 'falling rate of profit' thesis. On this question, see Sraffa's critique of Bortkiewicz in file D1/91 and Sinha (2014).

Standard commodities as units of measure for *w* and prices, then the two sets of *w* and prices cannot be compared. On the other hand, if he measured *w* and prices in the two systems with the Standard commodity of the first technique then it turns into an arbitrary unit of measure for the system of the second technique, and in this case the *w–r* relation for the second system would be non-linear. Thus it could cut the first straight line *w–r* several times. Thus the discovery of the re-switching phenomenon, as we know it, is not Sraffa's own but Besicovitch's—an accidental discovery that Sraffa was not even looking for:

> My suggestion was that, in the case of several intersections of the prices from 2 alternative methods, the two systems resulting must have the same value of R. The reason given being that the connection between w and r in the two systems being linear, the two straight lines cannot intersect more than once: & if they must have several points in common, the lines must coincide, & therefore also coincide with R.
>
> B's answer is that they are straight lines if each is in *its own* standard unit: but then they cannot be compared. Here they are both taken in the unit of *one* of the two systems: *that one* is a straight line, but (in that unit) the other is a curve – so, many intersections are possible. (D3/12/37:11, dated 14 June 1944)

In the 'Preface' to the *Production of Commodities by Means of Commodities* Sraffa wrote:

> While the central propositions had taken shape in the late 1920's, particular points, such as the Standard commodity, joint products and fixed capital, were worked out in the 'thirties and early 'forties. In the period since 1955, while these pages were being put together out of a mass of old notes, little was added, apart from filling gaps which had become apparent in the process (such as the adapting of the distinction of 'basics' and 'non-basics' to the case of joint products). (1960: vi)

Interestingly, the proposition regarding re-switching of techniques is not even mentioned—surely this was not just a slip or a case of forgetfulness on Sraffa's part. Sraffa is right in stating that during the period from 1955 to 1959, when he came back to his notes once again, not much of substance was added. However, it is important to note that in these notes one finds Sraffa's position on the condition of uniformity of the rate of profits and it being a non-price phenomenon, that is, not a phenomenon based on equilibrium of demand and supply, becomes stronger.

Notes of 1955–59

As we have seen in Chap. 3, during the late 1920s when 'the central proposition had taken shape' Sraffa was quite worried about the justification for the condition of uniform rate of profits in his system of equations. Although he had already come to the conclusion that the average rate of profits of the system could be discovered by solving for uniform rate of profits in the system, and which was his main concern, still his average was tied up with the solution of prices on the condition that industrial rates of profit were uniform—a condition that required justification. As we have seen, in early 1942 he assumed Marx's 'simple reproduction' where all the surplus is assumed to be consumed by the capitalists. However, when he began to analyze the effect of changes in wages on the value of the ratio of net output to non-wage capital he realized that he had to move from an 'inventory wage' concept to a 'money' or 'share in total net product' wage concept. The problem was how to maintain the assumption that capitalists consume all of the surplus when surplus is realized by reducing the share of wages in the total net output. If capitalists and workers consume different goods then wouldn't it create a disequilibrium situation and force the system to adjust the commodity mix of the net output even if the assumption that capitalists consume all the surplus is maintained? His preliminary answer was that he is only considering a paper transfer of income, and that is independent of how the income is disposed off. So by then Sraffa had realized that the income that is generated in production has to be accounted for independently of how it is disposed off. At this stage Sraffa was still holding on to the belief that the income measured by labor-values, that is, prices when $w = 1$, remains constant when the share of w in the net output moves from 1 to 0, as is the case with Marx's transformation of values to prices of production.

However, once he realizes that this proposition cannot be sustained then the concept of wages as a *share* of net output had to be given up too. Now the search for the unit of wages and prices that would ensure the constancy of capital–output ratio with respect to changes in the average rate of profits led Sraffa to the conclusion that the average rate of profits of any actual system can be discovered independently of the knowledge of prices. This liberated Sraffa from thinking that he needed to first ascertain total income produced and then ascertain the relationship of prices with the ratio in which that income is distributed. Now he could go directly from a given rate of wages to determining the average rate of profits. So prices must be such that the independently given average rate of profits is actualized. Now, if the actual system turns out to be a Standard system then Sraffa's thesis is proved irrespective of industrial rates of profit being equal or not. However, if the actual system is not in the Standard proportion then it so happens that prices that actualize the independently given average rate of profits are only compatible with uniform rate of industrial profits. But this is a *consequence* of the fact that the average rate of profits is determined independently of prices and not simultaneously with it:

> {…}, the rate of profits at the various levels of w will be $r = \mathrm{R}(1 - w)$. Individual prices will move in all directions with the variation of w, but here again prices will make no difference: r is a ratio between two quantities of the same composite commodity and can actually be discovered before knowing what those prices are. The rate of profits is embedded 'in the things' and no manipulation of prices could ever affect it. [There could be no more tangible evidence (convincing proof) of the rate of profits [being, as] a non-price phenomenon (effect)]. (D3/12/53: 32, 1955)

The fact that Sraffa has by now completely jettisoned the idea of a classical gravitation mechanism becomes clearer in yet another note of 14 February 1956 in relation to changes in *w*:

> The impulse towards price change is an internal one to each industry. It arises from its own internal conditions—not from those conditions *compared* with those of other industries. Hence the possibility of an *invariable* commodity. (D3/12/59: 24)

Here what is claimed is that with a change in w the average rate of profits of the system must change by the formula $r = \mathrm{R}(1-w)$. Now, if the direct to indirect labor ratios are not equal for all the industries in the system then some industries will have surplus and some deficit, which is solved by accompanying changes in the prices of commodities of those industries. In other words, given the condition of equal rate of profits, a surplus or a deficit implies that industrial 'equations' no longer hold and the equations can be re-established only through changes in prices. There is no mechanism through which these prices change. It cannot be observed because it does not happen over a period of time. And it is this logical relation that reveals why the Standard commodity is not just any *numéraire*. It is because, if there were an industry that would experience neither a surplus nor a deficit with a change in w, then the price of the product of that industry would not be affected and therefore it would be the ideal Standard by which the changes in prices, due to changes in w or r, of all other commodities could be measured. It is highly interesting that Sraffa clarifies this point by contrasting it with the classical case of *comparison* of differences in the rates of profit of industries and the accompanying mechanism of changes in prices due to changes in supply over a period of time. In this case, even if we assume constant returns to scale for all the industries as well as the condition that the use of total labor in the system remains constant all through the adjustment, a change in the commodity mix of the net output cannot be denied and therefore the idea of a Standard commodity becomes useless. It is because the change in prices in this case is not *logically* related to changes in wages but is rather due to an external factor, that is, due to the fact that the increase in quantities supplied of the commodities can only be sold at lower prices and the fall in the quantities supplied of commodities can only be sold at higher prices due to downward sloping demand curves for commodities.

This point gets further reinforcement from another note of the same period in which Sraffa is defending the socialist ideal of 'all incomes to labor' against arguments put forward by Hayek and Hicks (in other drafts of the same argument Joan Robinson's name is also included):

> If we now move in the opposite direction and, starting from the de facto level of wages, raise them until they absorb the whole net product of society and r = 0, we see that the distribution can be effected by a uniform rise of wages in all industries, through a readjustment of the prices of the products. The adaptation of the prices of commodities is what makes possible to reconcile the equality of the rate of surplus value in different industries and the equality of the rate of profits: [the equality of r holds at any moment, statically: the equality of *both* holds dynamically, in the sense that a change in either will change the other equally, till they both reach zero].This relation is obscured by the ingrained notion of economists that prices of commodities are handed down from somewhere, so that they are independent of the way in which the proceeds are distributed. An illustration (consequence) of this view is that two such opposite writers as v. H {von Hayek} and J.R. {J.R. Hicks} take it for granted that in a state in which the workers receive the whole product of industry this would inevitably result in the anomaly of higher wages in industries using much capital. (D3/12/54: 8)

Sraffa's argument appears to be as follows. Let us suppose we begin with an equilibrium situation with a positive uniform rate of profits in all industries. We also assume that the demand functions of all the capitalists and the workers are identical. Now, suppose a socialist government wins the election and orders that all the profits must be transferred to the workers. If this transfer takes place within every firm then industry wise the workers of the industries that use relatively more 'capital' (indirect labor) per worker would receive relatively higher rates of wages compared to the workers of the industries that use relatively less 'capital' per worker. This is the conclusion of economic theorists who think that, since market demand and supply conditions have not been disturbed, the old prices must prevail and thus a transfer of income from the capitalist class to the workers must amount to unequal wages for workers. Sraffa's point is that prices are determined by the equation system and therefore a transfer of income would *ipso facto* imply a change in the set of prices such that all wages are equal, which absorbs all the income, irrespective of market demand and supply conditions. As a matter of fact, the prices determined by Sraffa's equations would most likely represent *disequilibrium* of demand and supply since a change in prices would most likely affect quantities demanded even though quantities supplied have remained constant.

And finally, in a draft for the 'Preface' to the book, written in 1957, Sraffa makes it abundantly clear that his prices are not necessarily 'equilibrium' prices:

> This is not proposed as a complete system of equilibrium. The data assumed are not sufficient to determine either distribution or values. Only the effects of hypothetical, arbitrarily assumed extra data (such as wages, or the rate of profits) are discussed. {…} It is offered as a preliminary and there is no a priori reason why, on the basis of it, an equilibrium system should be built: there is some room left for it, as this is confessedly indeterminate; but the question is whether there is room enough for the marginal system. (D3/12/46: 20, dated 2 April 1957)

As a matter of fact, the original first sentence was written as: 'This is no system of equilibrium'. Then the 'no' was crossed out and in its place was inserted, 'not proposed as a complete'.

6

The Second Interlude

In Chap. 4, I mentioned that there are two decade-long breaks in Sraffa's notes. The second break came soon after 1944 and continued until 1955 (although in this case, a few notes written from 1945 to 1948 have survived). In the interim period, however, a major event happened. In 1951 the long awaited *Works and Correspondence of David Ricardo* in eleven volumes started to come out of the Cambridge University Press. Leaving aside the quality of Sraffa's editing work, which was universally hailed as the work that set the standard for such future works and brought Sraffa the great honor of being awarded the Söderström gold medal of the Royal Swedish Academy of Science,[1,2] a notable feature of this publication was the 'Introduction' to volume one written in collaboration with Maurice

[1] The letter to Sraffa by the secretary of the Royal Swedish Academy of Science stated that the medal was awarded 'in recognition of your eminent achievement in publishing the works of David Ricardo, thereby penetrating deeply into Ricardo's thoughts and presenting them in a clear critical analysis. Since its institution nearly sixty years ago, this medal has only been awarded seven times; among the recipients one could mention Gustav Cassel, Eli Heckscher, J.M. Keynes and Gunnar Myrdal. ' (B17/1: 6).

[2] In his review of this work, George Stigler (1953) wrote: 'Others may be uncomfortable as I at undiluted praise, and perhaps one should criticize Sraffa for the insertion of an erroneous "not" (VIII, 359) or argue the irrelevance of the splendid tale of Mr. — (III, 427ff.) in order to emphasize more subtly the superlative quality of the scholarship. But usual rules must bow to unusual events: here is a task that need not be performed again.' (p. 587).

A. Sinha, *A Revolution in Economic Theory*,
DOI 10.1007/978-3-319-30616-2_6

Dobb. This 'Introduction' brought about a change in the interpretation of Ricardo's *Principles* in a subtle but substantial way. As we have already noted in Chap. 4, there are no preparatory notes for this 'Introduction' available in Sraffa's files, only the final galley-proof. Given that, in Sraffa's own words, 'by the summer 1940, six volumes of the present edition had been set up in page-proof, while the volume of Speeches and Evidence had reached the stage of galley-proofs' (Sraffa 1951, p. ix), one would expect that Sraffa must have had at least a rough draft of the 'Introduction' ready by then. Moreover, given that Sraffa had a habit of writing several drafts of any piece he readied for publication, there is no doubt in my mind that there must have been several drafts of the 'Introduction' written over a number of years. As a matter of fact, in a response to Keynes's letter of 26 March 1943, in which Keynes showed his extreme frustration with the whole project dragging on for so long, Sraffa reported that 'of the Introductions, all those which must go in the middle of a volume are ready: the others (three of them) go at the beginning of volumes and can be printed later, on pages with roman numerals. On these I have done much work, and drafted parts over and over again: all the material is collected, but it is the drafting of the Introductions that has been holding up the whole thing.' (D3/11/65: 26, dated 31 March 1943). No sign of these 'drafts' are available in Sraffa's files. Had they been available to us it could have given us a direct glimpse of how Sraffa's interpretation of Ricardo evolved or changed over the two decades of the 1930s and 1940s. In any case, below I try to develop a sketch of the evolution of Sraffa's interpretation of Ricardo over time.[3]

Sraffa's Early Position on Ricardo's Theory of Value

As we have seen in Chap. 2, in 1925 Sraffa's understanding of Ricardo ('classical economics') was very much in line with Marshall's interpretation that Ricardo took supply functions as horizontal straight lines in the price quantity plane and therefore prices were independent of demand

[3] The arguments in this chapter have also been presented at various levels of developments in Sinha (2010a,c and 2016).

considerations. This implied that Ricardo was either assuming constant returns to scale in a partial equilibrium framework or also no substitution possibilities in a general equilibrium framework.

In an eight-page note on Marx's and Ricardo's theory of value written prior to 1928, Sraffa attributes to Ricardo the proposition that distribution between profits and wages does not affect value. Then he notes that the importance of Ricardo's theory for Marx is that a rise in wages leads to a fall in profits and it does not affect value. Then the importance of Ricardo's distinction between labor and wages is noted and it is claimed that all the wrong interpretations of Marx confuse labor with wages. Further on, Sraffa notes that what Ricardo calls profit Marx calls surplus value. (D1/21: 1–8). Clearly, at this stage a pure labor theory of value is attributed to Ricardo, at least in the sense that labor is the *sole cause* of changes in value and that changes in distribution do not affect it. In 1928 the position remains the same. For example, in a note titled 'The wages of Shepherds are capital' a footnote appears stating: 'note however that on Ricardo's theory this would not be true—values are independent of wages' (D3/12/7: 40) and again, 'If not Ricardo's proposition is true. Variations in wages do not affect values…' (D3/12/7: 94).

In his Lecture notes of 1928–31, Sraffa tells the story that Ricardo was a practical man and his interest in economic theory was purely driven by practical matters such as the 'corn law' controversies. He notes that in the 'Preface' to the *Principles*, Ricardo announces that:

> the principal problem in Political Economy is to determine the laws which regulate distribution', that is the distribution of 'the produce of the earth, all that is derived from its surface by the united application of labour, machinery and capital…among the three classes of the community, namely the proprietor of the land, the owner of the stock of capital necessary for its cultivation, and the labourers by whose industry it is cultivated.

And then Sraffa goes on to add:

> The wording of this definition is remarkable; it is intended {or} meant to apply to the distribution of the whole of the national income, but it only mentions the produce of the surface of the earth, and regards all capital and all the labourers as only engaged in its cultivation. Ricardo was a city man,

> in fact he was in his outlook a typical representative of the commercial and manufacturing classes and was not likely to over-estimate the importance of agriculture, as the French physiocrats did, so as to make it include all productive industry. This definition is in fact characteristic of Ricardo's main interest which was not so much distribution in general between all those who take part in it as distribution between land-lord on the one side and all the others on the other. As Professor Cannan has shown, the origin of the Ricardian theory of distribution is entirely found in the Corn Law controversy of 1813–15. Ricardo's scientific interest in economics developed when his main theory had already been established in his pamphlets. This theory of distribution was an extremely effective argument against the Corn Laws.'The divergence of interests with regard to the Corn Laws was a typical divergence of the interests of classes, and not of individuals. It was not a question of the rich against the poor, but of the land-owning class against the commercial and manufacturing class.' Ricardo's theory regarded as the fundamental problem, connected with the cost or production and value, the distribution between the landlord and the other classes; when this was done the division of their share between capital and labour would take place on entirely different principles, but changes in the proportions of this distribution would not materially affect value of the product. (D2/4/6: 6–8)

On the presupposition that Ricardo's theory was mainly designed to be used as a stick to beat the landlords, Sraffa at this stage believed that Ricardo remained ambivalent about whether cost of production included only labor or also use of capital and went on to more or less agree with Jacob Hollander's thesis of successive weakening (or at least ambivalence) of Ricardo's 'labor theory of value':

> Therefore Ricardo's theory lays great emphasis on the distinction between rent on one side and all other shares on the other; but he left in the background the question as to how the distribution of the other shares, that is, wages and interest, takes place, and the effects of the changes in the proportions of this division on the value of the product.What Ricardo's views were on this point is rather obscure, and it would be hard to say whether his theory of value based on the quantity of labour must be taken literally or interpreted as including the use {of} capital amongst costs. Probably, as Professor Hollander has shown in his book on Ricardo, he held different views at different times, and his changing views having been embodied in

successive editions of the principles, the result is that opposite passages from them can be quoted in support of both views.

But however the historical point as to the interpretation of Ricardo is settled, it is, I think, true to say that Ricardo's views on this point are not very important; they play a secondary part in his theory, and as the question had no practical importance in his time he certainly gave little thought to it. (D2/4: 9–10)

The 'Introduction': A Dramatic Shift

All this apparently changed dramatically in the 1951 'Introduction'. Now Sraffa claims that the theory of rent was designed to 'get rid of rent' 'in order to simplify the problem of the distribution between capitalist and labourer' (p. xxiii). The dominant story in the 'Introduction' runs on two parallel tracks. On the one track runs the concern for a theory of profits that is independent of prices and on the other track runs the concern for determining the effect on the rate of profits of a change in the rate of wages.

On the first track the story runs as follows: In *circa* 1914 and in the *Essay on Profits*, published in February 1915, Ricardo held the opinion that 'it is the profits of the farmer that regulate the profits of all other trades'. Malthus had opposed this view by asserting that 'the profits of the farmer no more regulate the profits of other trades, than the profits of other trades regulate the profits of the farmer' (p. xxxi). The 'rational foundation' of Ricardo's thesis, according to Sraffa, must have been the idea that only in agriculture it can be conceived that all the inputs, including real wages, and outputs are made of a single commodity, 'corn'. In such a case the rate of profits would be determined in physical terms in the 'corn industry' and if competition must equalize the rate of profits across industries then all other industries' prices must adjust such that they all receive the rate of profits determined in the 'corn industry' independently of prices. Malthus apparently had opposed this idea on the ground that '[i]n no case of production, is the produce exactly of the same nature as the capital advanced. Consequently we can never properly refer to a material rate of produce…' (p. xxxi).

It is Sraffa's contention that, due to Malthus's criticism of the 'rational foundation' of Ricardo's theory of profit, which, 'at the cost of considerable simplification', is able to determine the rate of profits of the system by completely by-passing the problem of measurement of heterogeneous capital and therefore the problem of a theory of value, Ricardo had to abandon this thesis and search for a general solution of the problem of determining the rate of profits in the system. As Ricardo wrote to James Mill on 30 December 1815, 'I know I shall be soon stopped by the word price' during the initial stages of the writing of the *Principles*. The 'labor theory of value' as the general theory of prices proposed in the *Principles* was, according to Sraffa, designed to solve this problem:

> It was now labour, instead of corn, that appeared on both sides of the account—in modern terms, both as input and output: as a result, the rate of profits was no longer determined by the ratio of the corn produced to the corn used up in production, but, instead, by the ratio of the total labour of the country to the labour required to produce the necessaries for that labour. (But while the theory that the profits of the farmer determine all other profits disappears in the *Principles*, the more general proposition that the productivity of labour on land which pays no rent is fundamental in determining general profits continues to occupy a central position). (p. xxxii–iii)

Sraffa reinforces the thesis of the corn-ratio theory of profits by citing Ricardo's letter of 13 June 1820 to McCulloch in which Ricardo writes: 'After all, the great questions of Rent, Wages, and Profits must be explained by the proportions in which the whole produce is divided between landlords, capitalists, and labourers, and which are not essentially connected with the doctrine of value' (p. xxxiii).

On the second track, Sraffa argues that as early as his *Essays on Profits* Ricardo had repudiated, although still in its agricultural form, Adam Smith's dictum that a rise in the price of corn, through its effect on wages, would raise all other prices. He had also pointed out that the exchangeable prices of all commodities rise or fall as difficulties of their production rise or fall. Thus improvements in agriculture or importation of cheap corn must lead to a fall in the price of corn vis-à-vis other commodities and therefore a fall in wages and consequently a rise in real profits. In his letter of the 30 December 1815 to James Mill, Ricardo went on to elaborate three points that must be clarified in order to understand the problem of value: '(a) the distinction between causes which affect the value of money and causes which affect the value of commodities; (b) the supposition of the invariability of the precious metals as a standard of value; (c) the opposition to the view that the price of corn regulates the price of all other commodities'. Sraffa goes on to state that 'these three things, which are so closely connected in his [Ricardo's] mind as to be almost identified, are what he calls "the sheet anchor on which all my propositions are built" (p. xxxiv).'

The crucial point in this context is that a rise or fall in wages would have no effect on exchange ratios of commodities if the ratios of direct to indirect labor-time are uniform across industries. Hence if the money-commodity happens to be one of the commodities produced within the system then a rise or fall in wages would have no impact on the prices. Thus it clearly refutes Adam Smith's dictum that a rise in wages would lead to a rise in the prices of all commodities. However, if the ratios of direct to indirect labor-time are not uniform across industries then a rise or fall in wages would affect all the prices to ensure an equal rate of profits across industries. Now, if these changes in prices are measured against a particular money-commodity then the question arises as to how to understand and ascertain the changes in price of a commodity due to changes in wages when the standard against which it is measured is itself affected by the same cause? But why this is a problem?

Sraffa's answer to this question is that:

> This preoccupation with the effect of a change in wages arose from his approach to the problem of value which, as we have seen, was dominated by his theory of profits. The 'principal problem of Political Economy' was in his view the division of the national product between classes and in the course of that investigation he was troubled by the fact that the size of this product appears to change when the division changes. Even though nothing has occurred to change the magnitude of the aggregate, there may be *apparent* changes due solely to change in measurement, owing to the fact that measurement is in terms of value and relative values have been altered as a result of a change in the division between wages and profits. This is particularly evident in the extreme case where the aggregate is composed of

> the same commodities in the same quantities, and yet its magnitude will appear to have changed as measured in value.
>
> The problem of value which interested Ricardo was how to find a measure of value which would be invariant to changes in the division of the product; for, if a rise or fall of wages by itself brought about a change in the magnitude of the social product, it would be hard to determine accurately the effect on profits (this was, of course, the same problem as has been mentioned earlier in connection with Ricardo's corn-ratio theory of profits.) On the other hand, Ricardo was not interested for its own sake in the problem of why two commodities produced by the same quantities of labour are not of the same exchangeable value. He was concerned with it only in so far as thereby relative values are affected by changes in wages. The two points of view of difference and of change are closely linked together; yet the search for an invariable measure of value, which is so much at the centre of Ricardo's system, arises exclusively from the second and would have no counterpart in an investigation of the first. (Sraffa 1951, p. xlviii–xlix)

Some Problems with Sraffa's New Position

The reader may have noticed that Sraffa's new thesis on Ricardo has an uncanny affinity with his own project. We have noted in Chap. 2 that in Summer 1927 Sraffa had identified the classical theory with an *essentialist* theory that reduced the 'ultimate cause' of cost of production to *labor*. From the 'Winter 1927–28' notes Sraffa embarked on his new and revolutionary project of removing the *essentialism* of the classical theory by building a non-causal theory of value on purely objective physical data. By 1944 Sraffa had concluded that for any given system of inputs and outputs, its rate of profits can be found without the knowledge of prices if the wage rate in terms of the Standard commodity is given from outside. Now a direct link can be drawn between these developments and Sraffa's hypothesis of a 'corn-ratio' theory as the 'rational foundation' of Ricardo's theory of profits. But not only that. The idea that Ricardo's concern for the 'invariable measure of value' relates to the problem of keeping the size of the pie constant when it is cut in various proportions relates to his problem of keeping the maximum rate of profits, '*R*', constant when wages and consequently prices change.

By now Sraffa's interpretation of Ricardo has become highly controversial. This is not a place to review this literature, however. In Sinha (2010a, b), which also contains a review of some of the literature on this controversy, I have made the case in detail that Ricardo's concern for the 'invariable measure of value' was not related to the problem of changes in the size of the pie when it is cut in different proportions but rather it was related to establishing the hypothesis that labor is the sole cause of *changes* in relative values or 'variations in wages do not affect value', which, as we have seen, was Sraffa's own position in 1928. Here I will briefly point out that this position still subsists in Sraffa's 'Introduction' although it is submerged under the new interpretation. Our object here is only to draw an arrow between Sraffa's notes and his new interpretation of Ricardo's *Principles.*

Let us begin with Sraffa's story on track one, that '[i]t was now labour, instead of corn, that appeared on both sides of the account—in modern terms, both as input and output: as a result, the rate of profits was no longer determined by the ratio of the corn produced to the corn used up in production, but, instead, by the ratio of the total labour of the country to the labour required to produce the necessaries for that labour'. Leaving aside the controversial issue of the 'corn-ratio' theory as Ricardo's pre-*Principles* theory of profits, the question is whether the 'labor-ratio' theory of profits is present in the *Principles.*

On my reading of Ricardo, it is not. In Section IV of his chapter on 'Value', Ricardo establishes that '[o]n account then of the different degrees of durability of their capitals, or, which is the same thing, on account of the time which must elapse before one set of commodities can be brought to market, they will be valuable, not exactly in proportion to the quantity of labour bestowed on them,–they will not be as two to one, but something more, to compensate for the greater length of time which must elapse before the most valuable can be brought to market' (Ricardo 1951, p. 34). But then what must be the ratio of exchange between the two commodities if not two to one? Ricardo has no answer to offer. After establishing that there is a reason why the labor-ratio theory of exchangeable value must be 'considerably modified', he no longer concerns himself with establishing what must be the 'modified' exchange-ratios which would have required him to establish the rate of profits in the system. Ricardo leaves the problem of, what Sraffa calls, the 'difference' between the labor-ratios and the 'modified' exchange-ratios unresolved and moves directly to the problem of 'change' by raising the question that given the 'modified' exchange-ratios, 'how will their relative value be affected by the rise in the value of labour?' (*ibid.*, p. 34).

Sraffa's proposed 'labor-ratio' theory of profits is based on Marx's notion of *absolute* labor-values of commodities—a notion that is absent in Ricardo's theory. As Ricardo clearly states:

> It is necessary for me also to remark, that I have not said, because one commodity has so much labour bestowed upon it as it will cost 1000*l.* and another so much as will cost 2000*l.* that therefore one would be of the value of 1000*l.* and the other of the value of 2000*l.* but I have said that their value will be to each other as two to one, and that in those proportions they will be exchanged. It is of no importance to the truth of this doctrine, whether one of these commodities sell for 1100*l.* and the other for 2200*l.*, or one for 1500*l.* and the other for 3000*l.*; into that question I do not at present enquire; I affirm only, that their relative values will be governed by the relative quantities of labour bestowed on their production. (*ibid.*, p. 47)

To leave no doubt that his theory does not deal with the notion of value in absolute-labor terms, Ricardo adds a footnote to this statement in the 3rd edition of the *Principles*:

> Mr. Malthus remarks on this doctrine, 'We have the power indeed, arbitrarily, to call the labour which has been employed upon a commodity its real value, but in so doing, we use words in a different sense from that in which they are customarily used; we confound at once the very important distinction between *cost* and *value*; and render it almost impossible to explain with clearness, the main stimulus to the production of wealth, which in fact depends upon this distinction.'
>
> Mr. Malthus appears to think that it is a part of my doctrine, that the cost and value of a thing should be the same;–it is, if he means by cost, 'cost

> of production' including profits. In the above passage, this is what he does not mean, and therefore he has not clearly understood me. (*ibid.*, p. 47)

Now, the major evidence that Sraffa provides in support of his 'labor-ratio' theory of profits in Ricardo is as follows (Sraffa 1951, *Works I*, p. xxxii):

> A rise in wages, from an alteration in the value of money, produces a general effect on price, and for that reason it produces no real effect whatever on profits. On the contrary, a rise in wages, from the circumstance of the labourer being more liberally rewarded, or from a difficulty of producing the necessaries on which wages are expended, does not, except in some instances, produce the effect of raising price, but has a great effect in lowering profits. *In the one case, no greater proportion of the annual labour of the country is devoted to the support of the labourers; in the other case, a large portion is so devoted.* (Ricardo 1951, pp. 48–49, italics added).

I have italicized the last sentence because this is what Sraffa cites as evidence in support of the above thesis. But the context makes Ricardo's meaning clear: a nominal rise of wages will have no impact on the rate of profits but a real rise of wages (or the value of wages), which amounts to a greater proportion of the annual labor of the country being devoted to the support of the laborers, will lower the rate of profits. There is no theory of the determination of the *rate* of profits by taking the ratio of the total labor of a country to the labor necessary to produce total wages here—all we get is a statement that a rise in wages would *cause* the rate of profits to fall. In any case, Sraffa's proposition would be valid only if total capital was equal to total wage advances. But it was the existence of non-wage capital and their differing time-structures that gave rise to the problem of the 'difference' between the labor-ratio theory of relative values and the 'modified' exchange-ratios in the first place, which renders the simple labor-value calculations invalid and thus any such method of calculating the rate of profits.

In addition, in a footnote to the above-cited quotation, Sraffa writes: 'See the statement that profits depend upon the "proportion of the annual labour of the country [which] is devoted to the support of the labourers", below, p. 48–49, and "the same conclusion" on p. 126 below' (f.n. 5, p. xxxii). Again, the reference to page 126 reads:

> Each man may, and probably will, have a less absolute quantity; but as more labourers are employed in proportion to the whole produce retained by the farmer, the value of a greater proportion of the whole produce will be absorbed by wages, and consequently the value of a smaller proportion will be devoted to profits. This will necessarily be rendered permanent by the laws of nature, which have limited the productive powers of land (Ricardo 1951, p. 126).

Here again, the statement simply refers to a fall in profits due to an increase in the difficulty of producing the given wage basket and not the determination of its rate.

Furthermore, the chapter 'On Profits' in the *Principles* presents its *problematique* as: 'The profits of stock, in different employments, having been shewn to bear a proportion to each other, and to have a tendency to vary all in the same degree and in the same direction, *it remains for us to consider what is the cause of the permanent variations in the rate of profit, and the consequent permanent alterations in the rate of interest*' (*ibid.*, p. 111, italics added). And so it is not surprising that we, yet again, do not find any theory of the *determination* of the rate of profits in this chapter except for an examination of the *cause* that brings about permanent variations or changes in the rate of profits. In other words, Ricardo's concern with the rate of profits is entirely about '*change*' and not about '*difference*'.[4]

Now let us move to track two of Sraffa's story. This track relies heavily on Ricardo's unpublished drafts of 'Absolute value and Exchangeable value', written only a few weeks before Ricardo's untimely death on 11 September 1823. Sraffa, however, does not provide any direct evidence

[4] In several conferences my argument has been challenged on the ground that 'how can one develop a theory of *change* in a variable without knowing how its value at a given point is *determined*?' The answer to this question is simple. A physicist may not have a theory to determine the speed of a projectile at any precise point but still have a theory to predict the rate at which its speed (whatever that might be) would be changing. Similarly, one can claim that the speed of a car would slow down after the application of the brake or an increase in the incline of the road, other things being equal—one does not need to know how to determine the speed of the car at any point of time to be able to make such predictions.

for his claim that 'in the course of that [division of national product between classes] investigation he [Ricardo] was troubled by the fact that the size of this product appears to change when the division changes'. In this context, Sraffa emphasizes that by *absolute* or *real* value Ricardo means the value of a commodity measured against the 'invariable measure of value':

> The idea of an 'invariable measure' has for Ricardo its necessary complement in that of 'absolute value'. This concept appears in the *Principles* at first (in ed. I) as 'absolute value' and later (in ed. 3) as 'real value', it comes out from time to time in his letters, and takes more definite shape in his last paper on 'Absolute Value and Exchangeable value'. In one of the drafts for that paper he writes: 'No one can doubt that it would be a great desideratum in political Economy to have such a measure of absolute value in order to enable us to know[,] when commodities altered in exchangeable value[,] in which the alteration in value had taken place'. (*Works I*, p. xlvi).

And then Sraffa immediately goes on to add:

> In another draft he [Ricardo] explains what he means by a test of whether a commodity has altered in value: 'I may be asked what I mean by the word value, and by what criterion I would judge whether a commodity had or had not changed its value. I answer, I know no other criterion of a thing being dear or cheap but by the sacrifices of labour made to obtain it.' (*Works I*, p. xlvi).

Thus the second (actually the earlier) draft makes it clear that the *real change* in value for Ricardo always means *change* in its labor content only. Now, when we put the two positions together, that is: (i) a change in 'absolute value' or 'real value' is the change measured against the 'invariable standard' and (ii) a change in 'absolute value' is a change in its labor content, then we come up with the inescapable conclusion that the changes in value of any commodity measured against the 'invariable standard' measures *only* the changes that are caused by changes in its labor content. Therefore, all the apparent changes in its exchangeable value caused by changes in wages or profits must *ipso facto* disappear (that is, become zero) when measured against the 'invariable standard'. This is the property of the 'invariable measure' that Ricardo was looking for. But this is not concerned with keeping the size of the net output constant with respect to changes in wages but rather showing that changes in wages have no impact on the exchangeable value of a commodity—precisely the position Sraffa held during 1928–31.

And this is consistent with Ricardo's position in the third edition of the *Principles*. In Section VI on 'an invariable measure of value', after arguing that the differences in the direct and indirect composition of capitals across industries render it impossible for any single commodity to be an 'invariable measure of value' for all the commodities with respect to changes in wages, Ricardo goes on to argue that if gold is *assumed* to be a commodity that is always produced by the same amount of labor and that its direct and indirect capital composition is somewhere in the middle of most of the other commodities then it can be argued that the changes in the prices of all other commodities due to changes in wages would be minimized and therefore legitimately ignored (that is, assumed not to exist):

> Neither gold then, nor any other commodity, can ever be a perfect measure of value for all things; but I have already remarked, that the effect on the relative prices of things, from a variation in profits, is comparatively slight; that by far the most important effects are produced by the varying quantities of labour required for production; and therefore, if we suppose this important cause of variation removed from the production of gold, we shall probably possess as near an approximation to a standard measure of value as can be theoretically conceived. May not gold be considered as a commodity produced with such proportions of the two kinds of capital as approach nearest to the average quantity employed in the production of *most commodities*? (Ricardo 1951, p. 45, emphasis added)

The point to be noted here is that Ricardo does not allude to the proposition that the 'average commodity' as the standard of measure would render deviations of prices due to changes in profits in such a manner that both positive and negative movements of prices would cancel each other out and leave the value of the net output constant. His concern is solely with *minimizing* the price movements due to changes in wages or profits so that they could be rendered small enough to be *ignored*; and that could be achieved by minimizing the difference in the composition of the two kinds of capital of most of the commodities from the composition of capital of the standard of measure. It is important to note in this context that Ricardo refers to the 'average' of '*most* commodities' and not *all* commodities. This is because Ricardo leaves out 'extreme' commodities from his consideration because the deviations in prices of those commodities from the 'average commodity' cannot be assumed to be small enough to be ignored. However, this would not create a problem if his concern was only to ensure that total deviation was zero.

Sraffa, however, relies more on Ricardo's later draft of 'Absolute Value and Exchangeable Value', in which Ricardo refers to a '*mean* between extremes of commodities produced on one side by labour and advances for much more than a year, and on the other by labour employed for a day only without any advances' but then Ricardo goes on to add, 'and the mean will in *most cases* give a much less deviation from the truth than if either of the extremes were used as a measure'(Ricardo 1951–55, vol. IV). Here again the 'most cases' refers to most of the commodities and not all commodities and 'truth', of course, refers to zero deviation. So the position in the third edition of the *Principles* and again in the draft on 'Absolute and Exchangeable Value' of 1823 remains consistent.

But, of course, Ricardo was wrong in assuming that changes in the distribution will have no effect on relative values if they were measured against an 'invariable measure of value' for the simple reason that changes in the distribution affect relative values of commodities and thus logically there cannot be any commodity against which the relative values of commodities could remain constant in the face of changes in distribution. Now we find that Sraffa, in his 'Introduction' endorses this conclusion: 'In this attempt to extend the application of absolute value to the second problem (that of distinguishing the two sorts of changes in exchangeable value) Ricardo was confronted with this dilemma: whereas the former application presupposes an exact proportionality between relative and absolute value, the latter implies a variable deviation of exchangeable from absolute value for each individual commodity. This contradiction

Ricardo never completely succeeded in resolving, as is apparent from his last paper.' (Sraffa 1951, p. xlvii).

The fact that Ricardo had come to realize that what he was searching for was a logical impossibility or a chimera is evident in his letter to Mill written six days before his untimely death: 'I have been thinking a good deal on this subject lately but without much improvement—I see the same difficulties as before and am more confirmed than ever that strictly speaking there is not in nature any correct measure of value nor can any ingenuity suggest one, for what constitutes a correct measure for some things is a reason why it cannot be a correct one for other' (*Works IX*, p. 372, dated 5 September 1823). The point to note here is that Ricardo thinks that there are properties that could constitute a commodity to be a 'correct measure' for *some commodities* but not for all. Clearly that property holds for those commodities that are produced by the identical composition of direct and indirect labor ratios and, since the assumption of the theory is that this ratio is not equal for *all* commodities, it is evident that what makes it the 'correct measure' for some also makes it the incorrect measure for others. Here it is clear that Ricardo's 'correct measure' is solely concerned with ensuring no deviation in value due to changes in wages and has nothing to do with the problem of keeping the size of the net output constant with respect to changes in wages, because in this case the idea of a measure being 'correct' for some commodities has no meaning.

Why the New Interpretation?

So the question is how and why a new interpretation was superimposed on an old one. The answer lies in Sraffa's notes of 1942–45. As we have seen, during this period Sraffa's main concern was to prove his 'hypothesis' that '*R*' remains constant with respect to changes in wages and the rate of profits. This hypothesis had nothing to do with the idea of keeping the size of the pie constant when it is cut in various proportions. Instead, the 'hypothesis' was designed to prove that the theory of the determination of the rate of profits based on marginal productivity of capital is wrong, because it proves that the rate of profits is independent of the productivity of social capital. It was in this context that Sraffa in 1942 had enlisted Marx's transformation of values to prices of production as a helpful aid for a proof of his 'hypothesis' rather than Ricardo's concern with his 'invariable measure of value'.

The idea of a proportional distribution of the net output between the capitalists and the workers takes center stage in Marx's theory of exploitation. In this case, $(V+S)$ can be separated out, even though V is treated as part of total capital investment, as the value of total net output, and S/V can be shown to represent the relative share of the two classes in the total value of the net output. This Marx is able to do on the basis of his definition of value as 'embodied labor' in commodities independently of its expression or 'appearance' as prices in relative terms, unlike Ricardo who recognized value only in relative terms. It is, however, important to note that Marx had presented the transformation of values to prices of production in, what Sraffa describes as, the context of 'difference' rather than the context of 'change'. In other words, Marx's transformation is an answer to precisely the question of 'why two commodities produced by the same quantities of labour are not of the same exchangeable value'. Unlike Sraffa's notes of 1942–43, Marx does not begin (in *Capital vol. III*, chs 8 & 9) with the case when rate of profits is zero and therefore labor-value ratios are identical to price ratios. Instead, he begins with positive surplus value and unequal organic composition of capital, and argues that the proposition that 'two commodities produced by same quantities of labour must be of same exchangeable value' stands in contradiction to the requirement of a competitive capitalist system that the returns to capital must be uniform. Marx's transformation of values to prices of production (*op. cit.*, ch. 9) was designed to resolve this contradiction by showing that what price mechanism does behind the scenes is to pool the total surplus value produced in the system and redistribute it to all of the individual capitals uniformly by systematically deviating price ratios (or exchangeable values) from their labor-value ratios. This is the answer to the question of 'why two commodities produced by the same quantities of labour are not of the same exchangeable value'.

As a matter of fact, in Marx's judgment Ricardo's preoccupation with variations in prices due to changes in real wages laid unnecessary emphasis on a secondary problem. Commenting on Ricardo's discussion on an 'invariable measure of value', Marx wrote: 'This section VI On an Invariable Measure of Value deals with the "measure of value" but contains nothing important. The connection between value, its immanent measure—i.e., labour time—and the necessity for an external measure of the values of commodities is not understood or even raised as a problem' (*TSV II*: 202). So for Marx, it was Ricardo's weakness that he had failed to distinguish between the notion of 'absolute value' and its 'form of appearance' in relative or price form. In *Capital III*, Marx devotes a short chapter (Chap. 11) exclusively to Ricardo's problem of changes in wages and its effect on relative prices and concludes by saying: 'This is a very secondary question compared with the other important points which have been dealt with in this part' (p. 306).

Yet, Sraffa in his notes of 1942–43 interprets Marx's transformation of value to prices of production in the context of 'change' and not 'difference'. The crucial point in all this for Sraffa is not the problem of keeping $(V+S)$ constant in the price regime with respect to changes in wages because it was clear to him that, once the price equations are written in physical input and output form, it is evident that there is enough room in the system of equations to put the constancy of the net output as a *condition* that must be met by the solution sets for various values of wages. But this condition was not enough to prove the constancy of '*R*' with respect to changes in wages. To prove this Sraffa had to measure prices and wages against the Standard commodity, which implied that there was no more room left for the additional condition of the constancy of the net output with respect to changes in wages.

There are two aspects of Marx's transformation of values to prices that were crucial to Sraffa: (1) the average rate of profits of the system can be determined independently of prices, that is, 'profit is a non-price phenomenon'; and (2) a commodity produced by the 'average organic composition of capital' will show no deviation from value. Now, if these two points could be proved to be correct then, as we have shown in the previous chapter, Sraffa's hypothesis regarding '*R*' being constant with respect to changes in wages and the rate of profits would *ipso facto* be proven. Now we can see that all these aspects of Marx's economics are brought to bear upon Ricardo's theory of profits and the problem of the 'invariable measure of value'. It is not for nothing that Sraffa acknowledges his debt to Marx for the idea of the 'maximum rate of profits' in his book (Appendix D).

The evidence from Sraffa's notes of 1942–43 does lend support to Pier Luigi Porta's long-standing thesis (see Porta 1986, 2012) that Sraffa's interpretation of Ricardo is highly influenced by Marx's transformation problem. It should however be noted that Sraffa had to abandon Marx's formulations on his way to his final position on the proof of the constancy of '*R*' with respect to changes in the rate of profits. As we have seen in the previous chapter, Sraffa categorically abandons the notion of wages as a 'share' in total net output and only maintains the given 'money-wage' concept, where money commodity is defined in terms of the Standard commodity. In this context, it is quite clear to Sraffa, and he makes it explicit in his book, that, for any given actual system which is not a Standard system, it cannot be maintained that the size of the net output would remain constant when wages, given in terms of the Standard commodity, are varied from their maximum to zero. Thus the Standard commodity does not solve Ricardo's problem of maintaining the size of the net output constant when wages vary from their maximum to zero, if indeed it was Ricardo's problem.

A Retreat?

In the 'Introduction' when Sraffa writes:

> The problem of value which interested Ricardo was how to find a measure of value which would be invariant to changes in the division of the product; for, if a rise or fall of wages by itself brought about a change in the magnitude of the social product, it would be hard to determine accurately the effect on profits (this was, of course, the same problem as has been mentioned earlier in connection with Ricardo's corn-ratio theory of profits.)

He conflates two issues: (i) a scientific requirement of having an 'invariable scale' with respect to changes in wages to measure the changes in the prices of other commodities due to changes in wages; and (ii) a supposed consequence of such a measuring scale, which may or may not be true, that such an 'invariable scale' must ensure that the size of the total net output remains constant before and after the changes in wages. In the drafts of *Production of Commodities by Means of Commodities* (*PCMC*) written in 1955, we find that Sraffa begins to interpret Ricardo's problem of the 'invariable measure of value' in terms of the first point only. For example, in his earliest draft, we find a reference to Ricardo's problem of 'invariable measure of value' in the following terms:

> In such a world, where everything moves in every direction; where wages can increase more than profits fall; where the value & indeed the composition of the nat{ional} rev{enue} can change merely because it is divided in different ways; where the prices of commodities rise or fall, & we cannot express in simple words (or any words) the conditions under which they rise or fall; where … one sympathises with Ricardo in his search for an 'invariable measure of value'. In a universe where everything moves we need a rock to which to cling to, a horizon to reassure us when we see a brick falling that it is not we who are going up—nor that we are falling when we see a balloon rising. (D3/12/52: 15, dated 18 March 1955)

And again in the later draft, Sraffa writes:

> If we observe the movements of the price of commodity *a* in terms of commodity *b* we shall never know how much of any fluctuation originates in the circumstances of *a* & how much of those of *b*. The attempt to eliminate this type of disturbance lies at the basis of R's suggestion that we take as standard a comm. that is equally distant from the two extremes, 'those much capital … & those much labour{'}[quote R. This criterion, we shall soon find, is inadequate and assumes a measurability of capital (or of 'time') which R himself elsewhere denies (let. To M^cC){]}. (D3/12/53: 4, dated 6 September 1955)

It should be noted that in the later draft even a passing reference to 'the value & indeed the composition of the nat{ional} rev{enue} can change merely because it is divided in different ways' is removed and Ricardo's problem is attributed only to the changes in the relative prices of the two commodities. These remarks were written in the context of *PCMC* and the construction of the Standard commodity. It appears from these comments that when Sraffa had written the 'Introduction' to Ricardo's *Principles* he had not yet come to the conclusion that the Standard commodity does not ensure the constancy of the size of the net output of the actual system with respect to changes in wages or the rate of profits. However, once he realized that, he begins to distance Ricardo's problem with the requirement of the constancy of the size of the net output and relate it directly to the property of the Standard commodity, which ensures that the price movements measured against this standard would always measure the changes that have come about in the price of the commodity measured, and not in the standard, due to changes in wages.

His new interpretation of Ricardo appears to have been designed to fit Ricardo into what he had called, the 'frame'. The reader would recall that in 1928 Sraffa had set himself the task of constructing 'a sort of "frame", a machine, into which to fit their {the classical economists} own statements in a homogeneous pattern, so as to be able to find what is common in them and what is the difference with the later {modern} theories.'

In his 1960 book, Sraffa acknowledges the fact that his new interpretation of Ricardo 'suggested itself as a natural consequence' only after 'the Standard system and the distinction between basics and non-basics had emerged in the course of the present investigation'. In the preparatory note written on 22 April 1957 it is further elaborated:

> In the Introduction to Ricardo's *Principles* I have attempted an interpretation of Ricardo's theory of value on the lines of the Standard system of basic products given in the present work. Ricardo's theory appears to have developed from one shape in which the means of production and therefore the basic products consisted exclusively of corn (or agricultural produce) and accordingly the rate of profit received by the farmer determined the rate of profits of all other ('non-basic') trades. This led him to extend this theory and regard labour as constituting the universal means of production, with the result that the rate of profits was now determined by the proportion of a day's labour that was required to produce the subsistence for a day.
>
> The evidence for the 'agriculture' theory such as found in Ricardo's writings as they have come down to us is fragmentary and had to be strengthened (completed) with a good deal of inference, or imagination was necessary to fill the gap. It was not possible to explain in that Introduction

that that interpretation was formulated after having reached the views advanced in this paper and on the basis of them; which may enable the readers of the Introduction to decide themselves whether I have not read more in the evidence than is warranted. (D3/12/74: 7)

7

The Book

Sraffa's book was finally published in 1960—it was indeed a long time coming! It is definitely among the shortest books, if not the shortest book, published in economics in modern era—it is less than 100 pages long in large typed scripts including four appendixes and an index. In Sinha (2010a), I described it as a piece of minimalist art in economic prose and have compared it with the music of Beethoven, which is known for its meaningful silences. To this description of the aesthetic of the book, I might here add some of its literary qualities. It seems to be consciously designed as a 'detective short-story'. With its abrupt beginning and equally abrupt ending, the book fits the genre of 'short-stories', but the story is of a detective nature. The 'crime' has been announced in the 'Preface' of the book and several clues to the solution of the puzzle are scattered throughout the book. However, unlike a detective story but more like a short story, no final solution is provided. The reader is left to figure it out for himself or herself.[1]

[1] Legend has it that both Sraffa and Wittgenstein were avid readers of detective stories. When Sraffa was interned at the Isle of Man in the 1940s, Wittgenstein sent him a detective novel with a note, 'I've had a book seller send you "The thin man", a detective story I told you about a few months ago. Read it and don't be ashamed of liking it even though you know that I liked it. …'. As a matter of fact, there is enough evidence to show that Sraffa enjoyed doing detective work and was extremely good at it.

A. Sinha, *A Revolution in Economic Theory*,
DOI 10.1007/978-3-319-30616-2_7

The book is entitled, *Production of Commodities by Means of Commodities*. The title is designed to convey a crucial aspect of the book, which emphasizes the *circular* nature of the production process in opposition to the *linear* nature of production emphasized by modern economic theory. The book also has a subtitle, *Prelude to a Critique of Economic Theory*. In other words, Sraffa is announcing at the outset that the theoretical position of his book is built upon the idea that 'method of production' of an economy represents a *circular* relation and that this approach is designed to construct a foundation to develop a *critique* of the modern economic theory, which is built on the notion of production as a *linear* relation.

The Preface

In the 'Preface' to the book, Sraffa begins with a clear declaration:

> Anyone accustomed to think in terms of the equilibrium of demand and supply may be inclined, on reading these pages, to suppose that the argument rests on a tacit assumption of constant returns in all industries. If such a supposition is found helpful, there is no harm in the reader's adopting it as a temporary working hypothesis. In fact, however, no such assumption is made. No changes in output and (at any rate in Parts I and II) no

---

For example, for a long time the authorship of the *Abstract* of Hume's *Treatise on Human Nature* was attributed to Adam Smith on the basis of Hume's letter of March 4, 1740 to Francis Hutcheson in which Hume refers to a Mr. Smith without attributing the authorship to him. Later, however, it came to be understood that it was a reference to the young Adam Smith who had supposedly authored the *Abstract* on Hutcheson's instructions. It was John Hill Burton, who, in his *Life of Hume* published in 1846, started the story about Adam Smith without directly attributing the authorship to him. Later John Rae (1895), in his influential *Life of Adam Smith*, carried the story further and attributed the authorship of the *Abstract* to Adam Smith. It was Sraffa, in collaboration with Keynes, who carried out a minute forensic analysis of all the extant evidence and came to the conclusion that the author of the *Abstract* was none other than David Hume himself and that the Mr. Smith of Hume's letter was not Adam Smith but rather a Mr. John Smith, Francis Hutcheson's Dublin publisher. [See Hume (1938) [1740], J.M. Keynes and P. Sraffa (eds.)]. Again, the anonymous continental merchant, who was a witness before Bullion Committee of 1810 and referred to as Mr.— in its report, was generally understood to be N.M Rothschild, as Cannan put it: 'An obvious conjecture is that this modest Mr. Blank was the great N.M. Rothschild'. Yet again, Sraffa's forensic analysis of all the available evidence and his acute detective work led him to the conclusion, which has since been confirmed, that Mr. — of the Bullion Committee was not Mr. N.M. Rothschild but rather a Mr. John Parish of Hamburg. [See 'Appendix' to *Works and Correspondence of David Ricardo, volume III*].

> changes in the proportions in which different means of production are used by an industry are considered, so that no question arises as to the variation or constancy of returns. The investigation is concerned exclusively with such properties of an economic system as do not depend on changes in the scale of production or in the proportions of 'factors' (Sraffa 1960, v).

Let us unpack the arguments made in this paragraph. (1) Those readers who are accustomed to think of 'price theory' in terms of 'equilibrium of demand and supply' would think that the propositions published in the book are based on an *implicit assumption* that constant returns prevail in all the industries. But why would Sraffa think so? It is because bringing in the idea of 'equilibrium of demand and supply' to his propositions would *logically* imply the assumption of constant returns. (2) However, his propositions do not rest on the assumption of constant returns. Therefore, thinking in terms of 'equilibrium of demand and supply' is not the correct way of approaching his book. (3) This approach—of not thinking in terms of 'equilibrium of demand and supply'—is so revolutionary or novel that the first reading of the book may not make any sense to the reader if he or she does not bring in the *illegitimate* point of view that constant returns and therefore the equilibrium of demand and supply are tacitly assumed. Hence, the reader may assume them as 'a temporary working hypothesis'. However, a correct understanding of the book must finally enable the reader to jettison this working hypothesis. (4) The idea of 'returns to scale', constant or otherwise, has meaning only in situations when changes in the output are contemplated. His propositions are, however, built on the idea that no such changes take place—neither in the outputs nor in the inputs for Parts I and II, that is, Chaps. 1–11, and only in the inputs in the last Chap. 12.

Point (3) is so important that Sraffa further elaborates it after couple of paragraphs:

> The temptation to presuppose constant returns is not entirely fanciful. It was experienced by the author himself when he started on these studies many years ago—and it led him in 1925 into an attempt to argue that only the case of constant returns was generally consistent with the premises of

> economic theory. And what is more, when in 1928 Lord Keynes read a draft of the opening propositions of this paper, he recommended that, if constant returns were *not* to be assumed, an emphatic warning to that effect should be made. (p. vi)

Here two historical milestones on the way to the present book are noted. As we have seen in Chapters 2 and 3, in 1925 Sraffa held the view that the classical economists assumed constant returns (as well as constant costs) and that is why their prices were independent of demand considerations. He went on to argue that this was the only legitimate assumption to make in the context of perfectly competitive markets. By 1928 Sraffa had already worked out the 1st and 2nd equation systems to which Keynes was responding. As a matter of fact, Sraffa had shown these equations to Pigou as well, and Pigou had responded by writing: '(2) Your equations seem to me capable of being subsumed as a special case of the general analysis. You in effect are simply supposing that each of the three (or n) commodities is being produced under conditions of constant returns. Of course, an elaborate scheme of demand and supply is not needed in this case: but this case can be treated as a limiting case of the more general theory. I don't suppose for a moment that I have half got your point, but may as well send it along on the off chance' (C 239, dated January 1928). Thus it must have been quite clear to Sraffa since early 1928 that the novelty of his *new* idea rested on *not* allowing any notion of constant returns in his equations, and that it is not easy for even the best economists to understand or make sense of his propositions without that assumption.

In spite of Sraffa's clear warning in the very first sentences of the 'Preface', all the neoclassical economists who have cared to comment on Sraffa's book have, to the best of my knowledge, consistently maintained that they cannot make any sense of the book without invoking the assumption of constant returns as implicit in it. For example, in Paul Samuelson's view, 'if a Sraffian denies constant returns to scale, the one-hundred page 1960 classic evaporates into a few pages of vapid chit-chat' (Samuelson 2000, p. 123). On the other hand, 'Sraffians', particularly Garegnani and his followers, argue that Sraffa *assumes* that his 'given outputs' are in 'equilibrium of demand and supply' and therefore no change in outputs is contemplated, hence there is no need for a consideration of returns to scale. For example, Garegnani (1990) writes: 'The outputs he [Sraffa] takes as given are *ex ante normal* outputs just like the neoclassical "equilibrium" outputs…' (p. 132). And Kurz claimed: 'The evidence put forward should suffice to see that it is pure fiction to contend, as Sinha does, that the system from which Sraffa begins his investigation into its mathematical properties is not characterised by *a balancing of effectual demands and levels of outputs*' (Kurz 2012, p. 1566, emphasis added).[2]

The difficulty in understanding the nature of Sraffa's contribution was acknowledged by even some early reviewers of the book who were not of strictly neoclassical persuasion. For example, in one of the earliest reviews of the book, Sir Roy Harrod wrote: 'The publication of this book is a notable event. ... A reviewer would be presumptuous if he supposed that he could give a final assessment of the value of its net product, or even single out what may prove to be its most lasting contributions. Before that result could be achieved, much prolonged consideration and reconsideration would be required.' (1961, p. 783). In another review, Maurice Dobb wrote: 'It can be confidently said that never in the history of economic theory has so much fundamental and formally refined thought, and of so path-breaking a character, been packed into so slender and elegant a volume. It is a book that will perhaps be misunderstood and remain unappreciated by many more than will understand it; few probably will wholly grasp even the major part of it, though many can and will gain illumination and inspiration from it in part.' (1961, p. 491).

We have seen in Chap. 3 that Sraffa had embarked on his system of equations in November 1927 to see if the classical theory of value could be rid of the notion of 'ultimate cause'. The idea was to build a non-causal theory, which would be akin to geometry. This led Sraffa to not allow any changes in the parameters of his equations because he reasoned that causal explanations can come into play only if there is *change*. So by keeping change out of the scope he was keeping the notion of causation out of reach. However, in 1931 when he was thinking about a

[2] This is a part of Kurz's critical comments on my thesis against the 'given *equilibrium* output' hypothesis presented in Sinha (2012). See Sinha (2013) for my response to Kurz's criticisms.

critique of the marginal productivity theory of interest, he thought that he would have to bring in the notion of *change* to his system of equations to follow their reasoning. It was only in 1942 when Sraffa hit upon the idea of constancy of '*R*' with respect to changes in the rate of profits, which he called his 'hypothesis', that he realized that a consequence of the proof of his 'hypothesis' would be to prove the marginal productivity theory wrong. This was remarkable because the 'hypothesis' could potentially kill two birds with one stone. On the one hand, it establishes the independence of distribution of income from prices within a non-causal objective theory, which, for Sraffa, were the essential aspects of classical economics. On the other hand, it also proves that the theory of distribution of 'modern' economics that is built on the notions of subjectivity and marginal change is flawed. Now we find both these points highlighted in the 'Preface':

> This standpoint, which is that of the old classical economists from Adam Smith to Ricardo, has been submerged and forgotten since the advent of the 'marginal' method. The reason is obvious. The marginal approach requires attention to be focused on change, for without change either in the scale of an industry or in the 'proportions of factors of production' there can be neither marginal product nor marginal cost. (p. v)
>
> It is, however, a peculiar feature of the set of propositions now published that, although they do not enter into any discussion of the marginal theory of value and distribution, they have nevertheless been designed to serve as the basis for a critique of that theory. (p. vi)

It is, however, important that the nuances of both the claims be noted at the outset. In the first quotation Sraffa refers to 'classical economists from Adam Smith to Ricardo'. It is obviously not a list of *two* economists but a reference to the *period* from 1776 to 1823. The reference is to all of the major economists of this period, which must include, at least, Malthus and J.-B. Say. Thus the stated 'standpoint' is extremely broad in nature. It only refers to a *method*, which admits no change in output. As we have argued in Chap. 1, the classical theory of 'natural' prices must logically begin with an empirical system of given output. However, in the classical theory, this empirical system is connected to the notion of natural prices via a *gravitation mechanism*, which crucially rests on the *assumption* of constant returns with no substitution possibilities in the method of production. But the above statement of Sraffa's claims that classical economics does not assume constant returns. This again, in my opinion, is evidence of Sraffa's attempt to fit classical economics in his 'frame'. Sraffa's point seems to be that the classical 'natural' prices can be derived from the empirical input–output data alone without any need for the notion of effectual demand and a 'gravitation mechanism'; hence this aspect of classical economics can be cut out of the frame.

This standpoint or the *method* that determines prices only on the basis of factual data is then contrasted with the method of modern economics, which essentially rests on *counterfactual reasoning*. This brings us to the second quotation from Sraffa. Here Sraffa states that the propositions of the book have been designed to serve as the *basis* for a critique of modern theory. In other words, the propositions themselves do not amount to a critique of modern theory—they are only supposed to constitute a foundation or a platform, on the basis of which a real critique could be launched in the future, as the subtitle of the book also suggests.

Now, coming back to the distinction between factual and counterfactuals, it is clear that counterfactual reasoning *must* refer to something that by definition does not exist—it has only hypothetical or notional existence. The method based on the 'marginal change' of modern economics is essentially based on *notional* changes, that is, counterfactuals, and not *real* changes on the margin.[3] That is why they are able to maintain the idea of marginal change given the system in *a* stationary state. The idea of *notional* changes, however, relates to functional relations between variables. Sraffa's point seems to be that the propositions of his book do not engage with a critique of functional relations directly, and therefore they cannot constitute a critique of the 'marginal method' by themselves. Although, as I have pointed out in the Preface to this book, Sraffa was

[3]This point was first flagged by Harcourt: '[I]t should be noted that prices in the marginal theory of value are related to notional instantaneous rates of change which can be thought of as occurring at the margins of the levels of production of the actual economic systems examined here. In other words, there need not be an actual marginal product in order to have a determinate system of prices which is based on marginal notions.' (Harcourt 1972, p. 179).

highly skeptical of all functional relations because they are based on the belief in complete determinism.

Before leaving the 'Preface' behind, one cannot fail to notice the absence of Marx in the list of classical economists whose 'standpoint' the book apparently represents, even though Marx is acknowledged in the 'reference to the literature' for, perhaps, the most important idea of the book, that is, the idea of 'maximum rate of profits'. As a matter of fact, in an earlier draft of the 'Preface' written on 16 September 1956, Sraffa does mention Marx's name: 'The skeleton (bare bone) of a system put forward in these pages ... to facilitate the interpretation of certain of the theories of the classical economists & of Marx, ...' (D3/12/71: 32b). However, Marx's name disappears from all the subsequent drafts. I doubt that political expediency could be the main cause of dropping Marx's name from the list, particularly in the late 1950s. The reason could be Marx's metaphysical attachment to the measure of value in terms of labor. Sraffa might have come to the conclusion that this aspect of Marx's thought was so fundamental to Marx's theory that it could not be cut out from his system to fit him in the 'frame', particularly when he had realized that he could not establish a one-to-one relationship between distribution in terms of wages and profits in an actual system with variable capital and surplus value of Marx's theory. The reader would have also noticed that in the above quotation 'classical economists' are mentioned in a generic manner without any names attached to them. This description also changes over time and is narrowed down to either 'classical economists (up to Ricardo)' (D3/12/46: 1, dated 6 January 1959) or finally 'from Adam Smith to Ricardo'. One clear implication of this narrowing down of the set is, most notably, to put J.S. Mill out. This could be because Sraffa considered J.S. Mill a transitional figure rather than a pure classical theorist. Another surprising omission is the Physiocrats. Even though the crucial idea of the book—that the method of production is a circular process—is attributed to the Physiocrats in the 'reference to the literature', the Physiocrats are absent from the list perhaps because they did not have a developed theory of value or prices. Therefore Sraffa thought they were better left out of the set.

The Subsistence System

Chapter I of the book deals with the 1st equations, that is, the case of a subsistence economic system. Sraffa begins with an example of two commodities, where year's operation (that is, the rotation periods for both the commodities are assumed to be equal and 'one year' in length) is tabulated as follows:

$$280\,\text{qr.wheat} + 12\,\text{t.iron} \rightarrow 400\,\text{qr.wheat}$$
$$120\,\text{qr.wheat} + 8\,\text{t.iron} \rightarrow 20\,\text{t.iron}$$

Labor does not show up in the description of the method of production since it is subsumed under inventory of goods as 'subsistence'. In this case, without any additional information one could derive the unique exchange ratio between the two commodities as 10 qr. wheat for 1 ton of iron that would ensure that this system would reproduce itself at the same scale. Sraffa further shows that this property of the system remains undisturbed even when the number of commodities is increased to n. The reason for it is simple. A subsistence system provides us with $n-1$ independent linear equations with $n-1$ unknown relative prices to be determined. This is because the condition of a subsistence system requires that the aggregate of its inputs used in the system must be equal to its outputs; thus the nth equation can always be derived from the $n-1$ equations. Sraffa then goes on to add a footnote to this condition:

> This formulation presupposes the system's being in a self-replacing state; but every system of the type under consideration is capable of being brought to such a state merely by changing the proportions in which the individual equations enter it. (Systems which do so with a surplus are discussed in §4ff. Systems which are incapable of doing so under any proportions and show a deficit in the production of some commodities over their consumption even if none has a surplus do not represent viable economic systems and are not considered). (Sraffa 1960, 5, f.n.1)

Samuelson (2000) highlights Sraffa's statement: 'but every system of the type under consideration is capable of being brought to such a state merely by changing the proportions in which the individual equations enter it' as an example of an implicit assumption of 'constant returns' in his entire book. Elsewhere I (Sinha 2007) have argued that Samuelson's interpretation is incorrect. In the above footnote Sraffa, instead of *assuming* constant returns, is highlighting a property of a subsistence system of this kind. A subsistence system of this kind can have historical viability only if its methods of production display constant returns, otherwise even a small vibration in the system would either lead it to historical oblivion or turn it into a 'surplus' producing system. For example, suppose the above system was observed when it was not in a self-replacing state, as depicted below:

$$280 \text{ qr.wheat} + 12 \text{ t.iron} \rightarrow 400 \text{ qr.wheat}$$
$$240 \text{ qr.wheat} + 16 \text{ t.iron} \rightarrow 40 \text{ t.iron}$$

Obviously this system is not producing enough wheat to reproduce itself at the same scale. The reader can verify that the exchange ratio between iron and wheat in this case also remains at 10 units of wheat for 1 unit of iron. This is because in a subsistence system the total value of inputs must be equal to the value of its outputs for every industry.[4] Thus the wheat sector will exchange 120 qr. of wheat (its surplus wheat) for 12 t. of iron and reproduce itself at the same scale. On the other hand, given the technique the iron sector can now combine 120 qr. of wheat with only 8t. of iron (the remaining 20 t. of iron in this time period goes to waste). Now when the iron sector's scale is reduced by half, there can be only three possibilities: (i) if the sector displays decreasing returns then its

[4] In a review of Sraffa's book, Sir Roy Harrod (1961) had suggested that Sraffa was implicitly assuming equilibrium of demand and supply in his price equations. In his response, Sraffa (1962) stated that '(...[even when] the system ceased to be in self-replacing state) the exchange ratio would remain the same but the ratio between the excess productions of the two commodities would be changed, so that the two would no longer be equal' (p. 477). In other words, the prices are determined by the methods of production and not the condition of equilibrium of demand and supply. As we shall see, Sraffa considered that this proposition had a general validity and was not only applicable to a 'subsistence system'.

output will be more than 20 t. of iron; (ii) if the sector displays increasing returns then its output will be less than 20 t. of iron; and (iii) if the sector displays constant returns then its output will be equal to 20 t. of iron. As Sraffa's remark in the parentheses explains, if case (i) happens to be true then this system is a type that always produces surplus and is dealt with in §4ff. of the book; if case (ii) happens to be true then this system is a type that always produces deficit and is not viable and not considered; and if case (iii) happens to be true then it is the *type* depicting a system of 'production for subsistence'. Therefore, any system of production, if it is of the *type* that depicts production for subsistence, 'is capable of being brought to such a state [self-replacing state] merely by changing the proportions in which individual equations enter it.' Clearly the remark in the footnote is a remark about the condition of historical viability of a system of a particular *type* and not about any given empirical system. No 'returns to scale' *assumption* is implied in the remark.

My response to Samuelson was based on my reading of the published footnote. However, in the course of my archival research for this book I discovered a draft of this footnote on a small slip of paper written in March 1956. This draft now confirms that my interpretation was correct:

> Note to p. 4
>
> (1) The statement in this form applies only to a system which is in a self-replacing state. But any system, to be consistent, must be capable of being brought to such a state merely by changing the proportions in which the several equations enter it. If this is not possible there may be a deficit or a surplus, but no equality. (D3/12/71: 5)[5]

[5] In his response to Samuelson, Garegnani (2007) had argued that Sraffa's footnote was actually not referring to the property of the 'subsistence system' as such but rather to the property of the 'equations': 'That of course is true, but it applies to proportions between *actual outputs* and not to proportions between *equations*, as Sraffa is careful to specify in the one word we italicized in this passage' (p. 196, Garegnani's emphasis). This, in my opinion, is simply untenable. Sraffa clearly states that 'every system of the type under consideration is capable of being brought to such a state'. Hence the reference is to the 'system', which is capable of being brought to such a state and not simply a mathematical operation on equations. Now, the draft of the footnote makes it quite clear that Garegnani's position was incorrect. If Garegnani's interpretation was correct then Sraffa's phrase 'If this is not possible' would be meaningless since such mathematical operations on the equations must always be possible (see Sinha 2015 for more details).

As we suggested at the beginning of the chapter, Sraffa's book is full of riddles for the reader. Here the word 'type' in the footnote contains the secret of the riddle, and the answer to the riddle, in Sraffa's own code, is provided in the parentheses. The fundamental point of this brief chapter is to establish that in this simple and restrictive case the exchange ratios of commodities are completely determined by the observed 'method of production' but not 'cost of production'. In other words, the prices are determined by a solution of a simultaneous equation system and *not* by individual industries calculating their cost. That is, when it comes to price determination, there is no arrow of causation from the left hand side of the equations to the right hand side of the equations.

Production with a 'Surplus'

After establishing the fact that in a subsistence economy the relative prices are determined solely by the objective data of the method of production used, irrespective of whether or not the system is in 'equilibrium', that is, self-replacing state, Sraffa in Chapter II introduces his 2nd equations. Once a 'surplus' is admitted in the system, it becomes, in Sraffa's words, 'self-contradictory'. What does 'self-contradictory' mean? It means that after deducting item by item all the inputs used for a given repetitive system, some commodities are left on the right hand side as surplus. Therefore we no longer have an equation system, as the right hand sides, either in terms of values or physical commodities, are not equal to the left hand sides. The problem is how to re-establish the equation system and to see to what extent the results derived from the subsistence equation system can be maintained for the surplus system as well. To re-establish the equation system one needs to assign or allot the surplus of the right hand side back to the left hand side one way or the other. So the problem is how to do that. Sraffa explains:

> The difficulty cannot be overcome by allotting the surplus *before* the prices are determined, as is done with the replacement of raw materials, subsistence, etc. This is because the surplus (or profit) must be distributed in proportion to the means of production (or capital) advanced in each indus-

> try; and such a proportion between two aggregates of heterogeneous goods (in other words, the rate of profits) cannot be determined before we know the prices of the goods. On the other hand, we cannot defer the allotment of the surplus till after the prices are known, for, as we shall see, the prices cannot be determined before knowing the rate of profits. The result is that the distribution of the surplus must be determined through the same mechanism and at the same time as are the prices of commodities.
>
> Accordingly we add the rate of profits (which must be uniform for all industries) as an unknown which we call *r* ... (p. 6)

Here Sraffa states that the 'surplus' cannot be allotted to the industries before prices are determined, with the emphasis on 'before'. But strictly speaking, it is incorrect. For example, let us suppose there was an all-powerful state that appropriated the surplus product and then decided to allot it all to one or all the industries in an arbitrary manner. In that case, the number of independent equations will fall by one and the relative prices would be completely determined as in the case of the subsistence system. For example, let us suppose our 'surplus' system is given by:

$$\begin{aligned} 280\,\text{qr.wheat} + 12\,\text{t.iron} &\rightarrow 575\,\text{qr.wheat} \\ 120\,\text{qr.wheat} + 8\,\text{t.iron} &\rightarrow 20\,\text{t.iron} \end{aligned}$$

In this case, if the state decides to allot all the surplus to the wheat industry then we can write the equation system as:

$$\begin{aligned} 575\text{p}_\text{w} - \left(280\text{p}_\text{w} + 12\text{p}_\text{i}\right) &= 175\text{p}_\text{w} \\ 20\text{p}_\text{i} - \left(120\text{p}_\text{w} + 8\text{p}_\text{i}\right) &= 0 \end{aligned}$$

Evidently, it is a system with one independent equation and it determines the price ratio as 1:10. So what could Sraffa mean by his statement that the surplus cannot be allotted *before* the prices are determined? Clearly what he means is that any such *deus ex machina* to allot surplus is not allowed. Similarly, the state could decree that 1 ton of iron must exchange with 10 quarters of wheat. That would, however, imply that 'a system' in a mathematical sense no longer existed. The rates of profits in the two (or n) industries could be independently determined without taking any other industry into account. In this case, it would turn out that the total surplus would be allotted to the wheat industry and the two industries would have 43.7 (approximately) and 0 per cent rates of profit respectively. So, again what could Sraffa mean by his statement that 'as we shall see, prices cannot be determined before knowing the rate of profits'? Clearly, he means that prices must be determined from within the system and not taken as 'given' from outside in any manner, which in effect destroys the integrated system. Therefore, the 'self-contradiction' must be resolved by the system from within. In this context Sraffa argues that an additional unknown, the rate of profits, must be introduced and the prices and the rate of profits must be determined simultaneously.

Now it is clear that the system of equations does not allow for more than one unknown to be introduced. Could it be this technical reason why Sraffa in his parenthetical remark adds that the rate of profits 'must be uniform for all industries'? But then, *apparently* there is no such technical requirement. Let us suppose, for the time-being, that the risks associated with investments in various industries differ, but we know the structure of those risks, such as industry 1 is twice as risky as industry 2 and so on and that industrial rates of profit reflect such risk differentials. In that case one will only need to introduce *a* rate of profits as an unknown and solve for unequal rates of profit received by individual industries. For example, let us suppose that in our above given surplus system the wheat industry receives a rate of profit twice as large as that of the iron industry because capital investment in the wheat industry is twice as risky as in the iron industry. In that case, our equation system can be depicted as:

$$(280p_w + 12p_i)(1 + 2r) = 575p_w$$
$$(120p_w + 8p_i)(1 + r) = 20p_i$$

This will solve for p_i/p_w and r. So clearly the statement that the industrial rates of profits 'must be uniform' appears to be a mysterious claim at this point because no explanation has been offered.

Apparently, the parenthetical remark is superfluous, because the statement: 'Accordingly we add the rate of profits ...' implies a uniform rate of profits for the system. As a matter of fact, in the draft of *PCMC* written on 28 March 1956 (and other drafts before it) Sraffa had drafted the above expression as: 'Accordingly we add the rate of profits, which we call *r*, as an unknown and the system becomes …' (D3/12/71: 5). It is only in the notes of 25 August 1956 that we find Sraffa inserting the parenthetical note in pencil in the margin of a typed script: '(which must be uniform for all the industries)' (D3/12/72: 4). Could it be the case that yet again we have been given a clue to the mystery in a parenthetical remark? The word to take note of in the parenthetical remark is 'must'. This has to refer to some kind of logical necessity because it relates to certainty, rather than an outcome of a mechanism based on causation, which Sraffa always held could never be certain. The reader will recall that during the period 1927–31 Sraffa had articulated the problem under the title 'Man from the Moon' in these words: 'The significance of the equations is simply this: that if a man fell from the moon on the earth, and noted the amount of things consumed in each factory and the amount produced by each factory during a year he could deduce at which values the commodities must be sold, *if* the rate of interest must be uniform and the process of production repeated. In short, the equations show that the conditions of exchange are entirely determined by the conditions of production' (D3/12/7: 65–67, emphasis added). It is significant that in the present context the qualifier 'if' is removed.

Sraffa then proceeds to add a uniform rate of profits as an unknown in the system, which now has *n* independent equations and *n* unknowns to solve for, i.e., $n-1$ relative prices and one rate of profits. Sraffa claims that *a* solution exists. One effect of the emergence of surplus is that commodities can be divided into two separate categories. There can now be some commodities that appear in the system only as outputs but do not enter the system as inputs. Such commodities can be characterized as *non-basics* whereas the commodities that enter the system both as inputs and outputs can be characterized as *basics*.[6] Any change in the conditions of production of the basics would have an impact on the prices of all the commodities through its influence as an input to the system.

[6] A non-basic can appear as an input in the production of non-basics but is not directly or indirectly an input in the production of all the commodities in the system.

On the other hand, any such change in the condition of production of non-basics can affect only its own price or the prices of limited goods to which it may be an input.[7] Sraffa *assumes* that at least one basic commodity exists in the observed system.

Following this, Sraffa writes:

> It is desirable at this stage to explain why *the ratios which satisfy the conditions of production* have been called 'values' or 'prices' rather than, as might be thought more appropriate, 'costs of production'.
>
> The latter description would be adequate so far as *non*-basic products are concerned, since, as follows from what we have seen in the preceding section, their exchange ratio is merely a reflection of what must be paid for means of production, labour and profits in order to produce them—there is no mutual dependence.
>
> But for a basic product there is another aspect to be considered. Its exchange-ratio depends as much on *use* that is made of it in the production of other basic commodities as on the extent to which those commodities enter into its production. (One might be tempted, but it would be misleading, to say that 'it depends as much on the Demand side as on the Supply side'.) (pp. 8–9, first emphasis added)

Two very puzzling points are made here: (1) Sraffa claims that the exchange ratios derived from the 'surplus' equation system by adding a *uniform* rate of profits as an unknown 'satisfy the *condition* of production'. What does Sraffa mean by 'condition of production' and how do these prices 'satisfy' it? (2) Sraffa says that the fact that the price of a basic commodity enters as cost in the production of all other commodities whereas other basic commodities' prices enter as cost in its price renders the idea of determining 'price' of a commodity by its 'cost of production' meaningless, since there is no one-way avenue of determining cost prior to and independent of prices.[8] Then in a parenthetical remark he adds

[7] Harcourt and Massaro (1964) describe basic goods as 'price determining' and non-basics as 'price determined'.

[8] Contrast this with Ricardo's response to Malthus cited in the previous chapter: 'Mr. Malthus appears to think that it is a part of my doctrine, that the cost and value of a thing should be the same;–it is, if he means by cost, "cost of production" including profits. In the above passage, this is what he does not mean, and therefore he has not clearly understood me.' (*op.cit.* p. 47).

that '[o]ne might be tempted, but it would be misleading, to say that "it depends as much on the Demand side as on the Supply side"'. The point to note is that Sraffa says that the price of a *basic* commodity 'depends as much on *use* that is made of it in the production of other basic commodities as on the extent to which those commodities enter into its production'. Here it is clearly stated that the price of a basic commodity *depends* on the internal structure of the system of production, that is, how much of it is *used* by the system and how much of other commodities it *uses* in its production. Hence the 'profit' element of the left hand side of the equations is completely left out of the description. This is what 'the condition of production' represents and it is claimed in point (1) that the prices determined on the basis of a *uniform* rate of profits are the prices that satisfy the 'condition of production'. In other words, these prices can be derived from the objective data of the method of production alone without bringing any more information, as was the case with the 'subsistence system'. The parenthetical remark is, yet again, a clue to warn the reader that how the profits are disposed off has no impact on prices and that is why it would be misleading to think of his solution of prices as a general equilibrium of demand and supply.

Immediately after this Sraffa goes on to add:

> A less one-sided description than cost of production seems therefore required. Such classical terms as 'necessary price', 'natural price' or 'price of production' would meet the case, but value and price have been preferred as being shorter and in the present context (which contains no reference to market prices) no more ambiguous. (p. 9).

After giving the clue that his prices were derived directly from only objective data of inputs and outputs and that they should not be interpreted as a general equilibrium solution of demands and supplies, Sraffa, in the above quotation, goes on to clarify his position vis-à-vis the classical position. As we have seen, the classical notion of 'natural price' relates to, at least in Sraffa's interpretation, the solution of his equation system. But these prices have significance within the classical tradition only because they are supposed to be the 'center of gravitation' of the 'market prices'. Sraffa, yet again, gives a clue in his parenthetical remark. He tells us that 'the present context'—that is, the context of the determination of prices by adding a *uniform* rate of profits—does not contain any reference to 'market prices'. Now, the classical notion of center of gravitation, of course, contains a *reference* to 'market prices', as it is supposed to be the center of gravitation of nothing else but 'market prices'. It is the notion of 'effectual demand' of classical economics that calls forth the notion of 'market prices'. Sraffa's parenthetical remark suggests that his context of price determination has no room for the notion of 'effectual demand'.

To further clarify a common mistake in Sraffian literature of identifying Sraffa's above statement with the full-blown classical notion of center of gravitation, one must remind oneself of Sraffa's understanding of the term 'natural price'. In a note, written most likely in winter 1928 soon after the two equations were written, Sraffa clarifies his understanding of the term 'natural price' in these terms:

> When A. Smith, etc., said *'natural'* he did not in the least mean the 'normal' nor the 'average', nor, the 'long run' value. He meant that physical, truly natural relations between commodities, that is determined by the equations, and that is not disturbed by the process of securing a greater share in the product. 'Exchange value' was the result of natural value disturbed permanently by the scramble for the surplus: it might itself be distinguished into 'market value' (daily fluctuating) and normal or average. (D3/12/11: 83).

This fits well with our interpretation of Sraffa's term 'price' *satisfying* the 'conditions of production'.

Sraffa further complicates the system by arguing that workers' remuneration may contain a part of the 'surplus' thus adding another unknown to the system as *wages*, paid *post factum* from the surplus product. In Chap. 5, we have already seen why Sraffa had broken from the classical tradition of treating wages as part of capital advanced. With this the system acquires one more unknown than the number of equations, and thus can move with one degree of freedom. One implication of treating wages paid *post factum* from the surplus is that it puts all the wage-goods in the category of *non*-basics. Sraffa takes pains to add that a physically given subsistence for workers could be incorporated as part of the technical-inputs and only the wages over and above the subsistence could be reckoned as taking part in the distribution of net output. He, however, refrains from 'tampering with the traditional wage concept'. Joan Robinson (1961, p. 54) correctly pointed out that 'we could hardly imagine that, when the workers had a surplus to spend on beef, their physical need for wheat was unchanged'. Sraffa himself had made similar arguments against the idea of splitting the wage into 'necessary for production' and 'surplus' in his notes of the 1940s. Still Sraffa thinks that the role of the basic wage-goods as 'necessary for production' could be maintained by imposing a lower limit below which wages could not fall.

At this stage Sraffa introduces this unknown as a *share* or a proportion of the value of total surplus. Hence the value of total surplus is now introduced as the *numéraire* or the unit against which all prices and wages are measured. Now, by definition, changes in the *share* of wages cannot change the size of the net output. Sraffa also *assumes* that either all the labor sources used in the system are homogenous or they can be reduced to a homogeneous measure by multiplying their amount by the existing scale of wage differentials. After which, he proposes to normalize the total homogeneous labor used in the system to 1.

Given all the assumptions, now we can present Sraffa's repetitive system (or what he calls in the book, a system in 'self-replacing state') in general terms as:

$$
\begin{aligned}
(A_a p_a + B_a p_b + \ldots + K_a p_k)(1+r) + L_a w &= A p_a \\
(A_b p_a + B_b p_b + \ldots + K_b p_k)(1+r) + L_b w &= B p_b \\
\cdots\cdots\cdots\cdots\cdots\cdots\cdots\cdots\cdots\cdots\cdots\cdots & \\
(A_k p_a + B_k p_b + \ldots + K_k p_k)(1+r) + L_k w &= K p_k
\end{aligned}
$$

where $A_a + A_b + \ldots + A_k \leq A; B_a + B_b + \ldots + B_k \leq B; \ldots ; K_a + K_b + \ldots + K_k \leq K$. And $[A - (A_a + A_b + \ldots + A_k)]p_a + [B - (B_a + B_b + \ldots + B_k)]p_b + \ldots + [K - (K_a + K_b + \ldots + K_k)]p_k = 1$.

This gives us (k + 1) independent equations to solve for (k + 2) unknowns (*n* prices, since now the *numéraire* is given by the aggregate net output, wages and the rate of profits). The system can be solved if one of the unknowns is given from outside. It should be noted that technically the system can be solved by taking one of the *p*s as given from outside, say either by the state or international prices for a small country. In that case both r and w would be completely determined and changes in the given p would make both r and w change. But Sraffa does not contemplate this possibility at all in the book. This again shows that the theoretical position of Sraffa is that *all* the ps should be determined from within the system and only the distribution of income can be taken to be given from outside. However, this is a theoretical position and not a technical one. At this stage of analysis, Sraffa's position is that *if* it is accepted that either wages or the rate of profits are given from outside of the equation system then the system can be solved for all the prices and the other distributional variable simultaneously. The question of either the existence or the uniqueness of the solution is not raised.

Movements in Prices

Accordingly, in Chap. 3, Sraffa introduces the problem of observing the effects of changes in w from 1 to 0 (which is its full range, given that w is a share of the net output) on prices and the rate of profits. When w is given the value of 1 then the system technically reverts back to the system of linear equations of the earlier 'subsistence system', as the rate of profits becomes zero. In this case the relative values or prices of commodities are equal to their labor-embodied ratios. Sraffa, however, adds, '[a]t no other wage-level do values follow a simple rule' (p. 12).

The next step is:

> Starting from the situation in which the whole of the national income goes to labour, we *imagine* wages to be reduced: *a* rate of profits will thereby arise. (p. 12, emphasis added)

Two points need to be noted here. (1) This whole exercise is an 'imagined' exercise. In other words, it is simply a mathematical exercise and therefore the 'effects' of these changes are not causal in nature.[9] (2) Sraffa claims that 'a' rate of profits emerges as a consequence; that is, either the

[9] Sen (2003, p. 1253) has also argued that '[t]he temptation to see Sraffa's contribution as a causal theory of price determination… must be resisted. …The sense of 'determination' invoked by Sraffa concerns the mathematical determination of one set of facts from another set.'

uniformity of the industrial rates of profit is assumed to be 'axiomatic' at this point or the reference is to the average rate of profits of the system as a whole. Sraffa goes on to explain that as long as the proportions of the means of production to direct labor of all the industries are equal, the industry-wise transfer of wages to profits would ensure the *condition* that the industrial rates of profit are uniform without affecting the prices. However, if the proportions of the means of production to direct labor are not equal for all the industries then by the same logic prices *must* be affected. It should be noted that the determination of equality or inequality of proportions can be made by measuring means of production by taking their values at any wage (say, $w = 1$), since, when proportions are the same, changes in wages have no impact on the prices and thus on the proportions so measured. From this it follows that if the proportions are not equal at one wage they will not be equal at any wage:

> It is clear that if the proportion were the same in all industries no price-changes could ensue, however great was the diversity of the commodity-composition of the means of production in different industries. For in each industry an equal deduction from the wage would yield just as much as was required for paying the profits on its means of production at uniform rate without need to disturb the existing prices.
>
> For the same reason it is impossible for prices to remain unchanged when there is inequality of 'proportions'. Suppose that prices *did* remain unchanged when the wage was reduced and a rate of profits emerged. Since in any one industry what was saved by the wage-reduction would depend on the number of men employed, while what was needed for paying profits at a uniform rate would depend on the aggregate value of the means of production used, industries with a sufficiently low proportion of labour to means of production would have a deficit, while industries with a sufficiently high proportion would have a surplus, on their payments for wages and profits. (Nothing is assumed at the moment as to what rate of profits corresponds to what wage reduction; all that is required at this stage is that there should be a uniform wage and a uniform rate of profits throughout the system.) (pp. 12–13)

Those readers who are accustomed to classical economics will notice that Sraffa's reasoning above is quite contrary to how classical economists reasoned. In the case of classical economics, a fall in wages, given unequal ratios of means of production to labor, would *result* in unequal rates of profit in the system, which in their turn bring about the gravitation mechanism and through adjustments of outputs and prices bring about, once again, a uniform rate of profits in the system. Sraffa's argument, on the other hand, has nothing to do with any such 'mechanism'. It is pure mathematical reasoning. Given that a uniform rate of profits must prevail, the *consequence* of this condition is that if prices remain constant then some industries *must* have 'surplus' and some 'deficit' upon paying all the 'costs' including profits. In other words, the system becomes 'self-contradictory', that is, the left hand side and the right hand side of the equations no longer remain equal. The only way the two sides of the equations can, once again, be brought to equality is by changing prices. Hence, 'it is *impossible* for prices to remain unchanged when there is inequality of "proportions"' (emphasis added).

It appears that the prices of industries that have a 'deficit' should rise because a rise in prices relative to its cost of the means of production would release more of its gross output to pay for profits. Similar logic would suggest that prices of the 'surplus' industries must fall to redress the balance. This, however, does not mean that industries with higher ratios of value of means of production to labor must be 'deficit' industries and industries with lower ratios of value of means of production to labor must be 'surplus' industries. It may so happen that the industries with high ratios of the value of means of production to labor at a given wage may be using one or more commodities as inputs which use commodities of very low proportions of the value of means of production to labor at that given wage. In such circumstances, a fall in wages might lower the value of the means of production of the given commodity to such an extent that it might turn out to be a 'surplus' industry and its prices would need to fall instead of rise as expected. In fact the movements of prices of all the commodities may turn out to be highly complicated due to the complexity of commodities being produced by means of commodities. As Sraffa puts it:

> To conclude this preliminary survey of the subject it may be pointed out that these considerations dominate not only the price relations of a product to its means of production but equally its relation to any other product. As a result,

> the relative price-movements of two products come to depend, not only on the 'proportions' of labour to means of production by which they are respectively produced, but also on the 'proportions' by which those means have themselves been produced, and also on the 'proportions' by which the means of production of those means of production have been produced, and so on. The result is that the relative price of two products may move, with the fall of wages, in the opposite direction to what we might have expected on the basis of their respective 'proportions'; besides, the prices of their respective means of production may move in such a way as to reverse the order of the two products as to higher and lower proportions; and further complications arise, which will be considered subsequently. (p. 15)

Here we have all the basic ingredients to prove that the 'period of production' approach to measuring capital and the attempt to measure 'capital intensity' independently of the rate of profits are incorrect. But instead of pursuing these matters immediately, Sraffa defers them to subsequent considerations in Chapters VI and XII respectively. What immediately follows is an investigation of the mathematical properties of the equation system, which leads him to the Standard system and the Standard commodity.

The 'Balancing' or the Average Industry

The mathematical reasoning of the necessity of movements of prices with respect to changes in wages, when the 'proportions' of means of production to labor are not uniform, reveals an important fact. Because these 'surplus' and 'deficit' industries are the results of varying proportions of means of production to labor, there would be a *critical* or *balancing* proportion of means of production to labor for which no 'surplus' or 'deficit' would emerge. In other words, if an industry that used this 'balancing proportion' of means of production to labor then in this industry the 'cause' of change in prices due to change in wages would be absent:

> There would be a 'critical proportion' of labour to means of production which marked the watershed between 'deficit' and 'surplus' industries. An industry which employed that particular 'proportion' would show an even

> balance—the proceeds of the wage-reduction would provide exactly what was required for the payment of profits at the general rate. (p. 13)

The important point about this 'critical proportion' is that if it is a balancing proportion at one set of prices then it must remain a 'balancing proportion' for the whole set of prices throughout the range of w from 1 to 0. This is because by definition a fall in wages releases in this industry exactly the amount needed to be transferred to profits to pay for the new general rate of profits on the *initial prices*, that is, the 'price effect' of a change in wages is absent in this industry.

What does it mean to say that the 'price effect' is absent in this industry? Since price is a relative term, that is, it is an exchange ratio between *two* commodities, and exchange values of all other commodities have changed, then clearly the exchange value of this particular commodity has also changed with respect to all other commodities. So does not this only mean that this particular commodity is simply introduced as a *numéraire*? The answer is no. This particular commodity has a mathematical property that no other commodity has. The 'price effect' of a change in wages on all other commodities causes the *ratio* of the value of its total output to the value of its aggregate means of production to *change*. However, for the commodity produced by an industry that employs the 'critical proportion', the *ratio* of the value of its total output to the value of its aggregate means of production remains *constant* with respect to changes in wages. In other words, with respect to changes in wages the prices of all other commodities change when *measured against their own aggregate means of production* except for the commodity produced by the 'balancing proportion'. In this case, its price remains constant when measured against its own aggregate means of production and that is why the 'price effect' is absent.[10]

Now the ratio of the value of total output to the value of its aggregate means of production of the 'balancing industry' must represent the *average* ratio of the value of total output to the value of its aggregate means of production of the system. Since the means of production of the 'balancing industry' uses all the basic-goods directly or indirectly (as all other commodities do), it must use all the commodities directly or indirectly

[10] On this issue, see also Bellino (2004).

as inputs in such proportion that the rise and fall in the prices of all the goods in the aggregate, relative to its own price, must cancel themselves out. If the *average* ratio of the total output to the aggregate means of production of the system could change with respect to changes in wages then no such 'balancing proportion' could exist.

But how to discover the 'balancing proportion'? Let us suppose that there exists a balancing proportion and that the means of production of this 'balancing proportion industry' are also produced by the same balancing proportion and the means of production of their means of production are also produced by the same balancing proportion and so on and on however far we traced them back. In this case, a commodity produced by such an industry will have no reason from its condition of production to change its price with respect to its aggregate means of production when wages move from 1 to 0. Sraffa then argues that, as a matter of fact, it can be shown that the condition of 'recurrence' of the same proportion at all the layers of the production of the means of production implies that such an industry must be the industry with 'balancing proportion'.

Now, to discover the condition of 'recurrence', Sraffa points out that, although the ratios of the values of total output to their aggregate means of production of industries are unequal for any positive wage, they must all be equal when the wage becomes zero, if the condition of uniform rate of profits is to hold—Sraffa calls this ratio '*R*', which is the *maximum rate of profits of the system*. It follows from this that the value ratio of the total output to its aggregate means of production of the 'average' industry must coincide with the maximum rate of profits of the system. Now, this is the *only* value-ratio that can recur as wages move from 1 to 0, since any other ratio would be a 'non-balancing' ratio and would be affected by the changes in wages.

The Standard System and the Standard Commodity

Now, '*R*' can be found by simply solving the system of equations given on p. 193 by putting $w = 0$. But Sraffa does not do that. In the next chapter titled 'The Standard commodity', he instead tries to find the physical composition or the weights of the inputs that must be used by the 'average' industry. The average industry, however, is simply a mathematical construct and it does not need to actually exist or produce *a* commodity. One may construct an 'industry' that produces a 'composite' commodity such that the mathematical properties of the average industry are met. We have already seen that one such mathematical property of the average industry is that its value ratio of the output to its aggregate means of production remains independent of changes in prices as wages move from 1 to 0. This property would clearly be met if the average industry produced a 'composite commodity' which uses the same 'composite commodity' as its input. In other words, it produces a set of commodities in the same proportion as it uses them as inputs. In such a case, a physical ratio of the output to the means of production would be well-defined without any knowledge of prices—prices could take any values without disturbing this ratio. Sraffa claims that this is the *only* physical composition that would meet the mathematical property of the average industry.

Since in our actual system each industry produces only one commodity, hence production of a set of commodities (that is, a 'composite commodity') can only be produced by a combination of industries or a system of production. Finding an 'average' industry is therefore equivalent to finding a system of production that produces the required 'composite commodity'. The question is whether such a system of production can be constructed.

Sraffa first begins with an example of an actual system of three basic commodities:

$$
\begin{array}{llllll}
 & 90\ \text{t.iron} + & 120\ \text{t.coal} + & 60\ \text{qr.Wheat} + & 3/16\ \text{labour} & \rightarrow 180\ \text{t.iron} \\
 & 50\ \text{t.iron} + & 125\ \text{t.coal} + & 150\ \text{qr.Wheat} + & 5/16\ \text{labour} & \rightarrow 450\ \text{t.coal} \\
 & 40\ \text{t.iron} + & 40\ \text{t.coal} + & 200\ \text{qr.Wheat} + & 8/16\ \text{labour} & \rightarrow 480\ \text{qr.Wheat} \\
\hline
\text{Totals} & 180 & 285 & 410 & 1 &
\end{array}
$$

He then shows that, if we reduce the coal industry by 3/5 and the wheat industry by 3/4 and then expand all the industries by 4/3, we obtain a system of production which is given by:

$$
\begin{array}{l}
120\,\text{t.iron} + 160\,\text{t.coal} + \ \ 80\,\text{qr.wheat} + 1/4\,\text{labour} \rightarrow 240\,\text{t.iron} \\
\ \ 40\,\text{t.iron} + 100\,\text{t.coal} + 120\,\text{qr.wheat} + 1/4\,\text{labour} \rightarrow 360\,\text{t.coal} \\
\ \ 40\,\text{t.iron} + \ \ 40\,\text{t.coal} + 200\,\text{qr.wheat} + 2/4\,\text{labour} \rightarrow 480\,\text{qr.wheat} \\
\hline
\text{Totals}\ 200 \qquad 300 \qquad 400 \qquad 1 \qquad 240\text{i} + 360\,\text{c} + 480\,\text{w}
\end{array}
$$

Here we can see that the system produces the three commodities in the same proportion as it uses them in aggregate. Sraffa calls this system the Standard system and the 'composite commodity' made up in the proportion of (1 t. iron:1.5 t. coal:2 qr. wheat) the Standard commodity. It is clear from above that in this case the *physical ratio* of the total output to the aggregate means of production is well-defined, it is completely independent of prices, and it is, in this particular case, equal to 1.2. In other words, the maximum rate of profits of this system is 20%. It is also clear that no *non-basics* can appear in the Standard system because all its outputs must show up as inputs as well. Even those non-basics that use themselves as inputs or are used as inputs in a small sub-set of non-basics must not appear in the Standard system because the Standard system is like the 'one industry' that produces a 'composite commodity' by using only the self-same 'composite commodity' as its means of production (Ricardo's 'corn'), and therefore the process of construction of the Standard system must eliminate all non-basics from the system of equations. Now, our actual and the Standard systems can be represented in value form as follows:

$$
\begin{array}{l}
(90p_i + 120p_c + \ \ 60p_w)(1+r) + 3/16\,w = 180p_i \\
(50p_i + 125p_c + 150p_w)(1+r) + 5/16\,w = 450p_c \\
(40p_i + \ \ 40p_c + 200p_w)(1+r) + 8/16\,w = 480p_w, \\
\hline
(180p_i + 285p_c + 410p_w)(1+r) + \ \ w \ \ = 180p_i + 450p_c + 480p_w
\end{array}
\qquad \text{(I)}
$$

$$
\begin{array}{l}
(120p_i + 160p_c + \ \ 80p_w)(1+r) + 3/16\,w = 240p_i \\
(40p_i + 100p_c + 120p_w)(1+r) + 5/16\,w = 360p_c \\
(40p_i + \ \ 40p_c + 200p_w)(1+r) + 8/16\,w = 480p_w, \\
\hline
(200p_i + 300p_c + 400p_w)(1+r) + \ \ w \ \ = 240p_i + 360p_c + 480p_w
\end{array}
\qquad \text{(II)}
$$

The system of equations (II) is derived from (I) by simple algebraic manipulations, hence the two systems are mathematically equivalent. Now, the second system meets the required property of the 'average' industry of the actual system (I). Thus if we put $w = 0$, then the 'Standard ratio' given by the physical ratio of the total output to the aggregate means of production of the Standard system gives us the average rate of profits of the actual system. Now, we can see that the average rate of profits is a physical property of the actual system and is completely independent of prices or the condition of a uniform rate of profits across industries. 'Even if' prices were such that the industrial rates of profit were not equal, the average rate of profit would not be disturbed.

Sraffa then goes on to show that it is not only the maximum rate of profits of the Standard system that can be derived from the physical proportion independently of prices but it is also possible to derive the average rate of profits for any level of positive wages, as long as we measure the 'given' wages in terms of the Standard commodity. It is clear that if the wages are given in terms of the Standard commodity, then in the Standard system the remaining net output available for total profits (after deducting the wages) and the aggregate means of production still remain in terms of one composite commodity, and therefore their ratio can be known without the knowledge of prices. From here Sraffa derives the famous relationship, $r = R(1 - w)$, for the Standard system when w is given in terms of the Standard commodity.

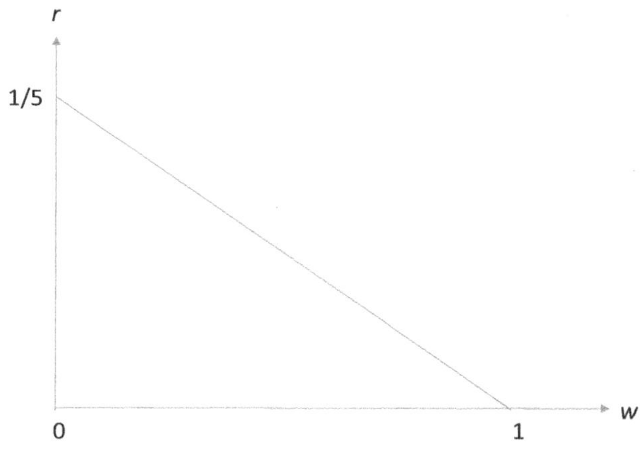

Fig. 1

After this, Sraffa goes on to state:

> Such a relation is of interest only if it can be shown that its application is not limited to the imaginary Standard system but is capable of being extended to the actual economic system of observation.
>
> ...
>
> But the actual system consists of the same basic equations as the Standard system, only in different proportions; so that, once the wage is given, the rate of profits is determined for both systems regardless of the proportions of the equations in either of them. Particular proportions, such as the Standard ones, may give transparency to a system and render visible what was hidden, but they cannot alter its mathematical properties.
>
> The straight-line relation between the wage and the rate of profits will therefore hold in all cases, provided only that the wage is expressed in terms of the Standard product. The same rate of profits, which in the Standard system is obtained as a ratio between *quantities* of commodities, will in the actual system result from the ratio of aggregate *values*. (pp. 22–23)

The first paragraph makes it clear that his equations refer to the *actual economic system of observation*. Hence, there is no doubt that the inputs and outputs are not necessarily assumed to be at the classical center of gravitation. The last paragraph of the quotation is most noteworthy. Here Sraffa clearly states that his reference to the rates of profits of the Standard and the actual systems is to the 'aggregates' or the 'average' rates of profits of the two systems. Further on, the straight-line relationship between wages and the average rate of profits, given that wage is expressed in terms of the Standard commodity, must hold in 'all cases', that is, for all the systems derived from rescaling the actual system. Now, the 'average' rate of profits can remain constant in the face of all the changes in the proportions of individual industries if and only if all the industrial rates of profit are equal. The point to note is that the construction as well as the determination of the average rate of profits of the Standard system does not require the condition of a uniform rate of profits in the real system—it is derived directly from the method of production given in physical terms. And since the Standard system represents the mathematical properties of the 'balancing' industry of the real system, it shows that the determination of the 'average' rate of profits of the real system does not require the condition of a uniform rate of profits in the system either. Now, the condition of a uniform rate of profits turns out to be a *consequence* of 'given' and uniform wages from outside the system. This is why, when Sraffa introduced the rate of profits in his equations on page 6, he declared that it *must* be uniform. (See Appendix to this chapter for a formal argument in support of this proposition.)

This also explains why in the 'Index' of the book the entry is: 'Rate of profits, assumed to be uniform for all industries 6; …' (p. 98). Clearly, anyone searching through the index for the 'rate of profits' cannot understand on page 6 itself that it refers to a logical necessity. He or she can only make sense of the condition at that stage as an 'assumption'. But it should be clear that Sraffa is very particular about the meanings of the words he uses and he knows very well that an *assumption* cannot be claimed to hold as a necessity such as the word *must* conveys. For example, in his review of Sraffa's book, M.W. Reder wrote: 'Every system must have at least one basic product, but no restriction is placed on the number of nonbasics.' (Reder 1961, p. 689). In the margin of his copy of the review, Sraffa wrote: '"must" ? ("is assumed to" not "must")'.

The point that the mathematical properties of the Standard system are the mathematical properties of the actual system was yet again emphasized by Sraffa in his draft response (written on 12 February 1961) to Eaton's[11] review of his book: 'First of all I am convinced that it {the Standard system} does represent a real property of the econ. system: and while this could be described in other ways, it should not be ignored, even if it did not find immediate application.' Further on, in the same response, Sraffa clarifies that the Standard commodity is nothing but the *average* commodity of the actual system:

> There are besides, many possible applications {of the Standard commodity}, which I have not mentioned in the book, in problems discussed by Marx. Take, e.g. the determination of a general rate of profits, from the rate of surplus value: Marx takes an average of the rates of profits obtained in the production of the different commodities on the basis of 'values', and

[11] John Eaton's (real name: Bodington) review was published in Italian in the journal *Società* and brought to Sraffa's notice by Maurice Dobb. See Bellino (2006) for the English translation of Eaton's review and the entire draft response of Sraffa.

> gets, as he acknowledges, an *approximately* correct result. An exact result could however be obtained by taking, instead of a simple average, a weighted average: & it can be shown that the appropriate weights can be derived directly from the proportions in which the comm{odities} enter the 'St{andard} com{modity}'. Similarly, in the application of M{arx}'s notion of the comm{odity} produced by 'a cap{ital} of av{erage} org{anic} comp{osition}': for an exact result the average must be found in the same way, in other words that comm{odity} is the St{andard} Com{modity}. (D3/12/111: 132)

One interesting implication of our interpretation is that the prices and the industrial rates of profit of an economic system are completely independent of the market structure. No matter whether an industry is characterized by perfect or imperfect competition or pure monopoly or oligopoly the price and its rate of profits are determined by the structure of all the interdependent industries and their combined productivity or the productivity of the system as a whole. Individual industries have no independent existence. This is why we find that the word *competition* (or any kind of market structure for that matter) simply does not appear in Sraffa's entire book. It is quite intriguing that a book devoted to the theory of value— by an author who had made significant original contribution to the theories of market structures—should remain absolutely silent about the market structure to which the theory applies. Now the reason for this silence appears to be simple: market structures are simply irrelevant to the problem of prices and the rate of profits of an economic system, if the distribution of income is given from outside. As we know, market structures affect the shape of the demand curves faced by the firms and the shape of the supply curves over a period of time. Given that both these variables are absent from Sraffa's equations, there is no room for market structure to play any role in his theory. This does not mean, however, that market structures are also irrelevant to the producers or the firms in the industries—market structures may affect the total profits of a firm but not the rate of profits of the industry. It should, however, be noted that in Sraffa's system the industries directly exchange their commodities with each other and it is assumed that there is no transportation and transaction costs involved in exchange. But, of course, in the real world a class of traders is always involved in making the transactions, particularly in the case of consumer goods when transaction takes place continuously over the entire period of the production cycle. Sraffa's theory abstracts from such institutional factors.

There is, however, one more wrinkle in the argument that still needs to be ironed out. What if rescaling the actual system could give rise to several Standard systems with differing average rates of profits? In that case, it must be admitted that the 'average' rate of profits changes as weights of the industries change. Hence, Sraffa needs to establish that the Standard system is *unique* to any given actual system, which he does in the next chapter.

However, before getting to that, we should take note of a few more notable remarks and points made by Sraffa in the current chapter. Soon after discovering the composition of the Standard commodity, Sraffa goes on to add:

> It can be said that in any actual economic system there is embedded a miniature Standard system which can be brought to light by chipping off the unwanted parts. (This applies as much to a system which is not in a self-replacing state as to one which is.) (p. 20)

We will come to the point of 'embeddedness' when we come to the proof of the uniqueness of the Standard system. Here an interesting clue to the problem of a 'uniform rate of profits' is yet again given in the parentheses. As we have seen, in Chapter II, p. 6, Sraffa introduces his 'surplus' equations in a 'self-replacing' state, which is defined as a state in which the gross outputs of all industries are *at least* as great as they are used in the aggregate as inputs in the system. Such systems were called 'repetitive' systems in the notes. Now without any warning, in a parenthetical note we are told that his construction of the Standard system also applies to 'non-repetitive' systems. As we have seen in Chap. 5, a 'non-repetitive' system is a snap-shot of a dynamic system when some industries might be contracting in size due to technical changes and so on. In this case, no *physical* surplus exists, as all the inputs cannot be deducted item by item from the outputs. Such situations are typically non-equilibrium situations and Sraffa's parenthetical note yet again is designed to nudge the reader to think about how a 'surplus' system could not be in a self-replacing state and how the condition of equal rates of profit could be applied to such a system when obviously it is not in an equilibrium state?

After showing that the average rate of profits derived as a ratio of *quantities* in the Standard system must also be equal to the average rate of profits of the actual system derived by the ratio of the aggregate *values*, Sraffa adds a small paragraph with a distinct number of its own, §32:

> Reverting to our example, if in the actual system (as outlined in §25 ff., with $R = 20\%$) the wage is fixed in terms of the Standard net product, to $w = 3/4$ there will correspond $r = 5\%$. But while the share of wages will be equal in value to ¾ of the Standard national income, it does not follow that the share of profits will be equivalent to the remaining ¼ of the Standard income. The share of profits will consist of whatever is left of the *actual* national income after deducting from it the equivalent of ¾ of the *Standard* national income for wages: and prices must be such as to make the value of what goes to profits equal to 5% of the value of the actual means of production. (p. 23)

Two points are made here. First, the job of prices in the *actual* system is to ensure an 'average' rate of profits, which is determined independently of the prices and not simultaneously with it. Once the Standard system and the Standard commodity are discovered, the problem no longer remains a simultaneous determination of prices and the rate of profits. The rate of profits is known, once wages are given, via the formula $r = R(1 - w)$. Now, this rate of profits could be applied to the actual equations and solved for prices—*the equation system now turns into linear equation system as was the case with the subsistence system.* The fact that the rate of profits can be known prior to the knowledge of the prices, and not simultaneously with it, was so important to Sraffa's theoretical project that, as Pasinetti (2001) has reported, he had penned down a couple of slogans for his book that said: 'The St. Syst. provides tangible evidence of the rate of profits as a non-price phenomenon' and 'A Dividend could be declared before knowing what is the price of the company's product' (H2/89: 56). Evidently, 'slogans' were designed to highlight the essence of the book.

Second, the attentive reader is quietly told that the Standard commodity does not solve what Sraffa had considered to be Ricardo's problem of the invariable measure of value in the 'Introduction' to Ricardo's *Principles*. It should be noted that the measure of wages in terms of the Standard commodity amounts to a move from using the net national income of the actual system as the *numéraire* to using the net national income of the Standard system as the *numéraire*. Hence the condition that the size of the net income of the actual system must remain constant with respect to changes in wages must be given up.

Uniqueness of the Standard System

In the next chapter titled 'Uniqueness of the Standard System' Sraffa takes up the question of whether rescaling of the actual system can give rise to more than one Standard system. First, he explains how a Standard system can be constructed from an actual system just like a sculpture is molded out of given clay. The first step in this process is that we make sure that *all* the basic commodities produced in the actual system are strictly greater in quantity than the aggregate use made of them in the system. If that is not the case, then the system must be rescaled (keeping the aggregate use of labor in the system constant) to bring it to a state in which all its outputs are produced in excess of their aggregate use in the system.[12] The second step is to chip off all the outputs by an equal percentage of their total output, leaving the input sides intact. Once any commodity whose total output becomes equal to its aggregate use as input, we stop the chipping-off process and once again rescale the system so that all the outputs are once again greater than their aggregate use as inputs. We keep

[12] We know that Sraffa had confronted this issue in relation to non-repetitive systems in his notes of 1943, where he thought that this can always be done if the number of equations was large. Besicovitch in his proof of the uniqueness of the Standard system showed Sraffa that this could always be done as along as physical surplus of one commodity was produced whereas no deficit of any other commodity was produced in the aggregate. But that this is also the case when some commodities show a deficit (that is, for a non-repetitive system) is not proved. It seems Sraffa thought that it must be the case as long as the system produces a 'surplus' in terms of value throughout the range of wages and that is why the clause of a large number of commodities was dropped.

repeating the process till the chipping-off process leaves *all* the outputs just equal to their aggregate use in the system—this, of course, is a subsistence system. Now, we expand all the outputs by the total percentage by which all the outputs were chipped off in this process. *Voilà*! We have our Standard system.[13] Here we can see that the Standard system is nothing but a *reshaping* of the actual system, as if it were embedded in the actual system and the sculptor simply brought it out by first chipping off the portions that were obscuring the shape and then adding the chipped-off clay proportionately so that the shape remains intact. The description of the process of construction of the Standard system leaves little doubt that there cannot be another Standard system embedded in the same actual system. But still, a mathematical proof of the proposition was required, which was provided to Sraffa by Besicovitch in September 1944 (D3/12/39: 42, dated 21 September 1944).

The mathematical proof that Sraffa provides in the book is as follows:

Step 1: Suppose our actual system of basic commodities is given by k equations. Our problem is to assign k multipliers to these k equations such that its aggregate means of production as inputs and aggregate outputs come out in the Standard proportion. Suppose these multipliers are given by $q_1, q_2, \ \ldots \ q_k$.

Step 2: Write down the vertical columns of the means of production of the inputs horizontally and multiply them with the maximum rate of profits of the system such as

$$\left(A_a q_a + A_b q_b + \ldots + A_k q_k\right)\left(1 + R\right) = Aq_{\mathrm{a}}$$
$$\left(B_a q_a + B_b q_b + \ldots + B_k q_k\right)\left(1 + R\right) = Bq_{\mathrm{b}}$$
$$\cdots\cdots\cdots\cdots\cdots\cdots\cdots\cdots\cdots\cdots\cdots\cdots\cdots\cdots\cdots\cdots\cdots$$
$$\left(K_a q_a + K_b q_b + \ldots + K_k q_k\right)\left(1 + R\right) = Kq_{\mathrm{k}}$$

With an additional *numéraire* given by

[13] Sraffa's procedure is an adaptation of Besicovitch's procedure, which relied on changing the proportions of the industries to its Standard proportions without keeping the total use of the labor constant in the system.

$$\left(L_a q_a + L_b q_b + \ldots + L_k q_k\right) = 1$$

This equation system can be reduced to a polynomial of *k*th degree in R. Therefore there can be k values of R with k different set of q's. However, if a positive value of R is associated with some negative value of q then that solution is *economically meaningless*, since a negative industry has no meaning. Therefore, one needs to prove that there can be only one positive value of R that is associated with all positive values of q

Step 3: Prove that there is always a positive value of the prices as wages move from 1 to 0. When wages are at 1 then prices are given by their labor embodied ratios. Hence, at $w = 1$, all prices are positive. Now if w is moved *continuously* from 1 to 0, all the prices would also move *continuously*. Therefore, for any price to become negative it must first go through zero. However, as long as wages and profits are positive, no price can become zero until at least one price of its means of production has become negative. Therefore, all prices must remain positive since no price can become negative unless some other price does so.

Step 4: Write down the price equation of the actual basic commodity system when wages are equal to zero.

$$\left(A_a p_a + A_b p_b + \ldots + A_k p_k\right)(1 + R) = A\mathrm{p}_{\mathrm{a}}$$
$$\left(B_a p_a + B_b p_b + \ldots + B_k p_k\right)(1 + R) = B\mathrm{p}_{\mathrm{a}}$$
$$\ldots\ldots\ldots\ldots\ldots\ldots\ldots\ldots\ldots\ldots\ldots\ldots\ldots\ldots\ldots$$
$$\left(K_a p_a + K_b p_b + \ldots + K_k p_k\right)(1 + R) = K\mathrm{p}_{\mathrm{k}}$$

Step 5: Suppose that there is a positive value of $R = R'$ with which is associated a set of positive values of q's given by $q_a', q_b', \ldots, q_k'$ and an all positive set of prices given by $p_a', p_b', \ldots, p_k'$. Further suppose that there is another value of $R = R''$ with which are associated all positive sets of q's and p's given by $q_a'', q_b'', \ldots, q_k''$ and $p_a'', p_b'', \ldots, p_k''$ respectively.

Step 6: Replace the generic price equations with the solutions associated with R' and multiply equations 1 to k by $q_a'', q_b'', \ldots, q_k''$ respectively:

$$q_a''(A_a p_a' + A_b p_b' + \ldots + A_k p_k')(1+R') = q_a'' A p_a'$$
$$q_b''(B_a p_a' + B_b p_b' + \ldots + B_k p_k')(1+R') = q_b'' B p_b'$$
$$\cdots\cdots\cdots\cdots\cdots\cdots\cdots\cdots\cdots\cdots\cdots\cdots\cdots\cdots\cdots\cdots\cdots\cdots\cdots\cdots$$
$$q_k''(K_a p_a' + K_b p_b' + \ldots + K_k p_k')(1+R') = q_k'' K p_k'$$

Step 7: Take the aggregate of the equations:

$$\begin{bmatrix} q_a''(A_a p_a' + A_b p_b' + \ldots + A_k p_k') \\ +q_b''(B_a p_a' + B_b p_b' + \ldots + B_k p_k') \\ +q_k''(K_a p_a' + K_b p_b' + \ldots + K_k p_k') \end{bmatrix} (1+R') = q_a'' A p_a' + q_b'' B p_b' + \ldots + q_k'' K p_k' \tag{1}$$

Step 8: Replace the q-equations with the solution associated with R'' and the set of q given by $q_a'', q_b'', \ldots, q_k''$ and then multiply each equation by $p_a', p_b', \ldots, p_k'$ respectively :

$$p_a'(A_a q_a'' + A_b q_b'' + \ldots + A_k q_k'')(1+R'') = p_a' A q_a''$$
$$p_b'(B_a q_a'' + B_b q_b'' + \ldots + B_k q_k'')(1+R'') = p_b' B q_b''$$
$$\cdots\cdots\cdots\cdots\cdots\cdots\cdots\cdots\cdots\cdots\cdots\cdots\cdots\cdots\cdots\cdots\cdots\cdots\cdots\cdots$$
$$p_k'(K_a q_a'' + K_b q_b'' + \ldots + K_k q_k'')(1+R'') = p_k' K q_k''$$

Step 9: Add them up. We get:

$$\begin{bmatrix} p_a'(A_a q_a'' + A_b q_b'' + \ldots + A_k q_k'') + \\ p_b'(B_a q_a'' + B_b q_b'' + \ldots + B_k q_k'') + \\ p_k'(K_a q_a'' + K_b q_b'' + \ldots + K_k q_k'') \end{bmatrix} (1+R'') = \begin{matrix} p_a' A q_a'' + \\ p_b' B q_b'' + \ldots + p_k' K q_k'' \end{matrix} \tag{2}$$

Step 10: The right hand sides of equations (1) and equations (2) are equal. Therefore, the left hand sides must also be equal. The terms under the large brackets on the left hand sides of the two equations are also equal, although arranged in a different order, except for the fact that they are multiplied by distinct numbers: $(1+R')$ and $(1+R'')$ respectively. Thus the two left hand sides can be equal if and only if the terms in the large brackets add up to zero. Now, if all the *p*'s are positive, then the terms in the large brackets can be zero if and only if some of the *q*'s must be negative. Similarly, if all the *q*'s must be positive then some of the *p*'s must be negative.

Step 11: This proves that if there is a set of positive values of *p*'s then there can only be one set of positive values for *q*'s and vice versa. Now it has already been shown that there exist a set of all-positive value for *p*'s and *q*'s.

In a footnote to Step 3, Sraffa adds: 'For a proof to be complete it is necessary to show in addition that the *p*'s representing prices of basic products cannot become negative through becoming infinite—unlike the *p*'s of non-basics which can do so. This is shown in the Note on Self-reproducing Non-basics (Appendix B)' (p. 28, f.n. 1). In Appendix B we are asked to contemplate a situation in which a non-basic commodity, say a type of 'beans', uses itself in its production at a very high rate, say to produce 110 units of 'beans' 100 units of 'beans' are required as input. In this case, it is clear that the 'beans' industry can never have higher rate of profits than 10%, if its price must be positive. Now, if the maximum rate of profits of the basic commodity system happens to be higher than 10% then, as wages fall and the rate of profits becomes 10%, at this rate of profits the price of 'beans' must become infinite and as rate of profits goes beyond 10% the price of 'beans' must go through infinity and become negative. At the 10% rate, if the 'beans' were used as the *numéraire* then all other prices must become zero. However, if a basic commodity is used as the *numéraire* then it is impossible for all the other prices to become zero because the commodity that is used as the *numéraire* must enter in the production of some other basic commodity. Therefore, the price of no basic commodity can go through zero and become negative.[14]

[14] Lippi (2008) has argued that Sraffa's 'proofs' are not complete from a classical mathematical point of view. He, however, concludes that Sraffa's results are valid and complete proofs of his mathematical propositions can be worked out. Velupillai (2008), on the other hand, argues that the mathematics Sraffa uses is the *constructivist* mathematics and not the formal-orthodox mathematics that

The point to note here is that the whole problem of 'beans' could be *logically* eliminated from consideration if Sraffa was *assuming* that his system was *already* in the classical 'center of gravitation', as Garegnani and his followers maintain. Because the mechanism that is supposed to bring the system to the classical 'center of gravitation' must ensure that 'beans' disappear from the system once the 'average' rate of profits of the system goes beyond 10%. But Sraffa goes on to add: 'The 'beans' could however still be produced and marketed so as to show a normal profit if the producer sold them at a higher price than the one which, in his book-keeping, he attributes to them as means of production' (p. 91). Here we get clear evidence for the fact that Sraffa is *not* necessarily dealing with the equilibrium condition. Moreover, he goes on to state that the *assumption* of the same price for both the inputs and the outputs could be broken for a *non-basic* commodity but not the condition of an equal rate of profits.

This completes the proof of the proposition that the industrial rates of profit in the equations of the actual system 'must be uniform'. The point that this proposition does not require the notion of equilibrium can also be gleaned from many of his remarks found in the archive. Here we give just one example. A German student named Soltwedel, who was asked by his diploma advisor to write an essay on Sraffa's book, wrote to Sraffa on 28 February 1968 asking for some help and clarification. In his letter, Soltwedel expresses his understanding of Sraffa's book in these terms: 'At the moment, I think the aim of your study {is} not to be a theory of distribution or a development of input output analysis, but rather a theory of price determination in input-output models, using the production system of closed Leontief model, given the physical amount of the surplus, economy in equilibrium and infinite elasticity of factor supply.' (C 294: 1, underlining and squiggly underlining by Sraffa). The reader should note that the squiggly underlining by Sraffa is a mark of extreme

the 'neo-Ricardians' use in their interpretation of Sraffa. Velupillai finds Sraffa's proofs to be complete from the 'constructivists' perspective. I think it would be natural for Sraffa to be attracted to the constructivist movement in mathematics given his closeness to early quantum physics and Marxist ideas that allow for *dialectical reasoning*, which is possible only if the tenet of the 'excluded middle' is rejected and hence the method of proof by 'contradiction' is disallowed. I am happy to note that Velupillai also thinks that 'there [is] no need for any kind of equilibrium assumption, …, in PCC [*Production of Commodities by Means of Commodities*]' (p. 277).

disapproval. In response to this Sraffa wrote: 'As regards your own interpretation, I must say frankly that you have gone astray the moment you speak of "equilibrium" or of "elasticity of factor supply": all the quantities considered are what can be observed by taking a photograph, there are no rates of change, etc.' (C 294: 3, dated 1 March 1968).

At this stage, it may not be out of place to point out that over the years three significant economists of the twentieth century also concluded that Sraffa's condition of a 'uniform rate of profits' is not necessarily based on the assumption of 'equilibrium' outputs. For example, Joan Robinson wrote in her review of Sraffa's book: 'It is this, not the austere style, that makes the book difficult. We are concerned with *equilibrium* prices and a rate of profit uniform throughout the economy, but we are given only half of the equilibrium system to stand on.' (Robinson 1961, p. 54, emphasis added). However, after much reflection and perhaps several conversations with Sraffa, in her posthumously published paper, she comes to the conclusion:

> To reconcile the two parts of Sraffa's analysis we may treat it as follows. The 'system' of production in use in an economy at a moment of time, and the stocks of inputs required to implement it, are set out in terms of a physical input-output table. *It does not represent a stationary state or an equilibrium position.* It is simply the position that has been reached, 'today', as a result of accumulation of stocks and of technical knowledge over the past history. (Robinson 1985, p. 164, emphasis added)

John Hicks also came to the conclusion that:

> Sraffa leaves us to find out what his prices are, but *I doubt if they are equilibrium prices.* They seem to be prices which are set upon products, by their producers, according to some rule. Now it is perfectly true that we are nowadays familiar with that method of price-fixing, by 'mark-up'; but when that method is used, the rate of profit that is used to establish the mark-up is conventional. Now it may be that Sraffa wants us to think of his rate of profit as being conventional; and that the uniformity of the rate of profit throughout his system, of which he makes so much, is just a uniformity of convention. (Hicks 1985, p. 306, emphasis added)

And finally, Amartya Sen, in his highly incisive understanding of Sraffa's project, wrote:

> In a work [Sraffa 1960] that is justly famous (and also, arguably, much misunderstood), Sraffa tried to explore whether the relationship between prices, productions, and distributions of income cannot be substantially explored without considering any changes—factual or counterfactual—and without, thus, invoking any 'marginal' concepts at all (since such concepts take the form of asking what would have happened if something had been one unit more or less).
>
> It is quite remarkable that Sraffa did establish a number of important relationships (e.g., those between the wage rate and the profit rate, and between relative prices and quantities) that could be expected on the basis of certain *given* characteristics (such as the same rate of profits and same wage rates in different enterprises). He did not go into the question as to why these characteristics (e.g., the same rate of profit in all enterprises) could be expected to hold, and it is possible to argue that such a justificatory inquiry would take one in the direction of equilibrium economics, involving the use of counterfactual considerations. But that was not the subject of Sraffa's investigation. (Sen 2004, pp. 583–84, emphasis in original.)

It is the hope of the present author that the arguments of this book would convince Professor Sen that the 'justificatory inquiry' into the condition of the same rate of profits does not need to take one in the direction of equilibrium economics.[15]

[15] Among the Sraffians, Roncaglia (1978, p. 16) did appreciate that 'there is no reason to believe that Sraffa's prices of production should equate quantity demanded and quantity supplied'. This position was based on his claim that Sraffa's system was like 'a photograph of the market place'. His thesis of the 'photograph of the market place' seems to be inspired by Sraffa's early note (D3/12/7: 115–119) mentioned in our Chapter 3, as Sraffa had allowed access to his early papers (1925–31) to Eatwell and Roncaglia to help them translate his 1925 paper during 1973–74 (see C 81). Roncaglia, however, did not manage to show how then Sraffa could take the rate of profits to be uniform and thus succumbed to holding the contradictory position that Sraffa's system was 'a photograph of the market place' and at the same time *assumed* to be at the center of gravitation. As he writes: 'In Sraffa's analysis, as in that of the classical economists and Marx, the analytic condition upon which determination of the prices of production (the "natural" prices of the classical economists) rests consists quite simply in an equal rate of profits in the various sectors. This assumption corresponds to the idea pondered by Smith and Marx among others, that the unity of the capitalist

What is Given, *w* or *r*?

Now we come to the question of the 'given wages' expressed in terms of the Standard commodity. It is quite clear that if the Standard commodity is chosen by the society as its 'money-commodity' then given 'money-wages' would *ipso facto* imply that wages are expressed in the Standard commodity. But, in my opinion, this cannot be true for any actual economy because an actual economy is constantly going through either changes in its total employment of labor or changes in its method of production or both. Therefore, its Standard commodity must continuously change. But no economy can function with a continuously changing money-commodity since one of the essential characteristics of money is to be a means of deferred payment. Therefore, one needs to find some way of converting given 'money-wages' to its equivalent in the Standard commodity at any moment of time. Of course, as Sraffa points out, one need not find the Standard commodity to express wages in terms of it. One can simply replace the *numéraire* equation with the condition $r = R(1-w)$ or alternatively $1/w = R/(R-r)$. In the 'reference to the literature' Sraffa suggests the similarity of the alternative expression of the mathematical property of the system with Adam Smith's idea of 'labor commanded' measure of value or wages as the 'invariable measure of value'. In the above expression, $1/w$ represents the quantity of labor that the Standard net product would purchase or command. Yet again, we see an attempt to put various aspects of classical economics in the 'frame'. But this digression does not solve our problem. We still need to know w in terms of the Standard commodity and actual wages cannot be taken to be given in terms of the Standard commodity. This, in my opinion, leads Sraffa to give up the idea of taking wages as 'given' and take instead the rate of profits as 'given' from outside because the purpose of 'given wages' for his theory was already accomplished by establishing the linear relation between w (in terms of the Standard commodity) and r (which must be uniform for all industries):

---

system is guaranteed by the free flow of capital from one sector to another in pursuit of the most advantageous utilization.' (Roncaglia 2000, pp. 34–35)

> The choice of the wage as the independent variable in the preliminary stages was due to its being there regarded as consisting of specified necessaries determined by physiological or social conditions which are independent of prices or the rate of profits. But as soon as the possibility of variations in the division of the product is admitted, this consideration loses much of its force. And when the wage is to be regarded as 'given' in terms of a more or less abstract standard, and does not acquire a definite meaning until the prices of commodities are determined, the position is reversed. The rate of profits, as a ratio, has a significance which is independent of any prices, and can well be 'given' before the prices are fixed. It is accordingly susceptible of being determined from outside the system of production, in particular by the level of money rate of interest. (p. 33)

It should be noted that the idea of variable wages as a share of net output was introduced on page 11 of the *PCMC* but the argument to switch from taking wages as 'given' from outside to taking the rate of profits as 'given' from outside takes place only after the deliberation on the standard system and the Standard commodity is complete. This is yet more evidence that points to the fact that Sraffa needed the analysis of the standard system and the Standard commodity to first ensure that the proposition regarding the determination of the average rate of profits of the real system independently of the determination of prices is established. Only then could it be argued that the average rate of profits of the empirical system may be taken as given from outside.

Still the maneuver to take the rate of profits as given from outside does not solve the problem because we do not know how the rate of profits is 'determined' by the 'given' rate of interest. Furthermore, the observed rates of interest may not be uniform as banks are expected to factor in the differential risks of lending to various industries. This brings us to the point made on p. 188 that *apparently* the industrial rates of profits could differ due to unequal risk factors. But this cannot be true because in Sraffa's equations the observed input–output data is for industries and not for firms in the industries. An industry can be judged more or less risky compared to another only on the empirical ground that investment in one industry is, on the average, more or less successful compared to the other. In other words, the industrial input and output data take into account all the successful as well as unsuccessful firms in the industry. Therefore, the rate of profits of the industries will not be affected by the risk factor. However, the successful firms in high risk industries would reap higher rate of profits compared to the successful firms in the low risk industries. Thus, uneven risks of investments in various industries may give rise to uneven rates of interest charged by the banks to hedge against the differential risks. Now, if the comparative structure of the risk factor is known then one can homogenize the uneven interest rates by taking the known risk factor into account.

But yet another problem looms. The problem with this way out is that in the real world labor is not homogeneous. In the first case, the heterogeneous labor could be homogenized in a simple manner. Let's suppose that the total wage bill for the whole economy is $100 and that industry *a* uses 5 units of labor and pays $60 in wages whereas industry *b* uses 5 units of labor and pays $40 in wages. If we set wages for homogeneous labor equal to $8 per unit of labor then all we have to do is count 5 units of labor of industry *a* to be equivalent to 7.5 units of homogeneous labor. But this exercise cannot be done if wages are unknown. Alternatively, we will need to make the assumption that the differential wage structure is 'given', although the homogeneous wages have to be determined. In any case, the most important problem is to first determine how the given interest rate determines the rate of profits and then how it, at the same time, determines wages, since if one of the distributional variables is fixed then the other is fixed too. In other words, the *theory of distribution* needs to determine the rate of profits and the wage rate simultaneously.

The 'Dated Labor' and the Period of Production'

In the next chapter (VI) Sraffa draws out the consequence of the complicated nature of price movements with respect to changes in wages due to the complicated interconnectedness of *basic* commodities in their production equations. Sraffa shows that when we reduce the price of a commodity to wages and profits paid in its successive layers of production such as: $L_a w + L_{a1} w(1+r) + \ldots + L_{an} w(1+r)^n + \ldots = Ap_a$, where symbols have their usual meaning, A is the total quantity of good '*a*' produced and 1 to n are the dates (or layers) going back in production cycles, then for any labor term of the period n a rise in the rate of profits would pull its value in two directions. This can be seen by replacing w with $w = 1 - r/R$ [given, $r = R(1-w)$] in the nth term of the equation: $L_{an}(1 - r/R)$ $(1+r)^n$. Clearly with the rise in r, the term in the first parentheses falls whereas the term in the second parentheses rises. In an example, Sraffa showed that if two commodities '*a*' and '*b*' are produced by an equal amount of labor but dispersed at different dates, for example, they differ in three of their labor terms while identical in all the others: '*a*' has 20 units of labor in excess of '*b*' for n = 8 whereas '*b*' has 19 units of labor in excess for n = 0 and 1 unit of labor in excess for n = 25. Now the difference between their prices in terms of the Standard commodity is given by: $p_a - p_b = 20w$ $(1+r)^8 - \{19w + w(1+r)^{25}\}$. The price of '*a*' rises relative to '*b*' as r moves from 0 to 9%, then it falls between 9% and 22% to rise again from 22% to 25%, for R = 25%. Such movements in prices clearly show that no measure of capital independent of the rate of profits is possible.

All of these complications notwithstanding, it can be unambiguously stated that, if the price of a commodity falls due to a rise in the rate of profits, its fall can never be greater than the fall in wages. To see that, take the reduction equation for good '*a*' given above:

$$\mathrm{L}_a w + L_{a1} w(1+r) + \ldots + L_{an} w(1+r)^n + \ldots = Ap_a.$$

It can be shown that a rise in r cannot lead to a greater fall in p_{a} than the fall in w. This proves that in the case of single-commodity production equations, the inverse relation between wages and the rate of profits is unambiguous. This brings Part I of Sraffa's book to close.

The rest of the book is mainly concerned with bringing more realistic elements of an economy into the equation system, such as fixed capital, land and the possibility of substitution in technique,[16] and satisfy-

[16] One of the complicated features of the economy, that Sraffa was working out quite consistently in his notes but is not included in the book, is the case of uneven rotation periods for industries. As we know, in the book, Sraffa states that '[w]e retain however the supposition of an annual cycle of production with an annual market' (p. 10). But, of course, the rotation period for an iron or coal

ing that the results obtained in the case of only circulating capital and single-product industries remain intact. We will not discuss Part II of Sraffa's book becuase it mainly deals with the technical issues arising due to joint-production (fixed capital and land) but adds little in terms of an understanding of the nature of his work. The reader is referred to Sinha (2010) for a brief account of Part II of Sraffa's book.

To Switch or to Re-Switch?

In Part III, which has only one small chapter titled 'Switch in Methods of Production', Sraffa first reverts back to single-product industries and then generalizes the result for joint-production as well. One consequence of the non-linear movements in prices with respect to changes in the rate of profits, as shown in the analysis of the 'dated labor approach', is that if there is choice of techniques available then the system may switch from one method of production to another and again switch back to the earlier method of production as the rate of profits continues to rise, and there can be several such back-and-forth switchings and re-switchings. For example, to take the simplest case, if there were two techniques available to produce a *non-basic* commodity then we could draw the non-linear price movements of this commodity when technique I is used and then do the same for technique II and superimpose these two price curves, which could cut each other several times. This shows that a technique that was deemed cheaper at a low rate of profits becomes dearer at a higher rate of profits compared to the other technique, but again becomes cheaper at yet higher rate of profits compared to the other technique. This proves that techniques by themselves cannot be classified in terms of 'intensity of capital' independently of the rate of profits.

Although this result has been hailed as Sraffa's crowning glory and the main result that the book was driving at, Sraffa himself apparently did not see it that way—and for good reason, as we have seen in Chap. 1. Fisher and Wicksell were on to this phenomenon before him and so

industry is not the same as the rotation period for the wheat industry. In his notes, Sraffa characterized 'industrial cycles', as opposed to 'agricultural cycles', where the rotation period is almost instantaneous. Apparently, he did not introduce this case in his book simply because of its mathematical complications.

Sraffa, who was well acquainted with their work, must have been aware that he had not discovered anything original here. Sraffa presents the possibility of re-switching in a 'matter of fact' manner in the first paragraph of the chapter as a minor extension of the analysis of price movements in the 'dated labor approach'. The main concern of the chapter, however, is not '*re*-switching' but rather the 'switch' in the methods of production. The problem is how to compare alternative techniques when the switch takes place in the processes of production of *basic* commodities. In the above example, we have carefully chosen a *non*-basic commodity so that the Standard commodity remains unaffected by the switches in the techniques. But if the switch is in the process of production of a *basic* commodity then before and after the switch the method of production would change, which must bring about changes in the Standard commodity. In this case we lose the common measure that could be applied to the movements of prices and wages in the two systems:

> If the product is a basic one, the problem is complicated by the circumstance that each of the two alternative methods of producing it implies a distinct economic system, with a distinct Maximum rate of profit. As a result we seem to lack a common ground on which the comparison between the two methods can be carried out: since, according as one or the other method is used, we are in one or the other economic system, and to any given rate of profits there will correspond, in each system, a different wage, even though in the same standard, and in different set of relative prices; as a consequence a comprison of the prices by the two methods becomes meaningless since its result appears to depend on which commodity is chosen as standard of prices. (p. 82)

The problem can be presented in this manner: At any given moment and given rate of profits we observe a method of production in use. If there were other methods of production available to produce the output mix that has been produced then the observed method of production must be the most efficient method at the given rate of profits. But how can we make such a claim without having any means of comparing the alternative methods of production? Sraffa's argument is that for such claims one only needs to take into account the condition of *a switch* (and not a re-switch) when the rate of profits is moved in either direction. And this can always be done.

Appendix[17]

Why Must Industrial Rates of Profits be Uniform in Sraffa's System of Equations?

Sraffa first begins with an example of an empirical system of production of three basic commodities:

$$\begin{array}{llll}
 & 90\text{ t.iron} + 120\text{ t.coal} + 60\text{ qr.Wheat} & & \rightarrow 180\text{ t.iron} \\
 & 50\text{ t.iron} + 125\text{ t.coal} + 150\text{ qr.Wheat} & & \rightarrow 450\text{ t.coal} \\
 & 40\text{ t.iron} + \ 40\text{ t.coal} + 200\text{ qr.Wheat} & & \rightarrow 480\text{ qr.wheat} \\
\hline
\text{Totals } 180 & 285 & 410 & 180\text{ i} + 450\text{ c} + 480\text{ w}
\end{array}$$

In price terms, this actual physical system can be written in equation form as:

$$\begin{array}{l}
(90p_i + 120p_c + 60p_w)\,(1+r_i) = 180p_i \\
(50p_i + 125p_c + 150p_w)\,(1+r_c) = 450p_c \\
(40p_i + 40p_c + 200p_w)\,(1+r_w) = 480p_w \\
\hline
(180p_i + 285p_c + 410p_w)(1+R) = 180p_i + 450p_c + 480p_w,
\end{array} \qquad \text{(I)}$$

where p's are the prices of respective commodities, r's are the rate of profits of the respective industries and R is the average rate of profit of the system. Let us first assume that all the industries receive the average rate of profits. In this case, equation system (I) can be written as:

$$\begin{array}{l}
(90p'_i + 120p'_c + 60p'_w)(1+R) = 180p'_i. \\
(50p'_i + 125p'_c + 150p'_w)(1+R) = 450p'_c \\
(40p'_i + 40p'_c + 200p'_w)(1+R) = 480p'_w, \\
\hline
(180p'_i + 285p'_c + 410p'_w)(1+R) = 180p'_i + 450p'_c + 480p'_w
\end{array} \qquad \text{(I')}$$

[17] This note is co-authored with Sanjay Reddy.

Notice that prices would change from equation system (I) if r's of system (I) are different from R. We know from the Perron-Frobenius theorem that a solution for R with all positive prices exist (in this particular case the reader can verify that R = 20%). Now we want to check: can industrial rates of profits be unequal?

Let us now suppose that they are unequal. In that case some industrial rates of profits must be greater than the average rate and some smaller than the average rate, R. Let us call $r_i = (R + \lambda_i)$, $r_c = (R + \lambda_c)$ and $r_w = (R + \lambda_w)$. Thus, equation system (I) can now be written as:

$$\begin{aligned}
&(90p_i + 120p_c + 60p_w)\ (1 + R + \lambda_i) = 180p_i \\
&(50p_i + 125p_c + 150p_w)(1 + R + \lambda_c) = 450p_c \\
&(40p_i + 40p_c + 200p_w)(1 + R + \lambda_w) = 480p_w, \\
\hline
&(180p_i + 285p_c + 410p_w)(1 + R) + \{(90p_i + 120p_c + 60p_w)\lambda_i + (50p_i + 125p_c + \\
&150p_w)\lambda_c + (40p_i + 40p_c + 200p_w)\lambda_w\} = 180p_i + 450p_c + 480p_w
\end{aligned}$$

The terms in the middle bracket must add up to zero by the definition of an average. Without loss of generality, we may assume that $\lambda_i > 0$ and λ_c and $\lambda_w < 0$.

Now rescale the iron industry by 4/3 and the coal industry by 4/5. We obtain a rescaled equation system I, which is a Standard system:

$$\begin{aligned}
&(120p_i + 160p_c + 80p_w)(1 + R + \lambda_i) = 240p_i. \\
&(40p_i + 100p_c + 120p_w)\ (1 + R + \lambda_c) = 360p_c \\
&(40p_i + 40p_c + 200p_w)\ (1 + R + \lambda_w) = 480p_w \\
\hline
&(200p_i + 300p_c + 400p_w)(1 + R^*) = 240p_i + 360p_c + 480p_w
\end{aligned} \qquad \text{(II)}$$

Now, given that by rescaling we have increased the relative weight of the iron industry and reduced the relative weight of the coal industry with the wheat industry's weight remaining the same, one must expect the average rate of profits of this system of equations to rise since we are assuming that $\lambda_c < 0$ and $\lambda_i > 0$. However, by inspection we can see that R^* = 20% = R. Since in this case we obtain the average rate of profits of the system directly from the aggregate equation, that R^* must be equal to R is also verified by the fact that R^* is independent of prices, and therefore even for the p' prices for which all the λ's are zero (equation system I'), the average rate of profits in the equation system II will remain R^*. Hence R^* (for the Standard system) must always be equal to R. Thus we have a contradiction. On the one hand, if the λ's take positive (the original system to which it corresponds) and negative values then the definition of an average tells us that in our example the average rate of profits of the Standard system R^* must be greater than R, but, on the other hand, that is clearly not the case. It follows that the λ's must take zero values. For this to be true is not only sufficient, but also necessary, for R^* to equal R, which we have already determined that it must.

To see that the λ's must be zero in another way we may note that the average profit rate must be the same when calculating the value of output in two different ways, viz. by valuing the output as the sum of the industry specific output values and by valuing the output as the sum of the industry-specific total input values marked up by the industry-specific profit-rates. Let us call this requirement the value of output identity. The first perspective in the value of output identity gives rise to the requirement that:

$$(200p_i + 300p_c + 400p_w)(1 + R^*) = 240p_i + 360p_c + 480p_w$$

The second perspective in the value of output identity gives rise to the requirement that:

$$\begin{aligned}&(120p_i + 160p_c + 80p_w)(1 + R + \lambda_i) + (40p_i + 100p_c + 120p_w)(1 + R + \lambda_c)\\ &+(40p_i + 40p_c + 200p_w)(1 + R + \lambda_w) = 240p_i + 360p_c + 480p_w\end{aligned}$$

$$\begin{aligned}&\rightarrow (120p_i + 160p_c + 80p_w)(1 + R + \lambda_i) + (40p_i + 100p_c + 120p_w)(1 + R + \lambda_c)\\ &+(40p_i + 40p_c + 200p_w)(1 + R + \lambda_w) = (200p_i + 300p_c + 400p_w)(1 + R^*)\end{aligned}$$

But we have already established that $R = R^*$. Thus,

$$\begin{aligned}&(120p_i + 160p_c + 80p_w)(1 + R + \lambda_i) + (40p_i + 100p_c + 120p_w)(1 + R + \lambda_c)\\ &+(40p_i + 40p_c + 200p_w)(1 + R + \lambda_w) = (200p_i + 300p_c + 400p_w)(1 + R)\end{aligned}$$

Grouping terms and simplifying, this implies that:

$$(120p_i + 160p_c + 80p_w)\lambda_i + (40p_i + 100p_c + 120p_w)\lambda_c$$
$$+(40p_i + 40p_c + 200p_w)\lambda_w = 0$$

An analogous relationship between the empirical system and the Standard system must hold for all rescaled systems of the Standard system (since the empirical system is nothing but one rescaled system of the Standard system), that is, multiplying the terms on the left hand side by arbitrary independent constants must leave the sum of the deviations from the average equal to zero. But this is possible only if $\lambda_i = \lambda_c = \lambda_w = 0$.

8

Epilogue

Had Samuelson not played tennis on the morning that Jacob Viner and Joseph Schumpeter lectured on Irving Fisher's critique of Böhm-Bawerk's theory of interest (see Samuelson 2000), he would have not made the mistake of asking his student David Levhari (1965) to disprove Sraffa's proposition regarding the 're-switching' of techniques, and the future of Sraffian economics would have been very different. This counterfactual speculation notwithstanding, the fact remains that Samuelson did set his student the task to prove Sraffa wrong and the history is now well-known. Samuelson and Levhari had to accept their mistake and acknowledge the robustness of Sraffa's 're-switching' proposition (see 'Symposium' in *Quarterly Journal of Economics* 1966). The long and at times acrimonious debate over this proposition between the neoclassicists and the Sraffians is most ably documented in Harcourt (1969, 1972) and Bliss et al. (2005) and there is no need to rehearse it here. As I have mentioned in the Preface, although this success was hailed as the crowning glory of Sraffa's great work, it, however, came at a very high price. The orthodoxy interpreted Sraffa's re-switching proposition as his main contribution to economic theory; they accepted its truthfulness and argued that the modern general equilibrium orthodox economics need not aggregate capital independently of prices. Hence

A. Sinha, *A Revolution in Economic Theory*,
DOI 10.1007/978-3-319-30616-2_8

Sraffa's critique of the orthodox theory was not fatal but rather 'minor' and therefore, the book on Sraffa could be closed.

Frank Hahn (1982) went a step further and claimed that Sraffa's theory could be incorporated within the orthodox inter-temporal general equilibrium theory as a special and a highly restrictive case (as Pigou had claimed in 1928) if a constant returns to scale assumption is incorporated in it. Hahn finds himself 'at a loss to understand Sraffa' when Sraffa claims that he makes no such assumption. According to Hahn, 'the only falsifiable entailment of the Sraffa economics is the postulate of a uniform rate of profit' (p. 359). Now, in the light of our interpretation in this book, it is clear that there must be something amiss in Hahn's understanding of Sraffa. The main problem lies in an attempt to *translate* one theoretical paradigm into another to 'make sense of it'. So let us follow Hahn to detect where the problem lies.

Hahn considers a case of two commodities and a two-time-period model. Call the two commodities 'x' and 'y' and the two time periods '0' and '1'. Production takes one time period (a harvest cycle). It begins at the beginning of time period 0 and the world ends at the end of period 1. Thus there is no production at the beginning of time period 1. We have four prices: $p^0{}_x$, $p^0{}_y$, $p^1{}_x$, $p^1{}_y$ and to which we add a wage rate w, which is paid to the workers at the beginning of the period 1. On the assumption of constant returns to scale, the equilibrium condition for producers is:

$$p^1{}_j = \Sigma a_{ij}\ p^0{}_i + a_{0j} w, i, j = x, y \qquad (8.1)$$

where a_{ij} are the fixed input coefficients given technology and a_{0j} is the amount of labor used in the production of 1 unit of j. Let us define a normalization equation as:

$$p_x^0 + p_y^0 + p_x^1 + p_y^1 + w = 1 \qquad (8.2)$$

Let us also define:

$$p_i^0 / p_i^1 = \left(1 + r_i\right), i = x, y \qquad (8.3)$$

Substituting (8.3) in (8.1), we get,

$$p^1_j = \Sigma a_{ij} p^1_i (1 + r_i) + a_{0j} w, i, j = x, y \quad (8.4)$$

Hahn claims that the equations described by (8.4) have exact Sraffa form except that they assume constant returns to scale and thus are written in terms of per unit of outputs, whereas Sraffa's equations would be for the real amount of outputs produced. On the basis of this Hahn goes on to claim: 'It will now be clear that Sraffa is considering a very special state of the economy where … the relative prices of 1976 wheat and barley are the same as those of 1977 wheat and barley. The neoclassical economist is quite happy with a more general situation' (pp. 363–64).

Hahn, however, is clearly mistaken here. If we write the equations (8.4) for x and y separately, we get:

$$p^1_x = a_{xx} p^1_x (1 + r_x) + a_{yx} p^1_y (1 + r_y) + a_{0x} w \quad (8.5)$$

$$p^1_y = a_{xy} p^1_x (1 + r_x) + a_{yy} p^1_y (1 + r_y) + a_{0y} w \quad (8.6)$$

These equations do not relate to industries because the rates of profit applied to the inputs are not the industrial rate of profits but rather the inter-temporal discount rates of those commodities (or their 'own rates of profit'). They will take 'Sraffa form' only if we *assume* that $r_x = r_y$, which also *ipso facto* implies that all industrial rates of profits in Sraffa's system *must* be equal. Thus, this is not Sraffa's assumption but turns out to be a condition that must apply when the inter-temporal price equations are translated into Sraffa-form.

Let us now imagine that we find the system of two equations after the end of period 0, or at the beginning of period 1, in Sraffa's Standard proportions. In this case we know that the maximum rate of profits of the system can be derived from the physical ratio of aggregate outputs to aggregate inputs. Now imagine that, given inter-temporal demand and supply functions, the general equilibrium prices of x and y in time 0 and time 1 are not proportional to each other. Thus the inter-temporal prices would give us the maximum rate of profits of the system which would be different from the physical ratio obtained independently of prices. The reason for this discrepancy is that the inter-temporal general equilibrium world is quintessentially linear. In this world 'x' in time 1 is not the *same* commodity as 'x' in time 0. In other words, there is no output which is also an input in the system and hence there is no *basic* commodity in the inter-temporal general equilibrium model. Now, the only *falsifiable assumption* of Sraffa's model is the assumption of at least one basic commodity in the system. Sraffa's theory evaporates in a world where there is no basic commodity. Perhaps this is the dividing line between the two theoretical paradigms.

If our interpretation of Sraffa's model is accepted, then the question arises as to how the system adjusts when it is not in equilibrium. Of course, if an industry is producing more than it can sell or less than there is demand for it then it cannot keep on year after year. In Sraffa's system the problem of realization of profit is not an issue. Whatever has been produced has to be accounted for. If an industry is not able to sell all it has produced then the excess supply goes into its inventory. However, the rise in the inventory must be accounted for as if it was bought by the industry itself at the prices determined by Sraffa's equations. It is only in the next time period that the industries could try to adjust their rise and fall in inventories or meet the unfulfilled demands by deciding to increase or reduce their outputs. Now, if constant returns do not apply to even one basic industry that decides to adjust its output then in the next time period all the prices would change, but they would again be determined by the new Sraffa-equations. Thus one can observe over a period of time movements in prices as a result of such quantity adjustments but they are a consequence and not a cause of the adjustment process. This suggests that a Sraffian price theory can be fitted into a Keynesian quantity adjustment mechanism without any need for an unnecessary assumption of fixed prices. This has brought us to the threshold of marrying Sraffa with Keynes—not an easy proposition given the role of psychology in Keynes's theory, but a good time to draw down the curtain on the current story.

References

Allen, H.S. 1928. The quantum theory. Supplement to *Nature* 3084: 887–895.

Bellino, Enrico. 2004. On Sraffa's standard commodity. *Cambridge Journal of Economics* 28(1): 121–132.

Bellino, Enrico. 2006. Banfi, Eaton, Dobb and Johnson review Sraffa's *Production of commodities. Storia del pensiero economico* III(2): 165–201.

Bellofiore, R. 2008. Sraffa and Marx: An open issue. In *Sraffa and an alternative economics*, ed. G. Chiodi and L. Ditta, 68–92. Basingstoke: Plagrave.

Bliss, C., A. Cohen, and G.C. Harcourt (eds.). 2005. *Capital theory*, 3 volumes. Cheltenham/Northampton: Edward Elgar.

Böhm-Bawrek, Eugen von. 1959[1884]. *Capital and Interest,* vols. 1–3. Trans. George D. Huncke and Hans F. Sennholz. Illinois: Liberation Press.

Bridgeman, P.W. 1927. *Logic of modern physics*. New York: Macmillan.

Burton, J.H. 1846. *Life and correspondence of David Hume*, vol. 1. Edinburgh: William Tait.

Cairnes, J.E. 1872. New theories in political economy. *Fortnightly Review* New Series, 11: 71–76.

Carter, S. 2014. From "pool of profits" to surplus and deficit industries: Archival evidence on the evolution of Piero Sraffa's thought. *Research in Political Economy* 29: 3–61.

A. Sinha, *A Revolution in Economic Theory*,
DOI 10.1007/978-3-319-30616-2

Clark, J.B. 1965[1899]. *The distribution of wealth: A theory of wages interest and profits*. New York: Augustus M. Kelley Booksellers.

Dardi, M. 2001. Why did Sraffa lose interest in imperfect competition? A comment on Marcuzzo. In *Piero Sraffa's political economy: A centenary estimate*, ed. Terenzio Cozzi and Roberto Marchionatti, 128–136. London/New York: Routledge.

De Cecco, Marcello. 1993. Piero Sraffa's "Monetary inflation in Italy during and after the war": An introduction. *Cambridge Journal of Economics* 17(1): 1–5.

De Vivo, G. 2003. 'Sraffa' path to production of commodities by means of commodities: An interpretation. *Contributions to Political Economy* 22: 1–25.

Dobb, Maurice. 1961. An epoch making book. *Labour Monthly* 10: 487–91.

Dupertuis, M.-S., and A. Sinha. 2009. A Sraffian critique of the classical notion of centre of gravitation. *Cambridge Journal of Economics* 33(6): 1065–1087.

Eatwell, J. 1987. Competition, classical. In *The new Palgrave dictionary of economics*. London: Macmillan.

Eddington, A.S. 1927. *The nature of the physical world*. New York: The Macmillan Company.

Edgeworth, Francis. 1925[1889]. The pure theory of monopoly, reprinted in *Collected papers relating to political economy*. London: Macmillan.

Fisher, Irving. 1907. *The rate of interest. Its nature, determination and relation to economic phenomena*. New York: Macmillan Company.

Garegnani, P. 1990. Sraffa: Classical versus marginalist analysis. In *Essays on Piero Sraffa critical perspectives on the revival of classical theory*, ed. K. Bharadwaj and B. Schefold. Delhi: Oxford University Press.

Garegnani, P. 2000. Savings, investment, and capital in a system of intertemporal general equilibrium. In *Critical essays on Piero Sraffa's legacy in economics*, ed. H. Kurz, 393–445. Cambridge: Cambridge University Press.

Garegnani, P. 2005. On a turning point in Sraffa's theoretical and interpretative position in the late 1920s. *The European Journal of the History of Economic Thought* 12(3): 453–492.

Garegnani, P. 2007. Professor Samuelson on Sraffa and the classical economists. *The European Journal of the History of Economic Thought* 14(2): 181–242.

Gehrke, C., and H.D. Kurz. 2006. Sraffa on von Bortkiewicz: Reconstructing the classical theory of value and distribution. *History of Political Economy* 38(1): 91–149.

Gilibert, G. 2003. The equations unveiled: Sraffa's price equations in the making. *Contributions to Political Economy* 22: 27–40.

Gilibert, G. 2006. The man from the moon: Sraffa's upside-down approach to the theory of value. *Contributions to Political Economy* 25: 35–48.

Hahn, F. 1982. The neo-Ricardians. *Cambridge Journal of Economics* 6(4): 353–374.
Hanfling, Oswald. 1984. *Wittgenstein's later philosophy*. London: Macmillan.
Harcourt, G.C. 1969. Some Cambridge controversies in the theory of capital. *Journal of Economic Literature* 7: 369–405.
Harcourt, G.C. 1972. *Some Cambridge controversies in the theory of capital*. Cambridge: Cambridge University Press.
Harcourt, G.C., and V.G. Massaro. 1964. Mr. Sraffa's production of commodities. *The Economic Record* 40: 442–454.
Harrod, R.F. 1961. Review of production of commodities by means of commodities. Prelude to a critique of economic theory. *The Economic Journal* LXXI: 783–787.
Hertz, H. 1899. *Principles of mechanics*. London: Macmillan.
Hicks, John. 1985. Sraffa and Ricardo: A critical view. In *The legacy of Ricardo*, ed. G.A. Caravale. New York: Basil Blackwell.
Hollander, J.H. 1904. The development of Ricardo's theory of value. *Quarterly Journal of Economics* 18: 455–491.
Hollander, S. 1973. *The economics of Adam Smith*. Toronto: University of Toronto Press.
Hollander, S. 1979. *The economics of David Ricardo*. Toronto: University of Toronto Press.
Hollander, S. 1992. *Classical economics*. Toronto: University of Toronto Press.
Hume, D. 1938[1740]. *An abstract of a treatise of human nature*, ed. and with an Introduction by J.M. Keynes and P. Sraffa. Cambridge: Cambridge University Press.
Jevons, H.S. 1957[1871]. *The theory of political economy*. New York: Kelly & Millman, Inc.
Kurz, H.D. (ed.). 2000. *Critical essays on Piero Sraffa's legacy in economics*. Cambridge: Cambridge University Press.
Kurz, H.D. 2012. Don't treat too ill my Piero! Interpreting Sraffa's papers. *Cambridge Journal of Economics* 36(6): 1535–1569.
Kurz, H.D., and N. Salvadori. 2001. Sraffa and the mathematicians: Frank Ramsey and Alister Watson. In *Piero Sraffa's political economy. A centenary estimate*, ed. T. Cozzi and R. Marchionatti, 254–284. London/New York: Routledge.
Kurz, H.D., and N. Salvadori. 2005. Representing the production and circulation of commodities in material terms: On Sraffa's objectivism. *Review of Political Economy* 17(3): 69–97.
Levhari, David. 1965. A nonsubstitution theorem and switching of techniques. *The Quarterly Journal 6 Economics* LXXXIX: 98–105.

Lippi, Marco. 2008. Some observation on Sraffa and mathematical proofs with an appendix on Sraffa's convergence algorithm. In *Sraffa or an alternative economics*, ed. G. Chiodi and L. Ditta, 243–259. New York: Palgrave Macmillan.

Marcuzzo, Cristina. 2001. Sraffa and Cambridge economics, 1928–31. In *Piero Sraffa's political economy: A centenary estimate*, ed. Terenzio Cozzi and Roberto Marchionatti, 81–100. London/New York: Routledge.

Marshall, A. 1949[1890]. *Principles of economics an introductory volume*, 8th edn. London: Macmillan and Co. Limited.

Marx, Karl. 1968[1905–10]. *Theories of surplus value part II*. Moscow: Progress Publishers.

Marx, Karl. 1991[1894]. *Capital*, vol. III. London: Penguin Classics.

Marx, Karl, and F. Engels. 1969. *Selected works*. Moscow: Progress Publishers.

McGuinness, Brian. 2002. *Approaches to Wittgenstein*. London: Routledge.

McGuinness, Brian. 2008. *Wittgenstein in Cambridge letters and documents 1911–1951*. Oxford: Blackwell Publishing.

Menger, C. 2007[1871]. *Principles of Economics*. Trans. J. Dingwall and B.F. Hoselitz. Auburn: Ludwig von Mises Institute.

Monk, R. 1990. *Ludwig Wittgenstein the duty of genius*. London: Vintage.

Naldi, Nerio. 2000. Piero Sraffa and Antonio Gramsci: Their friendship between 1919 and 1927. *European Journal of the History of Economic Thought* 7(1): 79–114.

Naldi, Nerio. 2001. Piero Sraffa's early approach to political economy: From the gymnasium to the beginning of his academic career. In *Piero Sraffa's political economy*, ed. T. Cozzi and R. Marchionatti, 23–40. London: Routledge.

Pareto, Vilfredo. 1971[1906]. *Manual of Political Economy*. Trans. Ann S. Schwier. London/Basingstoke: The Macmillan Press Ltd.

Pasinetti, L. 1998. Piero Sraffa: An Italian economist in Cambridge. In *Italian economic papers*, vol. III, ed. L. Pasinetti, 365–383. Oxford: Oxford University Press.

Pasinetti, L. 2001. Continuity and change in Sraffa's thought: An archival excurses. In *Piero Sraffa's political economy*, ed. T. Cozzi and R. Marchionatti, 139–156. London: Routledge.

Pears, D. 1969. *Ludwig Wittgenstein*, 1st ed. New York: The Viking Press.

Pears, D. 1985. *Wittgenstein*, 2nd ed. London: Fontana Press.

Pegou, A.C. 1922. Empty economic boxes: A reply. *Economic Journal* 32(128): 458–465.

Planck, Max. 1931. *The universe in the light of modern physics*. London: George Allen and Unwin Ltd.

Poincaré, Henri. 1952[1902]. *Science and Hypothesis*. Trans. W.J.G. New York: Dovar Publication.

Porta, P.L. 1986. Understanding the significance of Piero Sraffa's standard commodity. A note on the Marxian notion of surplus. *History of Political Economy* 18(3): 443–454.

Porta, P.L. 2012. Piero Sraffa's early views on classical political economy. *Cambridge Journal of Economics* 36(6): 1357–1383.

Rae, John. 1895. *Life of Adam Smith*. London/New York: Macmillan & Co.

Reder, M.W. 1961. Review of Sraffa's *Production of commodities by means of commodities. American Economic Review* LI: 688–695.

Ricardo, David. 1951[1821]. *On the principles of political economy and taxation*, 3rd ed. Cambridge: Cambridge University Press.

Ricardo, David. 1951–55. *The works and correspondence of David Ricardo,* ed. Piero Sraffa, vols. I–II, IV, VI–IX. Cambridge: Cambridge University Press.

Robinson, Joan. 1961. Prelude to a critique of economic theory. *Oxford Economic Papers* 13: 53–58.

Robinson, Joan. 1985. The theory of normal prices and reconstruction of economic theory. In *Issues in contemporary macroeconomics and distribution*, ed. George R. Feiwel, 157–165. Albany: SUNY, Albany Press.

Roncaglia, A. 1978. *Sraffa and the theory of prices*. Chichester: John Wiley & Sons.

Roncaglia, A. 2000. *Piero Sraffa his life, thought and cultural heritage*. London: Routledge.

Samuelson, P.A. (2000a). Sraffa's hits and misses. In *Critical essays on Piero Sraffa's legacy in economics*, ed. H.D. Kurz. Cambridge: Cambridge University Press.

Schefold, B. 2000. Paradoxes of capital and counterintuitive changes of distribution in an intertemporal equilibrium model. In *Critical essays on Piero Sraffa's legacy in economics*, ed. H. Kurz, 363–391. Cambridge: Cambridge University Press.

Schefold, B. 2008. Savings, investment and capital in a system of general intertemporal equilibrium—An extended comment on Garegnani with a note on Parrinello. In *Sraffa or an alternative economics*, ed. G. Chiodi and L. Ditta, 275–294. New York: Palgrave Macmillan.

Schrodinger, E. 1952. *Science and humanism physics in our times*, 2nd ed. Cambridge: Cambridge University Press.

Schumpeter, J.A. 1954. *History of economic analysis*. New York: Oxford University Press.

Sen, Amartya. 1978. On the labour theory of value: Some methodological issues. *Cambridge Journal of Economics* 2(2): 175–190.

Sen, Amartya. 2003. Sraffa, Wittgenstein, and Gramsci. *Journal of Economic Literature* 41(4): 1240–1255.

Sen, Amartya. 2004. Economic methodology: Heterogeneity and relevance. *Social Research* 71(3): 583–614.

Senior, Nassau. 1836. *An outline of the science of political economy*. New York: Kelley.

Sinha, Ajit. 2006. A comment on Sen's "Sraffa, Wittgenstein, and Gramsci". *Journal of Economic Behavior and Organization* 61: 504–512.

Sinha, Ajit. 2007. Sraffa and the assumption of constant returns to scale: A critique of Samuelson and Etula. *Contributions to Political Economy* 26: 61–70.

Sinha, Ajit. 2009. Sraffa and the later Wittgenstein. *Contributions to Political Economy* 28: 47–69.

Sinha, Ajit. 2010a. *Theories of value from Adam Smith to Piero Sraffa*. London/New York/New Delhi: Routledge.

Sinha, Ajit. 2010b. In defence of Adam Smith's theory of value. *European Journal of the History of Economic Thought* 17(1): 29–48.

Sinha, Ajit. 2010c. A note on Ricardo's invariable measure of value. *Cahiers d'économie politique*, N° 58, 133–144.

Sinha, Ajit. 2012. Listen to Sraffa's silences: A new interpretation of Sraffa's *Production of commodities. Cambridge Journal of Economics* 36(6): 1323–1339.

Sinha, Ajit. 2013. The new interpretation of Sraffa's prices: A response to Hienz Kurz. *Cambridge Journal of Economics* 37(6): 1449–1453.

Sinha, Ajit. 2014. On Marx's law of the falling rate of profit: Disentangling some entangled variables. *Review of Radical Political Economics* 46(2): 184–189.

Sinha, Ajit. 2015. A reflection on the Samuelson-Garegnani debate. *Economic Thought* 4(2): 48–67.

Sinha, Ajit. 2016. A comment on Sraffa's "classical economics". *Cambridge Journal of Economics* (forthcoming). doi: bew026.

Smith, Adam. 1981[1776]. *An inquiry into the nature and causes of the wealth of nations*, vols. I and II. Indianapolis: Library Fund.

Sraffa, Piero. 1993[1920]. Monetary inflation in Italy during and after the war. Trans. Wendy J. Harcourt and C. Sardoni. *Cambridge Journal of Economics* 17(1): 7–26.

Sraffa, Piero. 1922. The bank crisis in Italy. *Economic Journal* 32(126): 178–197.

Sraffa, Piero. 1925. Sulle relazioni tra costo e quantita prodotta. *Annali di Economia*, vol. 2: pp. 277–328. English Translation by John Eatwell and A. Roncaglia in *Italian economc papers*, vol. 3, ed. L.L. Pasinetti. Oxford: Oxford University Press.

Sraffa, Piero. 1926. The laws of returns under competitive conditions. *The Economic Journal* 36(144): 535–550.

Sraffa, Piero. 1951. 'Preface' and 'introduction'. In *Works and correspondence of David Ricardo*, vol. I, ed. P. Sraffa. Cambridge: Cambridge University Press.

Sraffa, Piero. 1960. *Production of commodities by means of commodities.* Cambridge: Cambridge University Press.

Sraffa, Piero. 1962. Production of commodities: A comment. *The Economic Journal* 72(286): 477–479.

Sraffa, Piero. n.d. *Piero Sraffa papers.* Wren Library, Trinity College, Cambridge.

Stigler, G.J. 1953. Sraffa's Ricardo. *American Economic Review* 43(4:1): 586–599.

Symposium 1966 on reswitching of methods. *Quarterly Journal of Economics* 80(4): 503–583.

Uhr, C.G. 1962. *Economic doctrines of Knut Wicksell.* Berkeley/Los Angeles: University of California Press.

Velupillai, Kumaraswamy. 2008. Sraffa's economics in non-classical mathematical modes. In *Sraffa or an alternative economics*, ed. G. Chiodi and L. Ditta, 275–294. New York: Palgrave Macmillan.

Walras, L. 1954. *Elements of pure economics* (4th definitive edition), ed. W. Jaffé. London: Allen and Unwin.

Wicksell, Knut. 1934. *Lectures on political economy, vol. one, general theory.* London: George Routledge and Sons Ltd.

Wicksteed, Philip. 1914. The scope and method of political economy in the light of "marginal" theory of value and distribution. *The Economic Journal* 24(94): 1–23.

Wittgenstein, L. 1974[1922]. *Tractatus Logico-philosophicus.* Trans. D.F. Pears and B.F. McGuinnes. London/New York: Routledge.

Wittgenstein, L. 1958. *Blue and brown books,* ed. R. Rhees. Oxford: Blackwell.

Wittgenstein, L. 1953. *Philosophical investigations.* Oxford: Basil Blackwell.

Von Wright, Georg Henrik. 1955. Ludwig Wittgenstein, A biographical sketch. *Philosophical Review* 64(4): 527–545.

Von Wright, Georg Henrik. 1974. *Causality and determinism.* Durham: Duke University Press.

Index

Note: Page number followed by 'n' refers to footnotes.

A. Sinha, *A Revolution in Economic Theory*,
DOI 10.1007/978-3-319-30616-2

The manufacturer's authorised representative in the EU is Springer Nature Customer Service Centre GmbH, Europaplatz 3, 69115 Heidelberg, Germany. If you have any concerns regarding our products, please contact ProductSafety@springernature.com

Printed and bound by CPI Group (UK) Ltd, Croydon, CR0 4YY
30/09/2026
02225216-0005